ABANDONED OHIO

RUSTBELT DERELICTS

JACOB JOSEPH

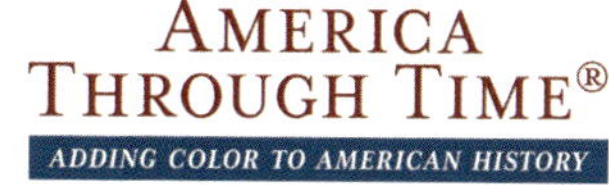

America Through Time is an imprint of Fonthill Media LLC
www.through-time.com
office@through-time.com

Published by Arcadia Publishing by arrangement with Fonthill Media LLC
For all general information, please contact Arcadia Publishing:
Telephone: 843-853-2070
Fax: 843-853-0044
E-mail: sales@arcadiapublishing.com
For customer service and orders:
Toll-Free 1-888-313-2665

www.arcadiapublishing.com

First published 2022

Copyright © Jacob Joseph 2022

ISBN 978-1-63499-379-1

Typeset in Trade Gothic 10pt on 15pt
Printed and bound in England

CONTENTS

ABOUT THE AUTHOR

JACOB JOSEPH comes from an automotive journalism background. Taking photos of cars at international shows is always a good time, but abandoned buildings offered a bit of variety, and a whole new set of photography challenges. An American-Israeli dual citizen and U.S. Army veteran, Jacob has seen a lot of the world, but upon returning to Cleveland, the city where he grew up, he felt inspired to document the area's many abandoned buildings. His love of architecture extends to buildings that aren't even abandoned, at least sometimes.

INTRODUCTION

Curiosity has always been the driving force behind my desire to explore abandoned buildings. I'd see a crumbling old building and I had to see what it was like inside, what artifacts were left over from the previous occupants, and if there were any interesting architectural features. The places I've explored have been surprisingly different from one another, with each one offering up something I'd never seen in any other building. I think that's why I still feel such a strong need to explore. Curiosity drives my desire to see what new thing the next building will reveal.

When I began taking photos, I started with the buildings that I saw all the time and had been curious about, in some cases, for years. The photos in this book are in more or less chronological order, but sometimes there are repeat visits. The chronology of the photos isn't especially important anyway, so sometimes they aren't.

These photos were all taken with my trusty Nikon DSLR, which has miraculously survived any number of bumps and knocks against walls and fences, thanks to my especially ungraceful style of ingress for abandoned buildings. I tend to prefer long exposures to using a flash for dark places, and that's probably going to be pretty obvious when you see the pictures. That means lugging a tripod along with me most of the time, but it's worth it, as I firmly believe the tripod is an extremely underrated piece of equipment. My last piece of necessary equipment is at least one other person. I never go exploring alone, and I don't recommend that anyone else do either. A lot of things can happen in an abandoned building, which would require at least one person to be able to call 911. Be smart.

1

CLOSE TO HOME

This chapter features buildings that I'd seen a lot before I ever went inside. They fed my curiosity before I ever decided to take up this hobby. The "READ MORE BOOKS" graffiti was specifically placed to be visible from a very busy section of highway, right in the middle of Cleveland. The building was an older industrial one, which had most recently been used for sort of textile manufacturing. An old ladder was leaning against one exterior wall around the back of the building when we got there, and we figured that would be the best way in. It was a little nerve wracking, since we didn't really know what condition the ladder was in, but we made it. Later, when exploring the boiler room, we found a giant hole in the wall at ground level that we could have just walked through. As you can see, one photo was taken at midday, and the others at dusk. This was the result of two separate visits—we used the giant hole to get in the second time. The building has since been completely renovated and is now a school.

Also included is the old Cleveland Aquarium, abandoned since the mid-eighties. I have what I believe to be a vague memory of visiting with my dad in what must have been the final days of the aquarium, but coming back, it didn't look at all familiar, so I'm perfectly willing to accept that I might have just imagined it. The location of the building is very odd and unique. It's located inside a park, which remains open. There's even a parking lot right next to the old aquarium, presumably from when it was still open, but it now serves as parking for the park. The building was easy to get into, but we were conspicuous doing it. We went in the morning on a cold day though, so nobody was around to see us.

Rounding out the chapter is another building that I'd seen a lot of before I went in. I pass by it every time I go downtown or to the west side of Cleveland. It's a fairly old building, from the last half of the nineteenth century, but as you can see, parts of it are quite a bit newer. We did some rummaging around in the basement, and the most recent documents we were able to find were from the seventies, so we're assuming it's been abandoned since then. I'm not entirely sure when the roof collapsed on the middle section, but it has been at least ten years. That whole middle section was full of rubble until fairly recently, when it was cleared out so the location could be used for shooting the movie *The Land*. I've always found the roofless portion oddly fascinating, although the nearly 150-year-old basement is the stuff of nightmares. With almost no light down there, I've included the only decent photo I've ever been able to get of the space.

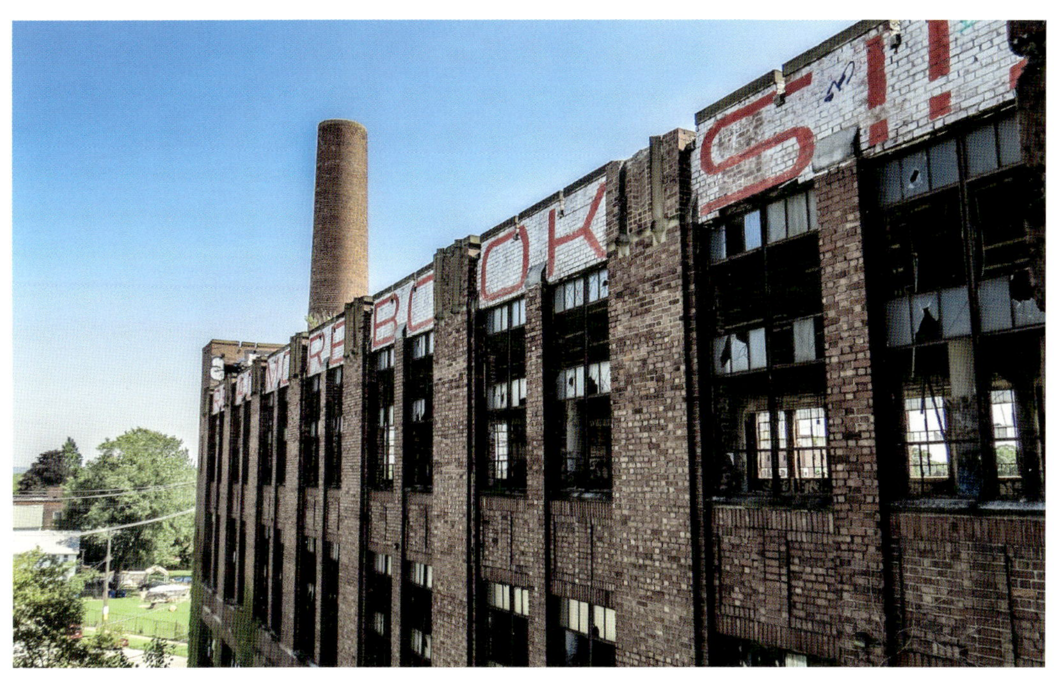

It's not easy to read from this angle, but the graffiti says: "READ MORE BOOKS!!!" The building has since been converted into a school.

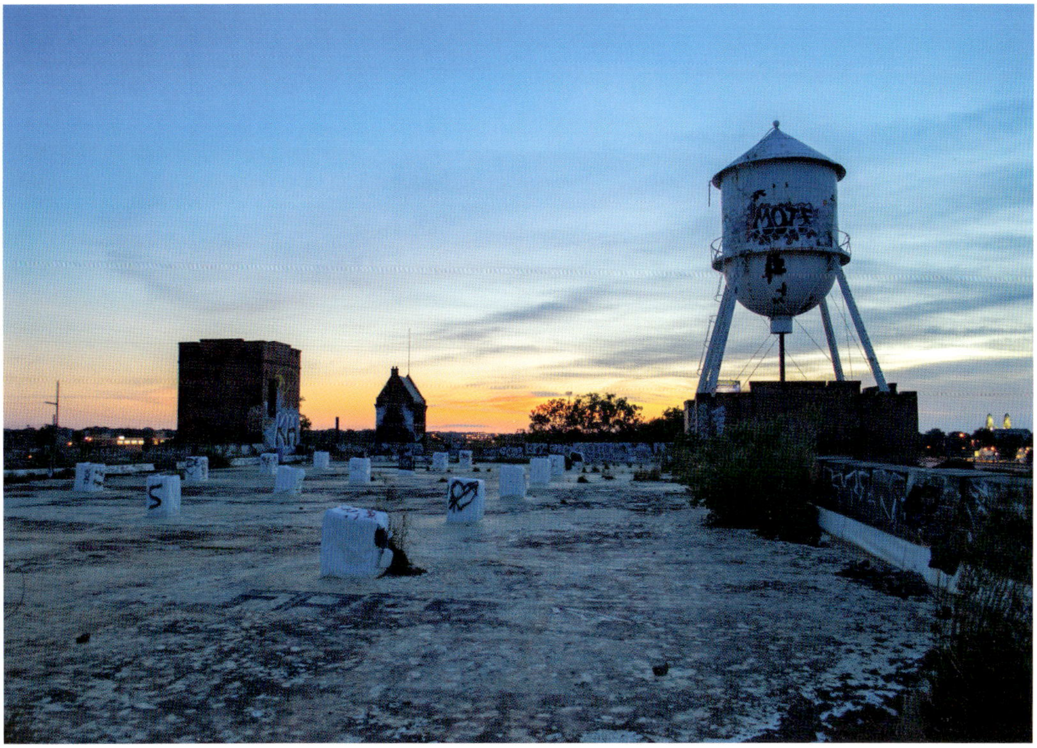

My exploring buddy decided to climb this water tower while we were there. I decided to pass, but I'm still glad that it survived the renovation. They have painted over the graffiti, however.

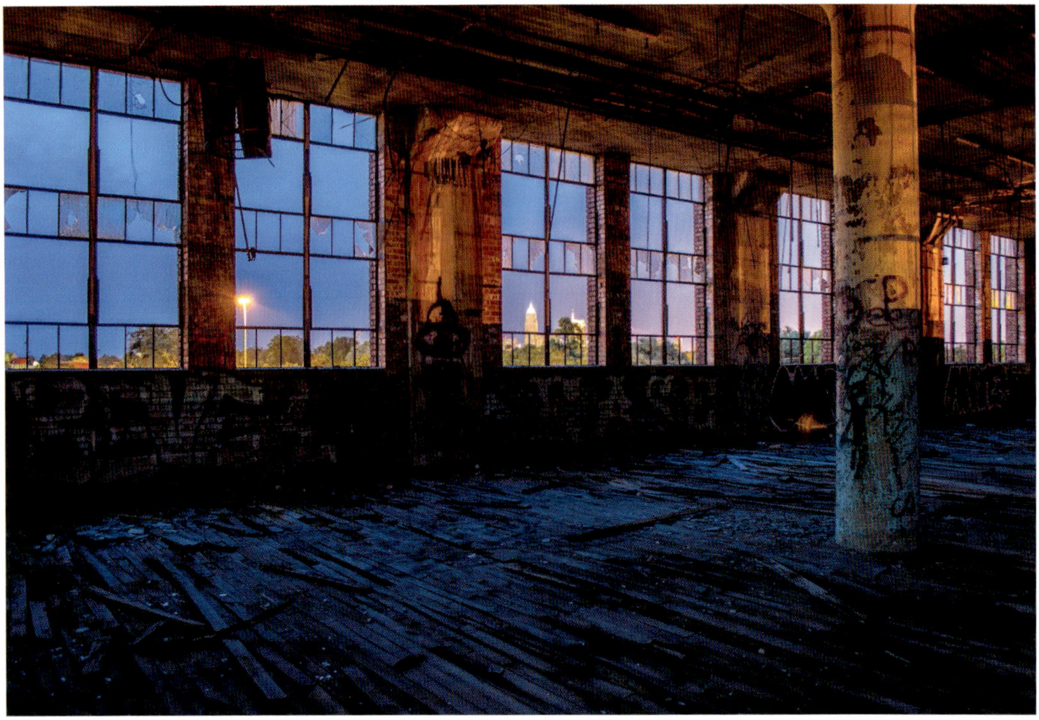

I took photos looking out of all the different windows on this floor. This was the only one where the light was just right.

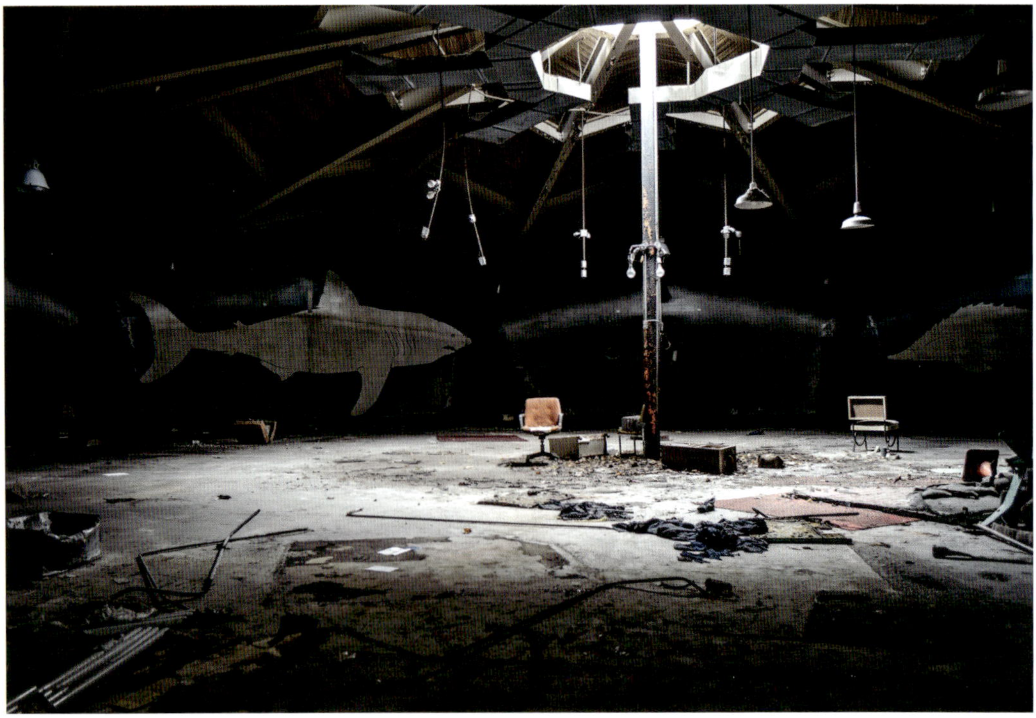

This was the main hall of what was a small aquarium. I remember it seeming a lot bigger, but I was six when it closed, so that's no surprise.

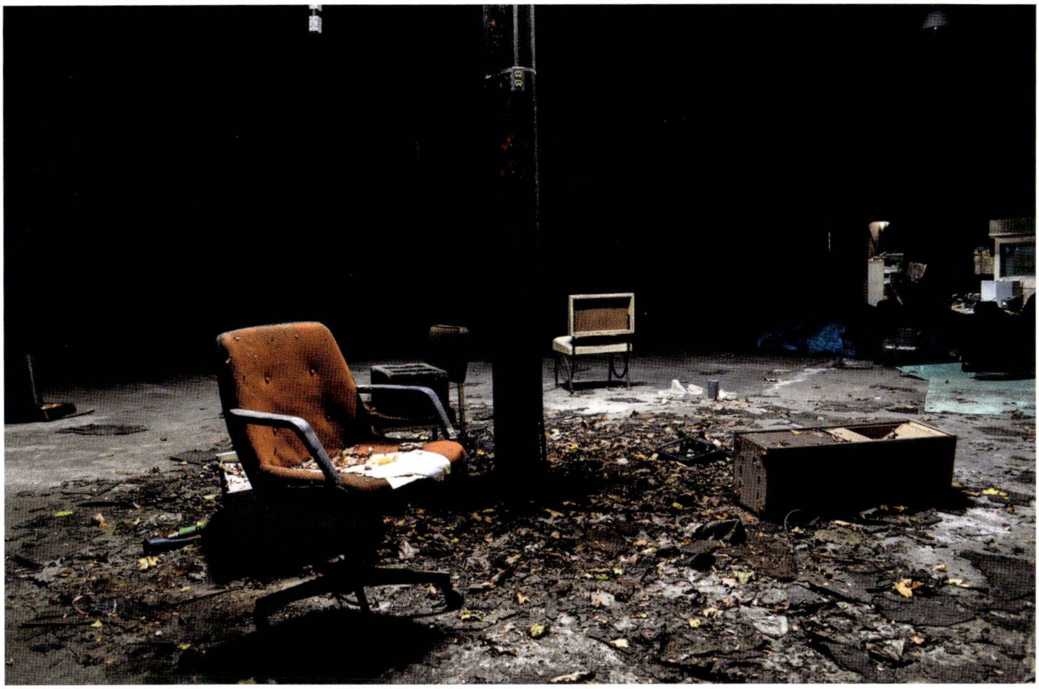

The middle of the main hall of the aquarium. It was dark in the hall, but the hole in the roof had the effect of creating a spotlight on a grouping of random furniture in the middle of the room.

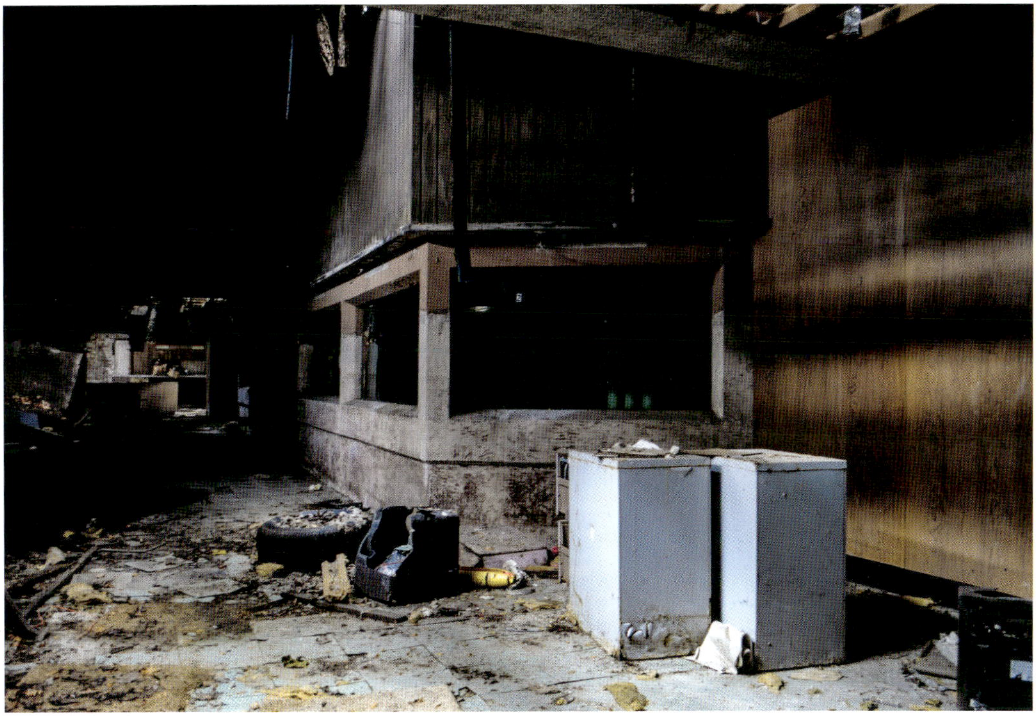

An old tank with some really thick glass. Someone did eventually manage to break it, but not until after we'd been there.

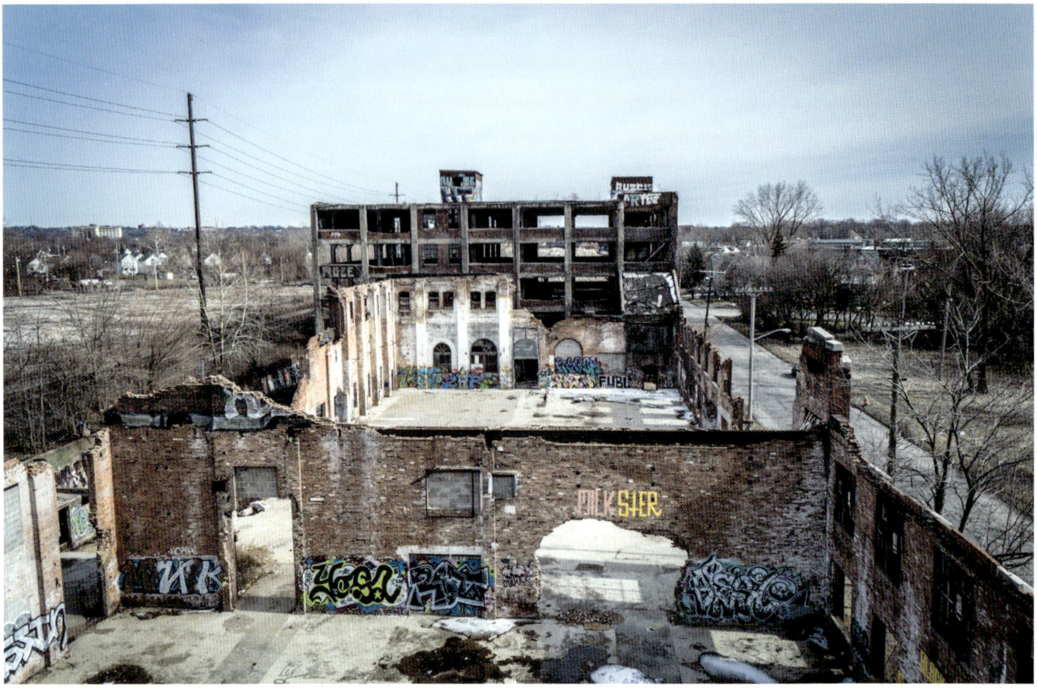

Taken from the third floor of the older part of the building. This whole area was covered in rubble (presumably from the roof collapsing) when I first went. But it was cleared out because the building was used to shoot some scenes for the movie *The Land*.

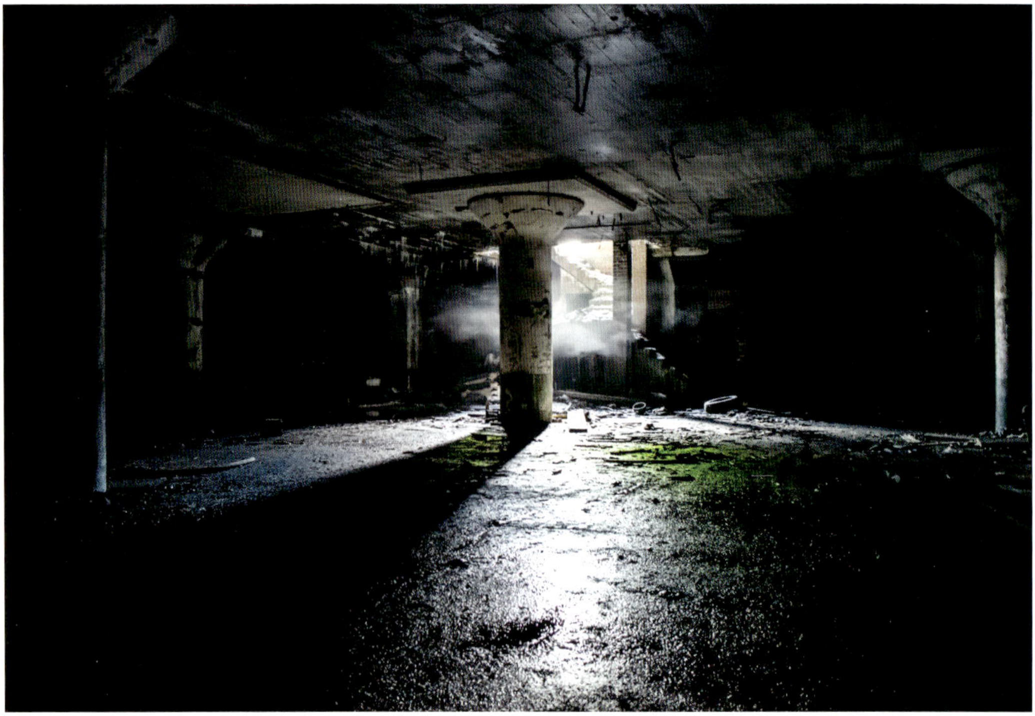

From the basement of the newer part of the building. I don't know what the cause of the mist was.

2

HAPPY ACCIDENTS

These are locations that I stumbled upon purely by accident, usually while looking for something else. The old farmhouse was not the intended destination of our outing the day we found it. We had driven out to explore an old motel, which turned out to be pretty uninteresting, and just happened to drive by this place on the way. It looked like the set of a horror movie, and once inside, that impression wasn't diminished even slightly. It was fascinating, and by far the spookiest place I've ever explored. I always wanted to go back and take some more photos, since I didn't have my tripod with me for the first trip, but it burned to the ground before I had the chance.

There are a few photos of buildings that had more to offer, aesthetically speaking, from the outside than the inside. The first is an abandoned mall, and the color of this photo hasn't been altered in any way—it was just that gray.

One of these was a large retail store, abandoned long enough that we couldn't say for sure what had been sold there. But I included the picture to illustrate how strange the things found in abandoned places can be. An assortment of lamps and a painting of a vase of flowers—did these have anything to do with whatever the building had been before? Were they intentionally being displayed like this for some reason? I've found myself asking these sorts of questions often while exploring places like this, and I usually ask them while laughing.

We found the small neighborhood clinic when we were exploring a bigger industrial building nearby, which turned out not to be very interesting, but had a decent view of the city. As we were standing around, admiring the view, we saw a building with an overgrown parking lot, and decided to give it a shot. The door was unlocked, and we walked right in. This is, I believe, the newest abandoned building I've ever been in. It was kind of an odd feeling, being in this building that was probably built after I was born but already abandoned. It was fascinating all the same.

We found a very large abandoned middle school in the middle of the night, on the way home from the Masonic Hall (also in this book). It was in decent shape a couple of years ago when the photos were taken but has since been trashed. We spent a lot of time walking through all the classrooms, most of which still had all the teachers' decorations up. Several even had farewell messages from the students to their teachers written on the chalkboards. But there was very little light in the whole building. Even the top floor had boards over the windows, so I have very few photos.

Rounding out the chapter is a complex of buildings in Youngstown, clearly abandoned for a very long time. Most of the buildings were just shells, with no floors left on the upper levels, which is why there are so many exterior shots. These were the furthest-gone abandoned buildings I've been to, and they also contained my favorite graffiti I've ever found.

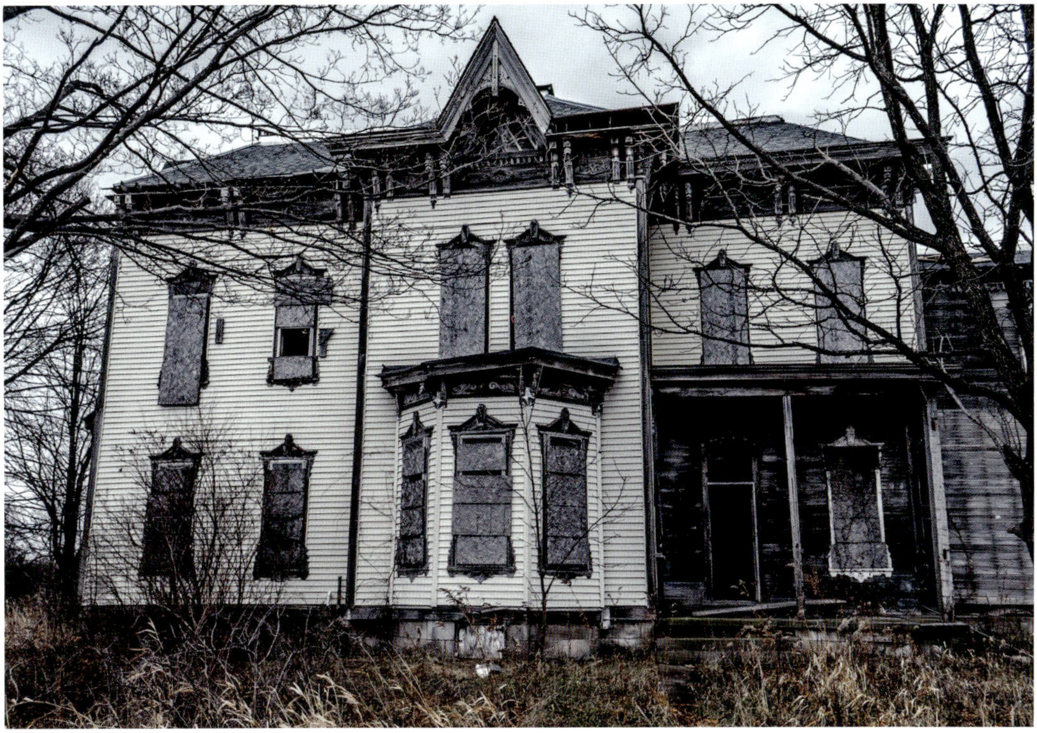

I played around with some edits to see if I could make this look any spookier than it looked already. I couldn't.

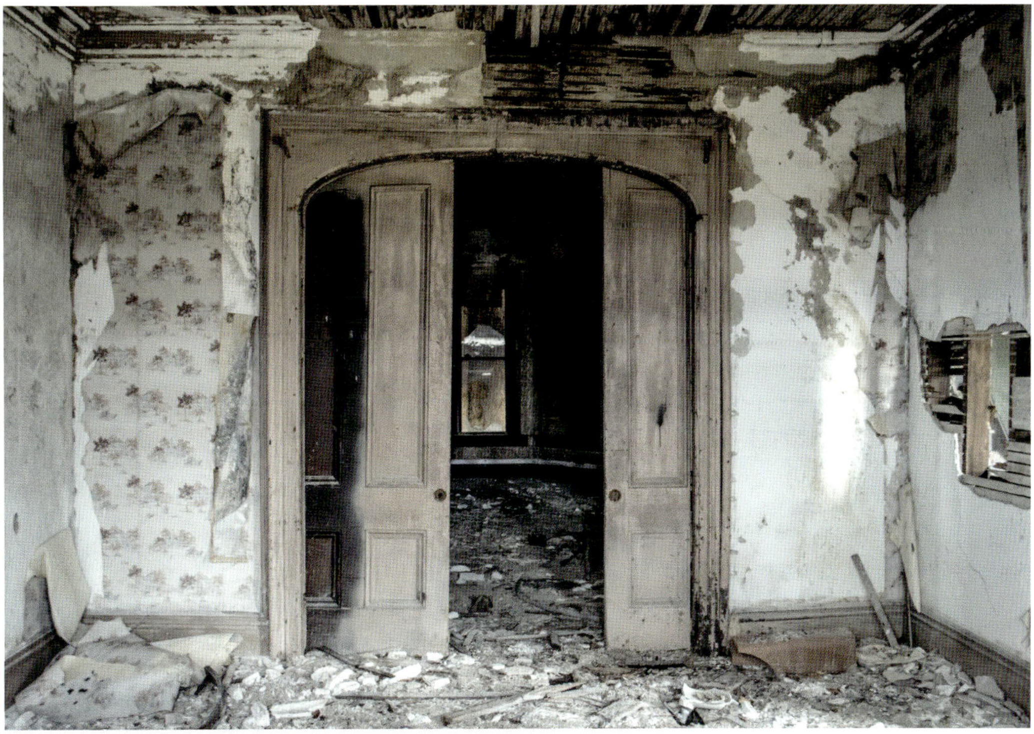

These pocket doors didn't really want to budge, and from the look of the paint on them, they hadn't in a long time.

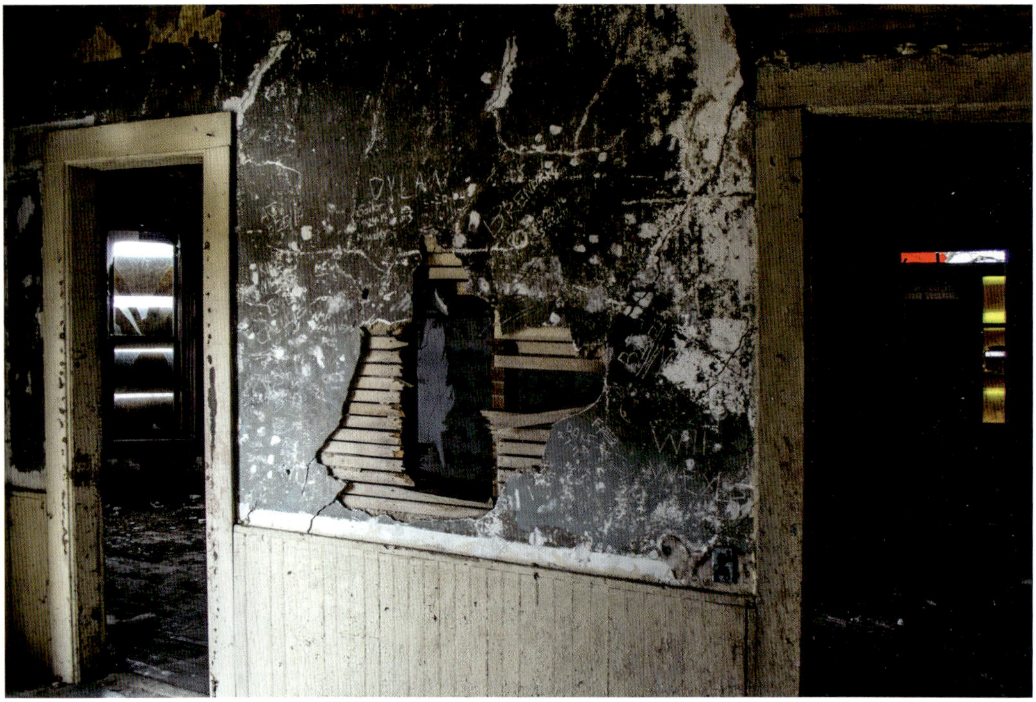

With the windows boarded up, there wasn't a lot of great light inside this house. Inside the side entrance, where the door was missing, was one of the only places easy to photograph.

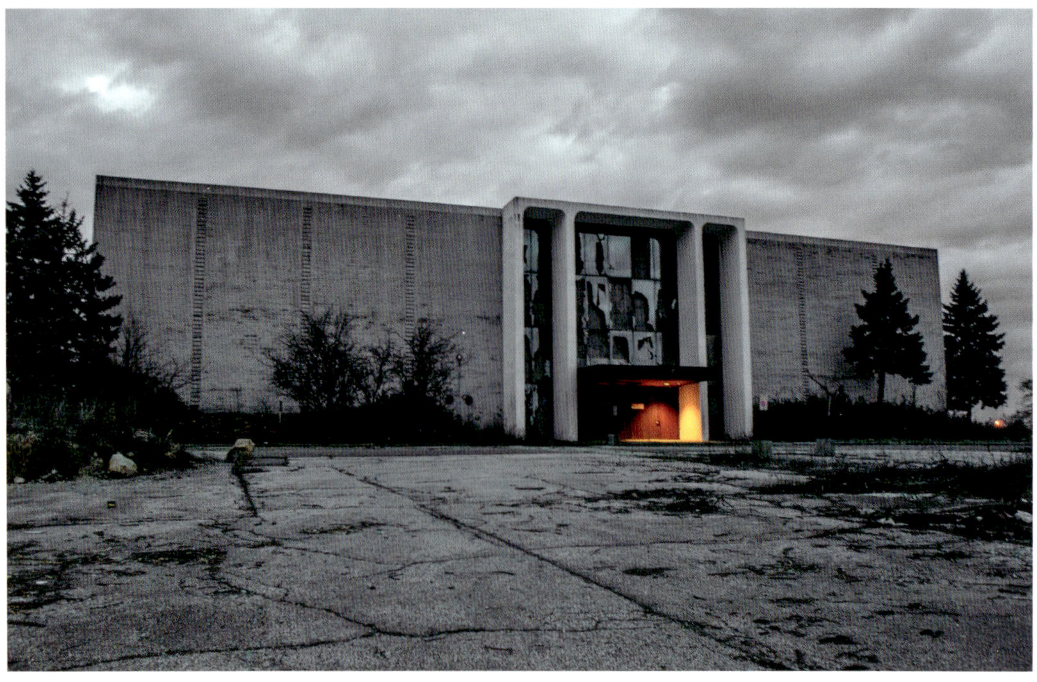

We didn't explore the inside of this building; we didn't even try. We were just in the area and decided to take a look at the outside. As we drove past, I saw this one light left on, years after the mall had closed, so I had to take a photo.

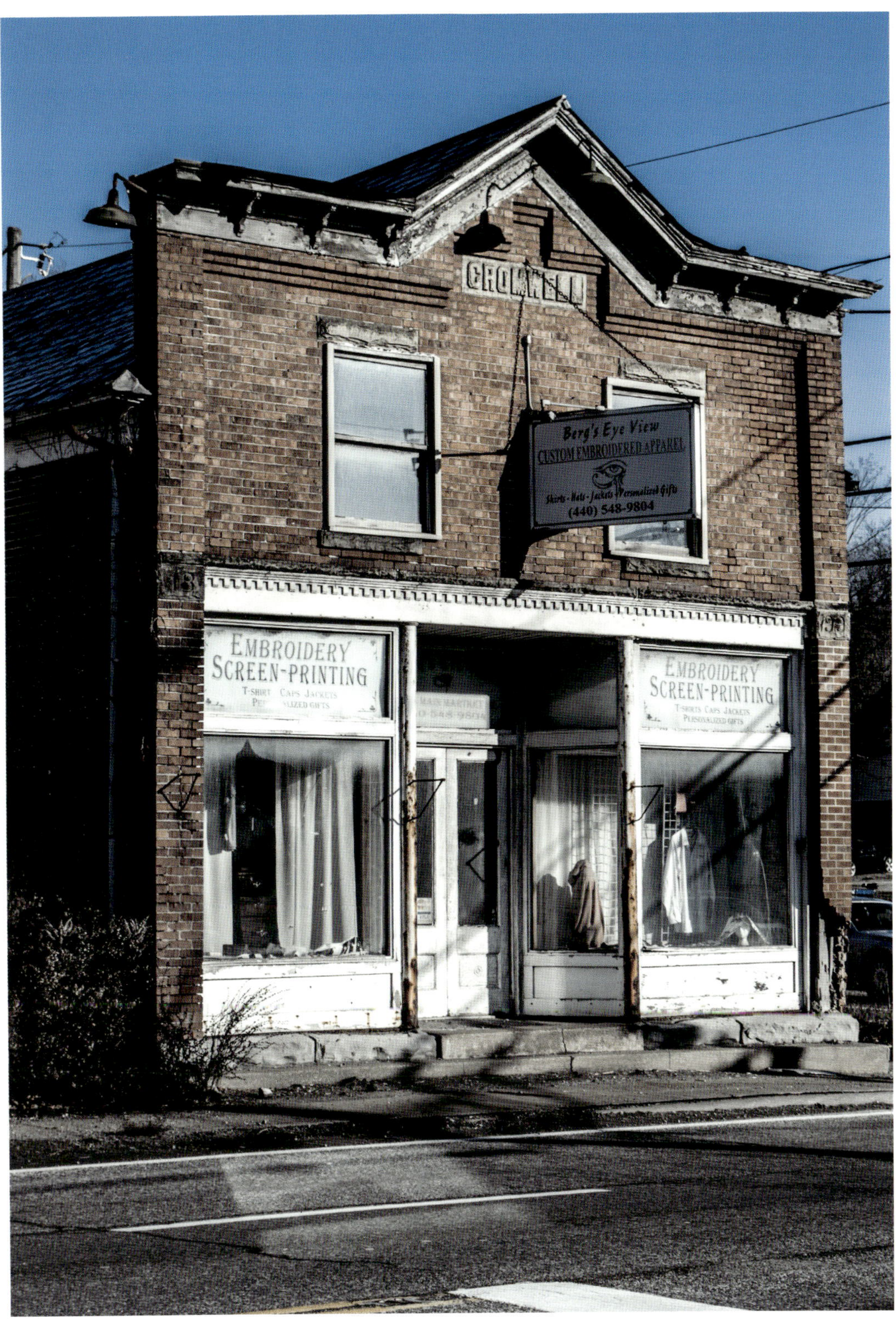

I used to drive past this building a lot, and I always found it charming, in spite of its condition. I finally went and snapped a photo, only a couple of months before it was torn down.

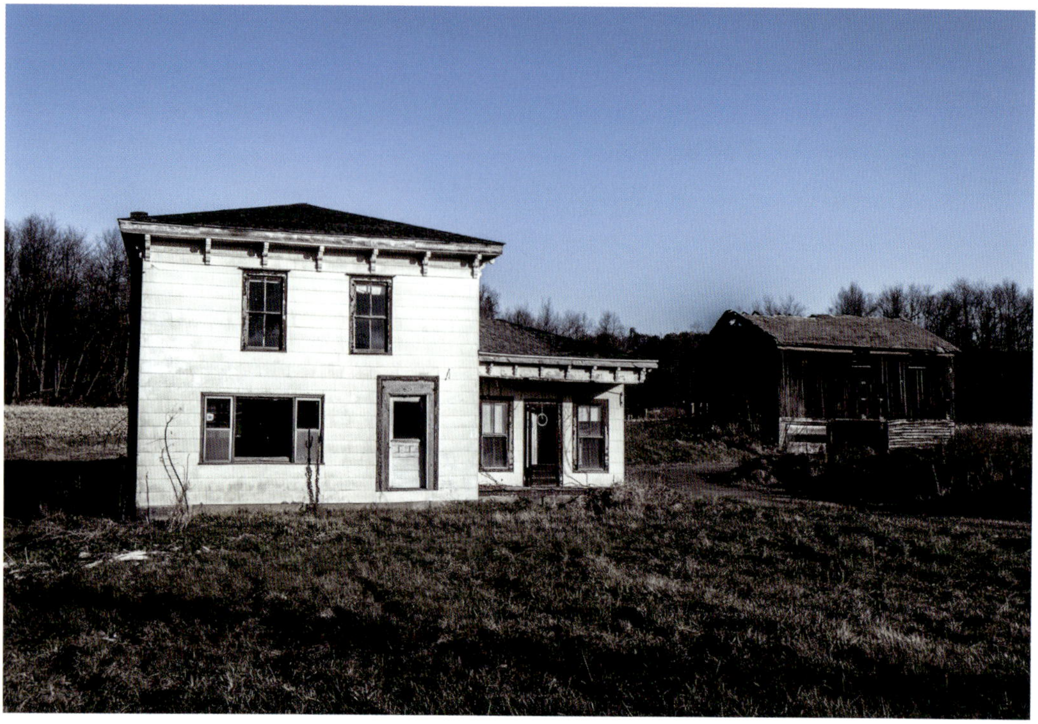

This farmhouse was on the outskirts of a small town, where it was likely one of the oldest buildings in the area. It was reasonably well preserved for being abandoned, too. It's a shame it couldn't be saved.

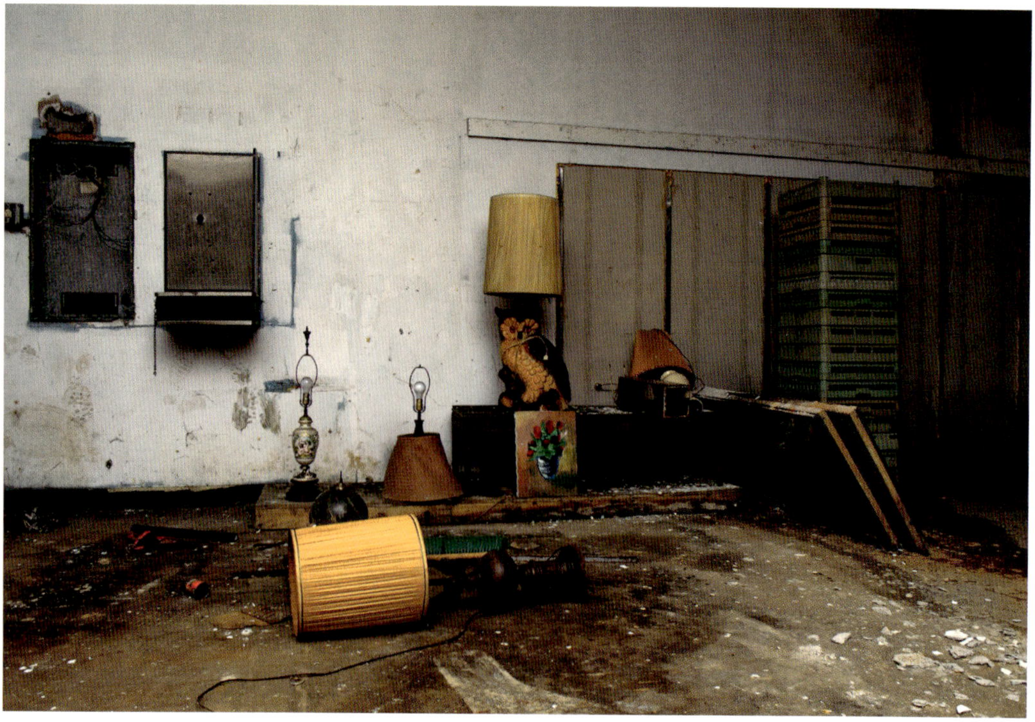

Someone, somewhere, is decorating their house with found items like these. It's probably not a great look.

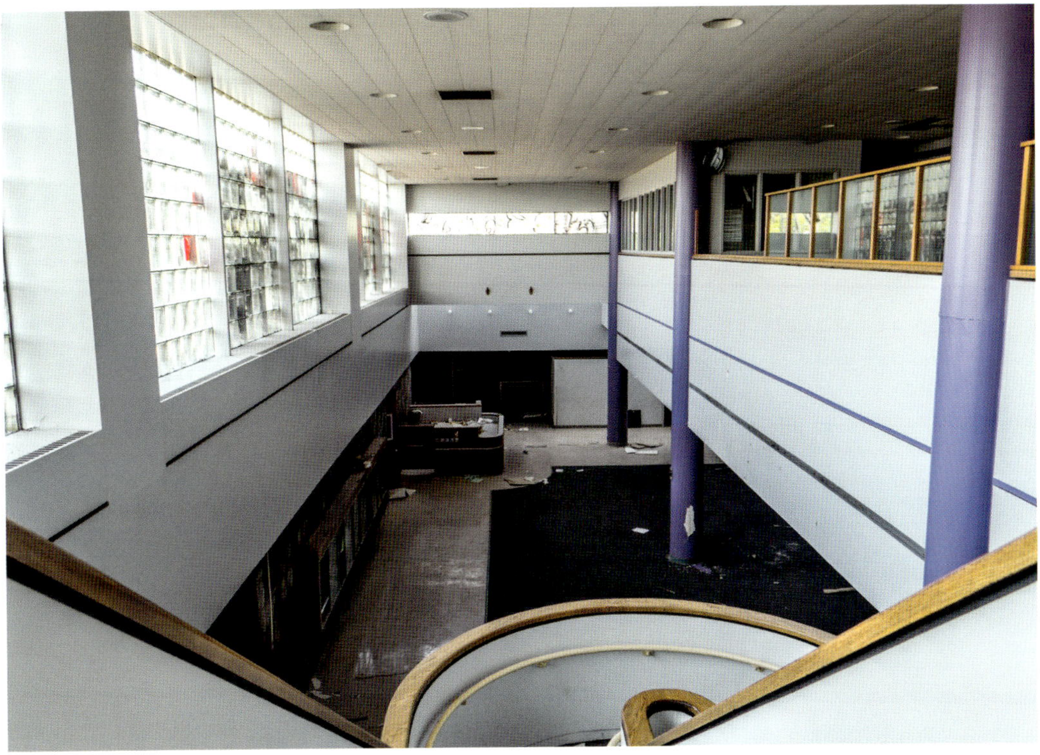

The bright colors and modern architecture of this put me in mind of my elementary school.

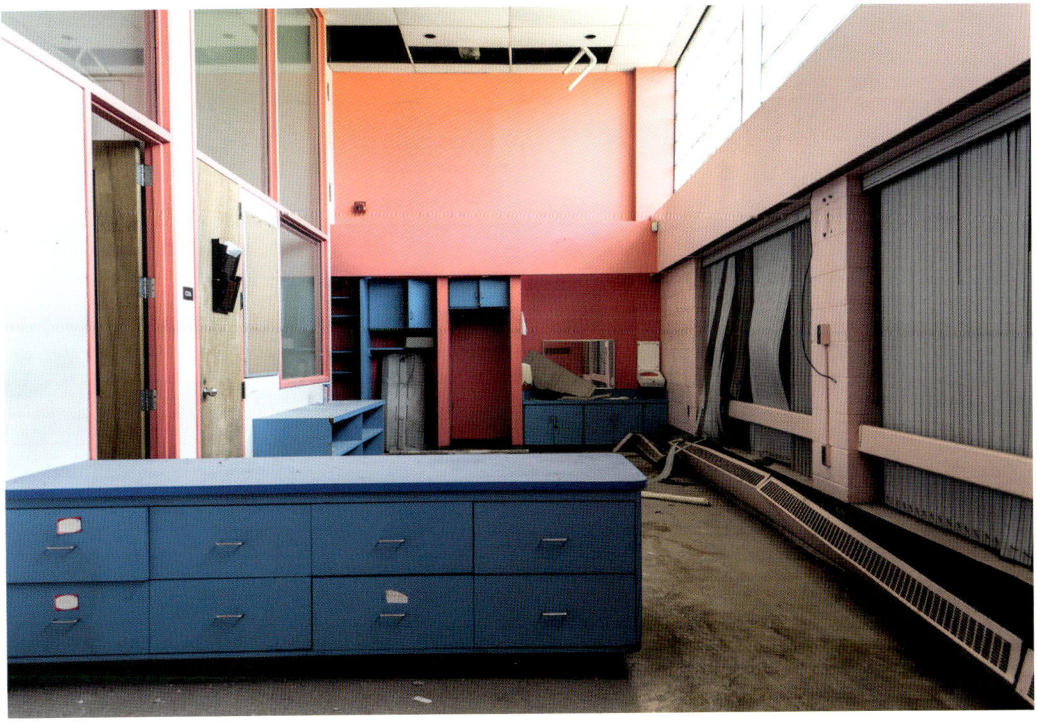

This room was so unrelentingly pink. I had to have a photo of it.

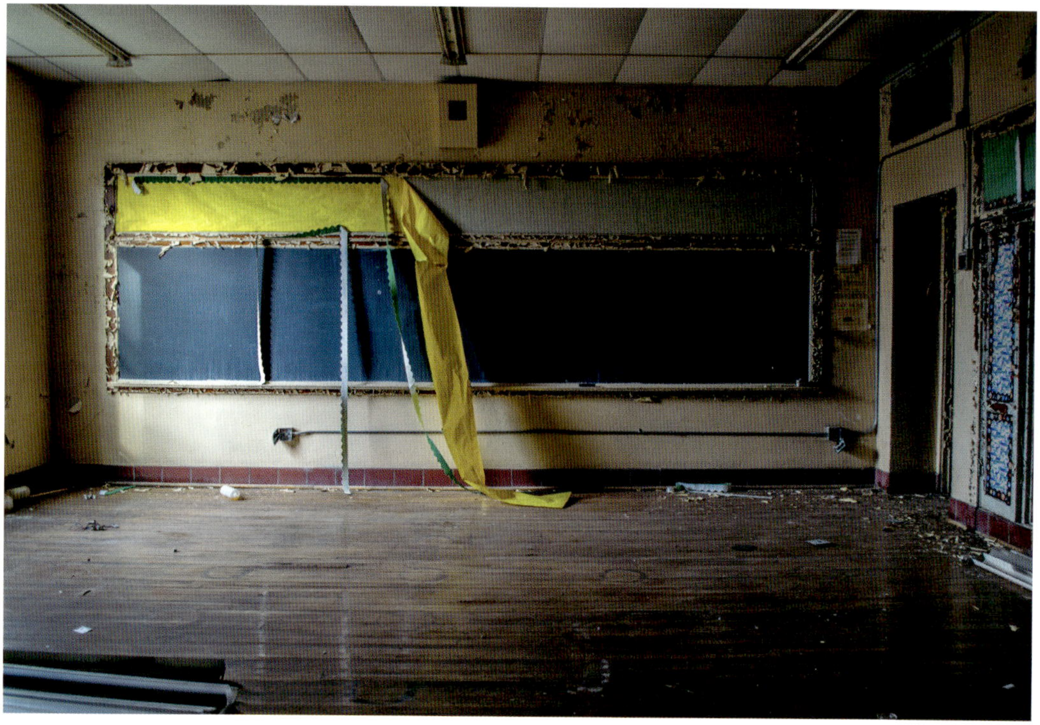

The boards over the windows in this place made it difficult to get decent pictures of most of the classrooms, but some were still in pretty good shape.

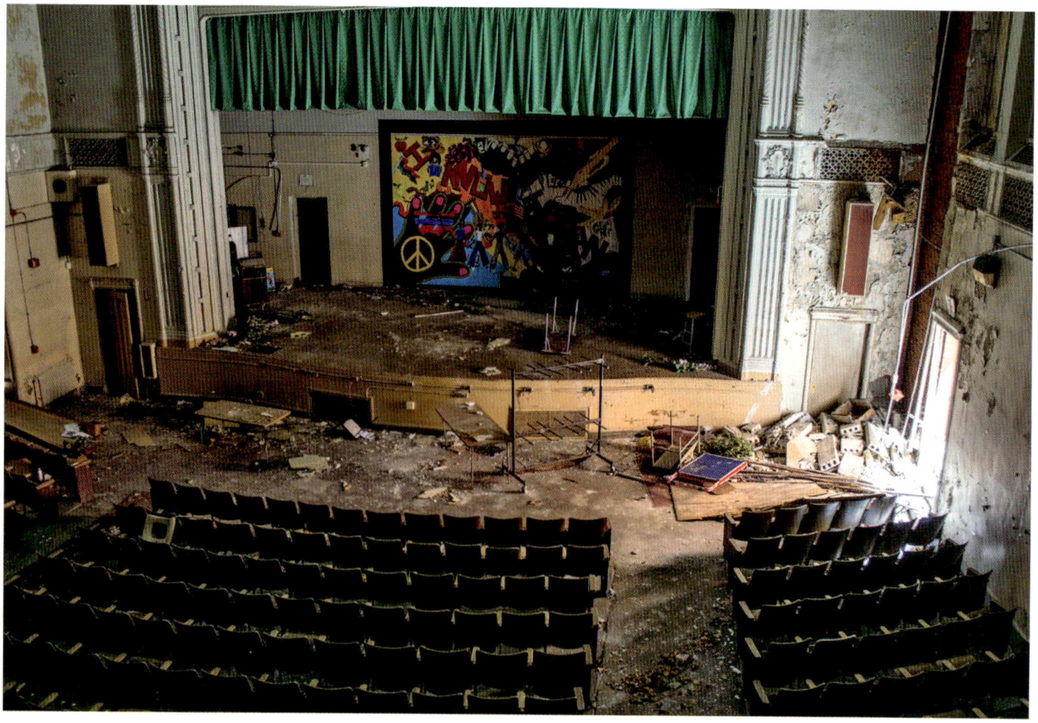

After seeing a huge rat down on the ground floor of this auditorium, I found it a lot more relaxing up in the balcony.

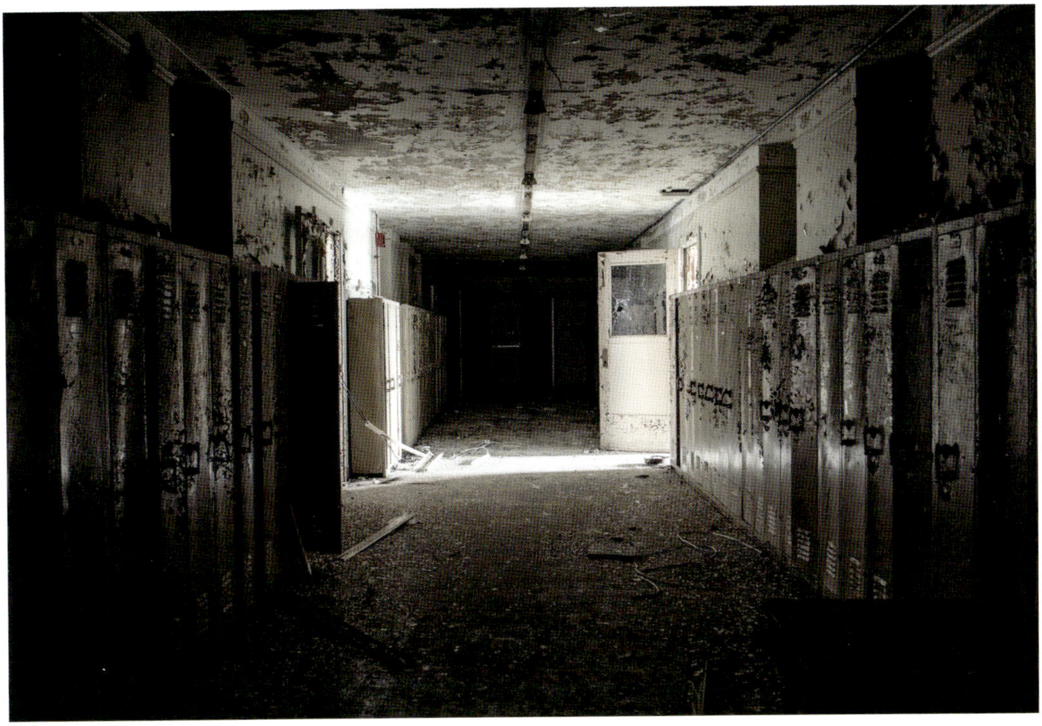

A lot of times, an abandoned building will have so little light in it that it actually becomes disorienting. I only managed to this much light in the photo by a long exposure.

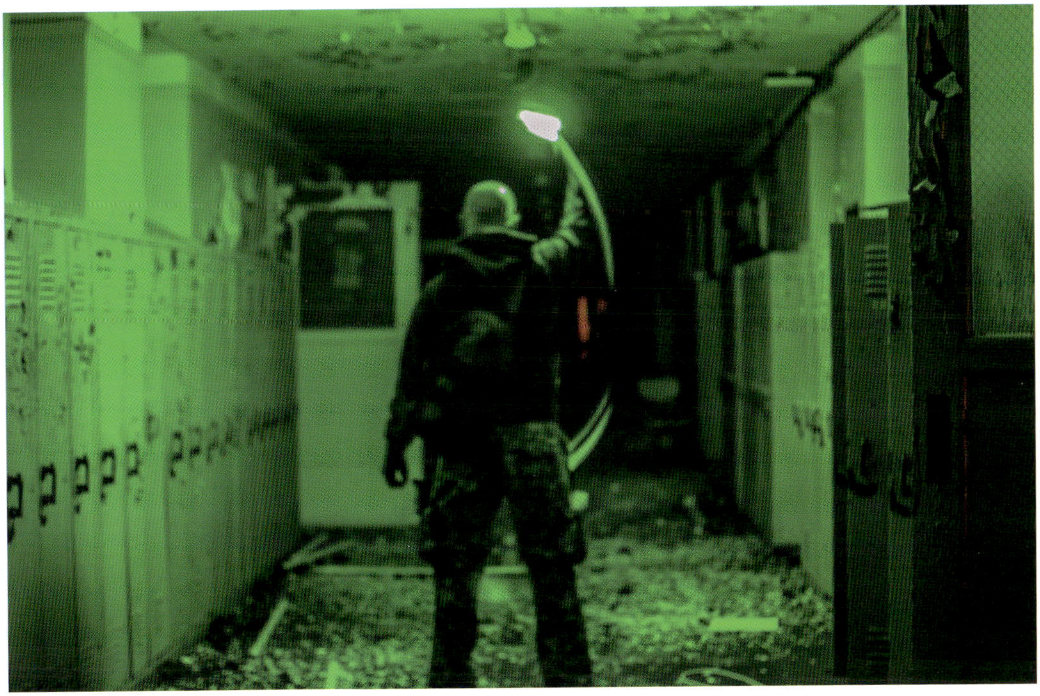

I took this photo of myself using a tripod and a remote. The focus is therefore a bit off, but sometimes you just have to make do with self-portraiture.

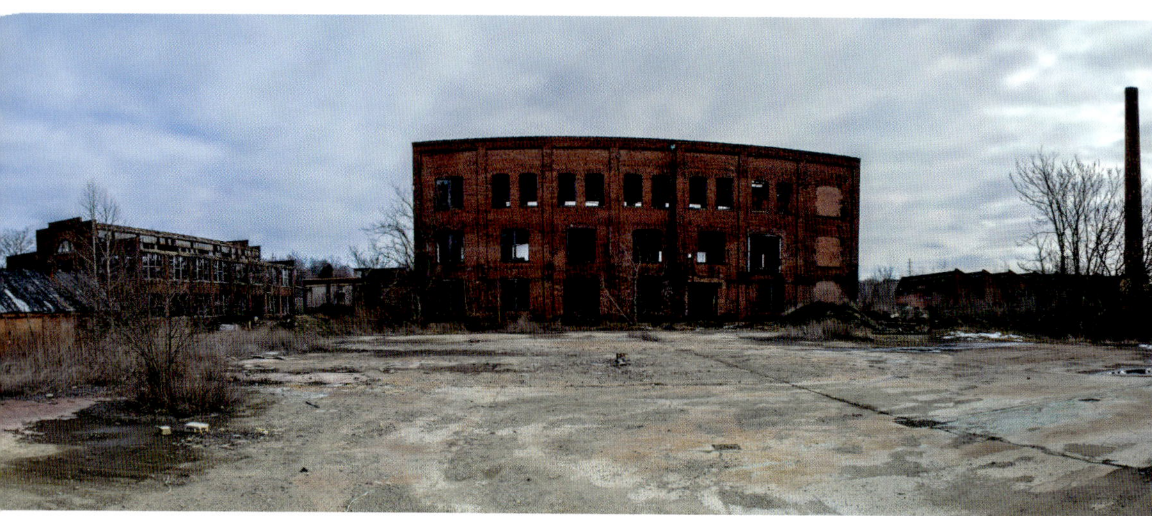

These are, if you can't tell, three separate photos stitched together. This complex was absolutely huge, and individual photos were failing to capture the enormity of it.

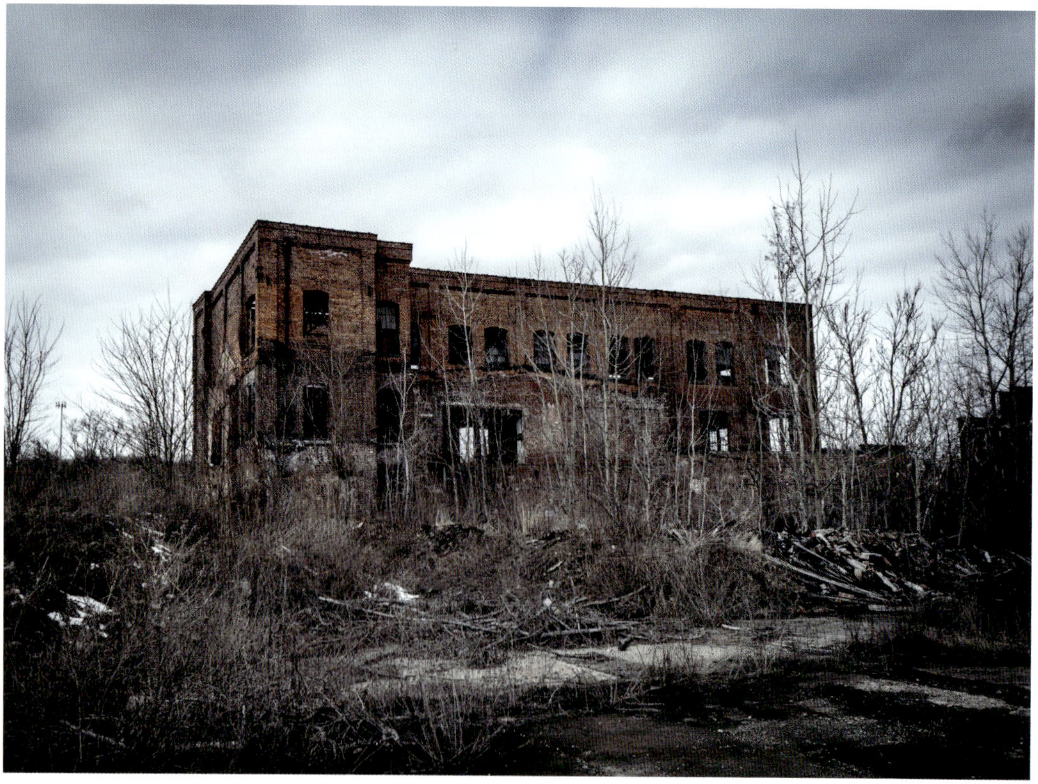

This building was very far gone. Only the ground floor was accessible, and there wasn't a lot to see there.

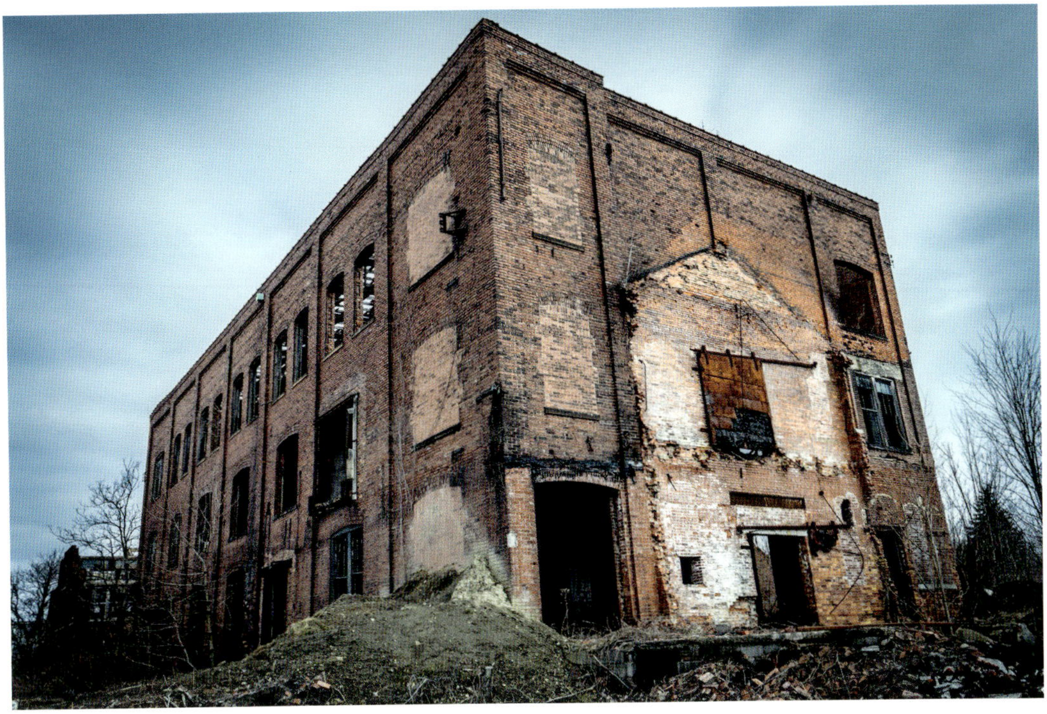

For as big as this place was, there was so much that showed how much bigger it used to be. The remnants of walls, doors to nowhere, and big piles of rubble were everywhere.

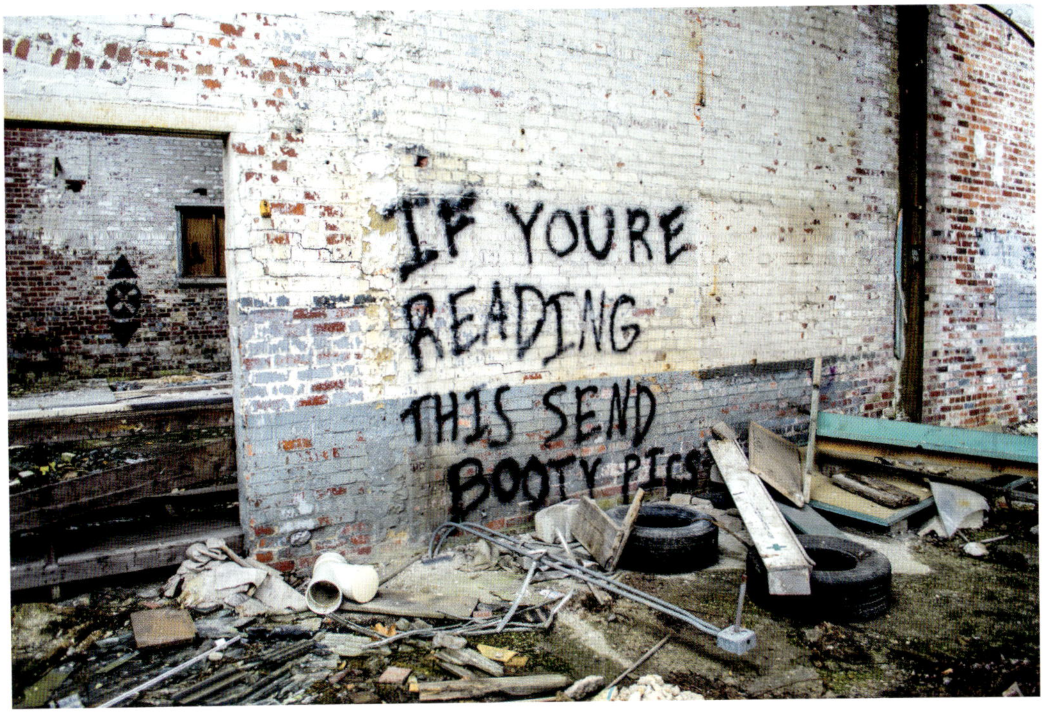

It seems like nearly all of the graffiti you see in abandoned buildings is crude drawings of penises, so this was a refreshing change.

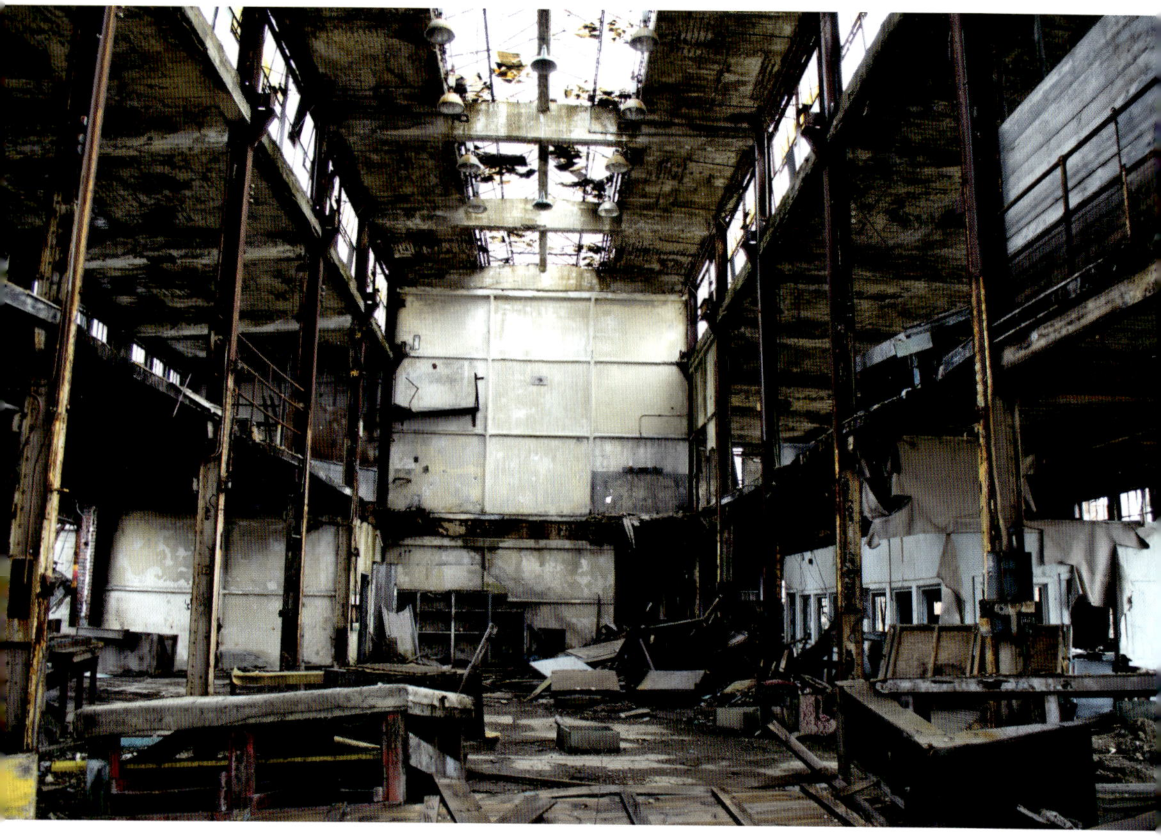

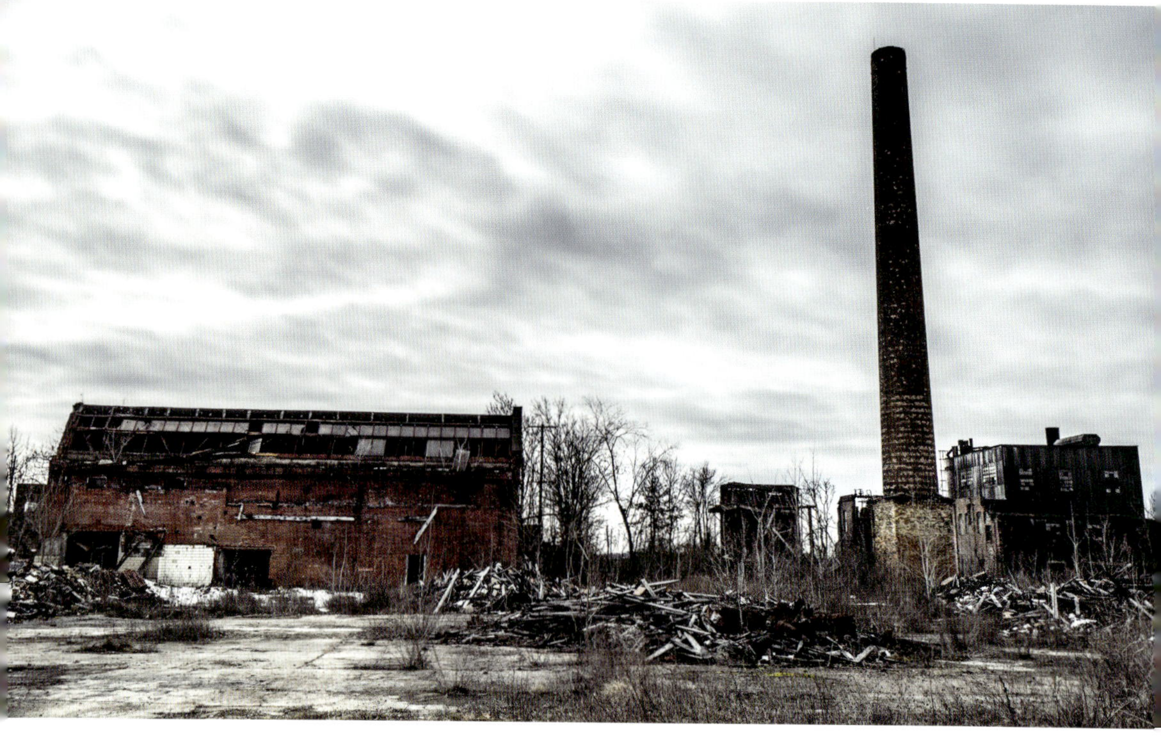

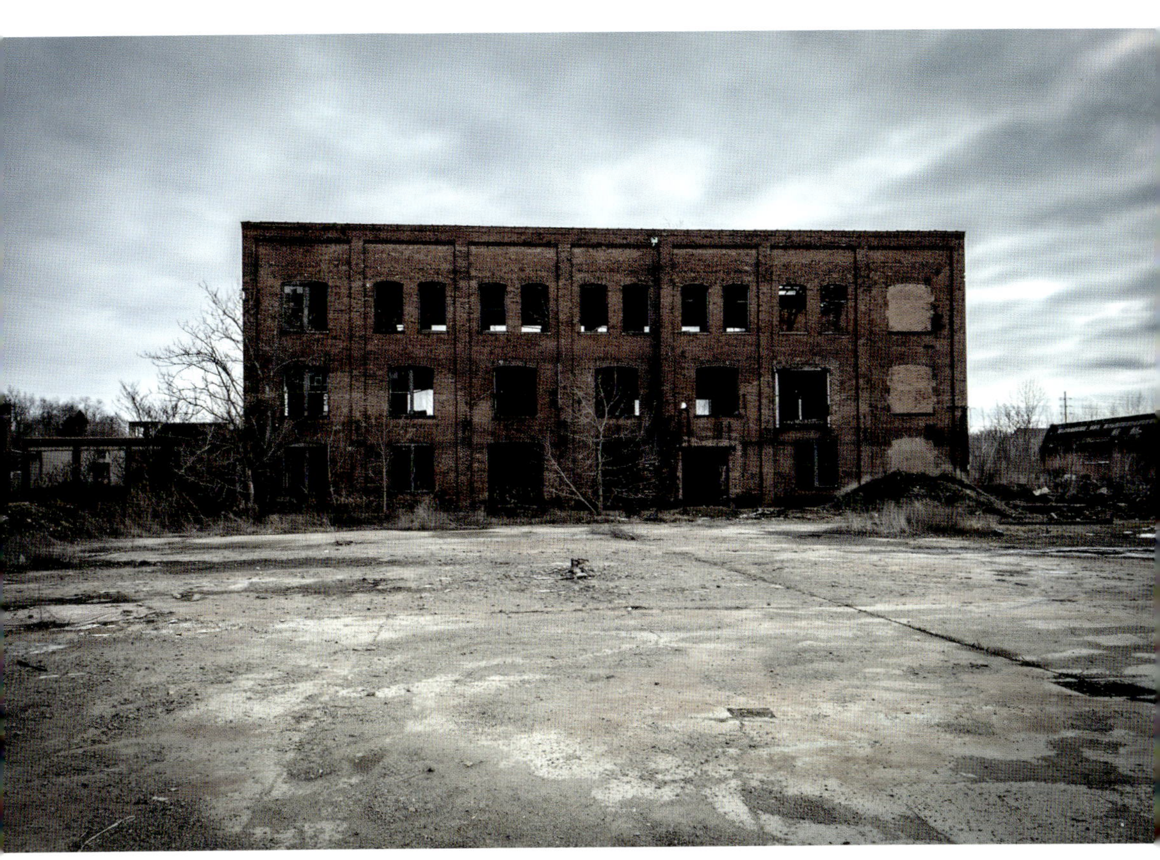

We got lucky with the weather here. The clouds add so much drama.

Opposite above: The most intact building in the complex was still far gone.

Opposite below: There was a basement room connected to the base of the smokestack here that was still intact. But it was open to the elements and the rest of the building around it was gone.

3

MINED GOLD

This chapter features the well-researched spots, ones that required a lot of homework, either to locate or to discover the existence of in the first place. I didn't necessarily do all the homework; it was my exploring partners in several cases, and some of it was quite extensive.

One of these was an office building that closed in 1992 and was something of a time capsule. It was very well preserved, owing in part to the fact that it was so difficult to get in. We had to squeeze through a gap in the fence, scale a wall, and climb through a window. The supply closet was stocked, and there was even a can of instant coffee in the break room. It looked like everyone had just gone home for the day and never came back. But as is sometimes the case with well-preserved places, it didn't even look abandoned, just closed. I took a picture of a typewriter, a rare find and the only photo in the book taken in Pennsylvania. The building has since been demolished.

The photos from the department store might not look like they all come from the same place, but I can assure you that they do. It had been abandoned for some time, and so part of what makes it hard to tell is simply the level of decay. It was an older building, and the water damage on the lower floors was extensive. In fact, the display you see in the photo was pretty close to all that was left that could identify the place as a department store. It was several stories tall, in the fashion of the old-style downtown department stores. Many of the upper floors were offices, and possibly even apartments in a couple of parts. Near the top floor, we found an old computer, and the associated piles of tape reels in the last image. It was a strange and incongruous sort of building, and I wish I'd had a chance to see it before it was so far gone.

The small motel is one of several abandoned in the area. This isn't quite a rural area, but it's also not in the city. It was a little surprising to see what seemed like evidence of someone living there, although they were long gone by the time we stopped by. The room with the open door in the third picture contained what was possibly the worst smell I've ever discovered while exploring an abandoned building—and that's obviously saying something.

Also featured in this chapter is a very small elementary school located not far from the motel. It had about ten classrooms and must have dated back to a time when the community was smaller. I grew up in a populous suburb, so this was an interesting place to walk around and imagine what it must have been like to attend such a tiny school.

We also visited a furniture factory, although very little evidence of that remains today. I don't know how long it's been abandoned, but it has clearly been a long time. We were stopped by the police while exploring here. It was the first and only time that has happened to me. And really, it would be accurate to say we introduced ourselves to the police. They had pulled into the area in front of the building and were looking at our cars, so we figured it would be better for everyone if we didn't make them come in and find us. They just told us to be careful and sent us on our way.

The old engine factory was an interesting building to get into. I had received a tip that you had to park under a bridge, walk along some railroad tracks, and then at a certain point there was a hidden hole in the fence. I'll admit, the treasure hunt aspect made it more fun. The building itself was enormous—possibly the biggest in terms of land area of anywhere I've explored. Parts of it were fairly old as well. There are stories that it's haunted, although some of this might have come from it being used as a haunted house during the Halloween season at one point, which is why the room in the second photo is painted black. Legend says during the Spanish Flu epidemic, people were dying faster than they could be buried. At the time, the building was occupied by an ice company, and the city ended up using the basement to store bodies of flu victims until they could be interred properly. It is even said—although we're sliding further down the plausibility scale here—that the unclaimed bodies were all buried in a mass grave on the property. I can't speak to the historical accuracy of the story, and I don't believe in ghosts, but it certainly was creepy to be there at night. It has since been converted into condos.

Right down the street from the engine factory was another abandoned building. It was a hotel, located conveniently close to the railroad. But it was very far gone, and not even accessible, so I had to be satisfied with an exterior shot. It was torn down shortly after.

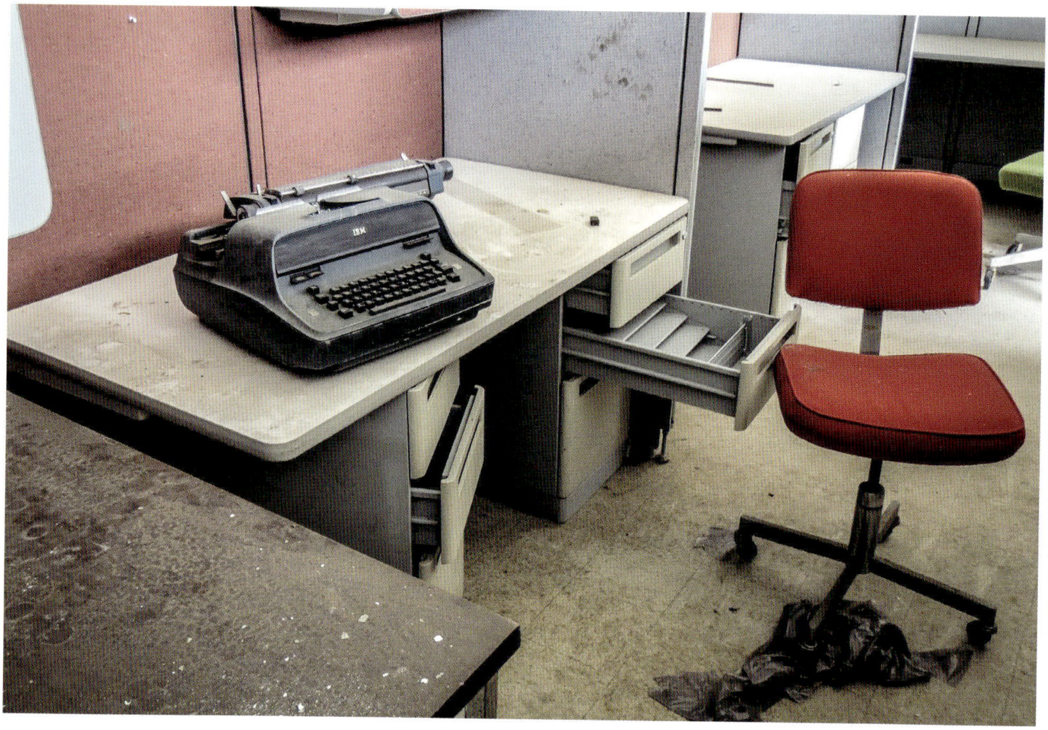

This was one of many typewriters we found here. There were also a couple of computers, which were fairly ancient in computer years. By the time this place closed in 1992, it would have been well behind the times.

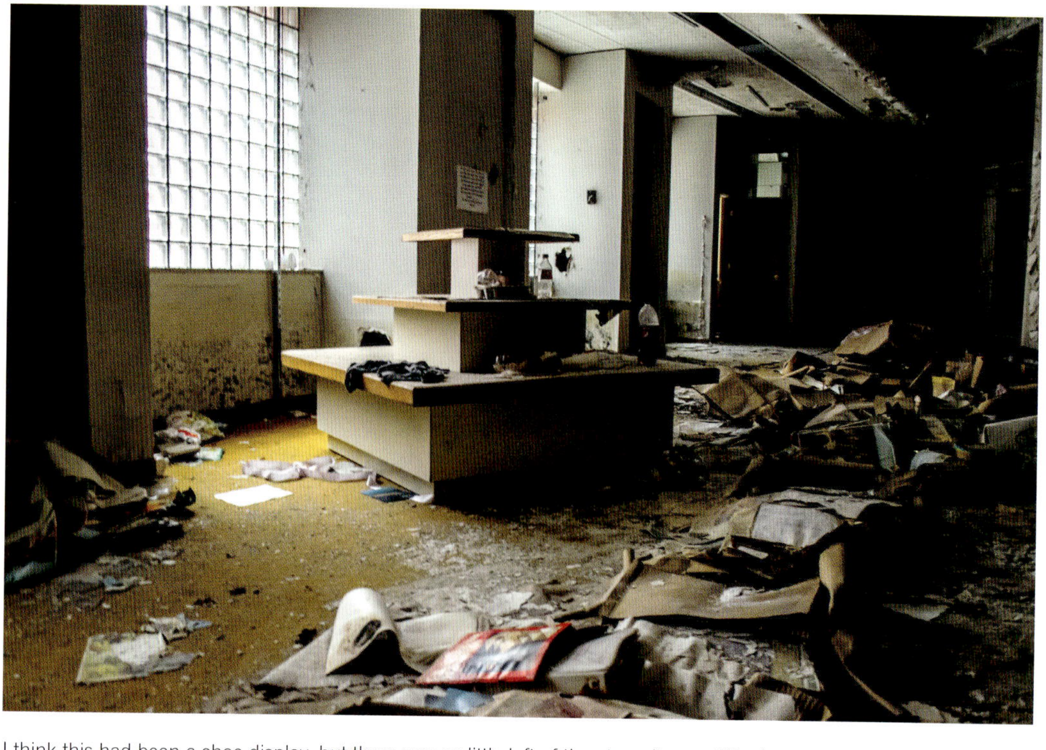

I think this had been a shoe display, but there was so little left of the store, it was difficult to say.

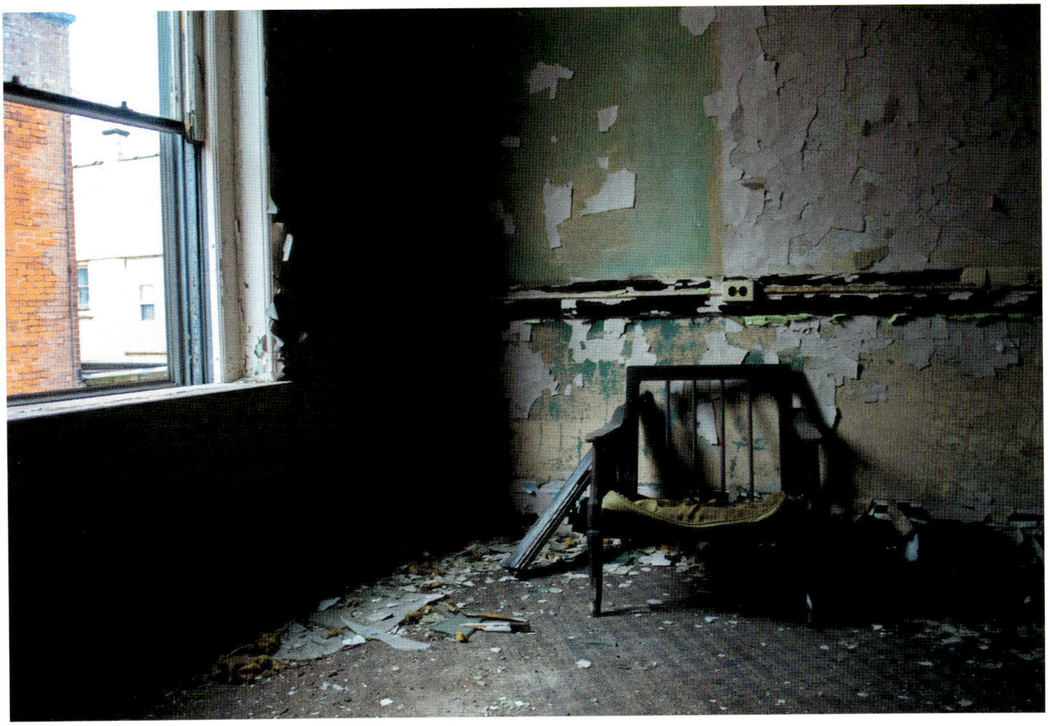

This looked as though maybe people had been living there at some point. The furniture we found suggested it was just offices.

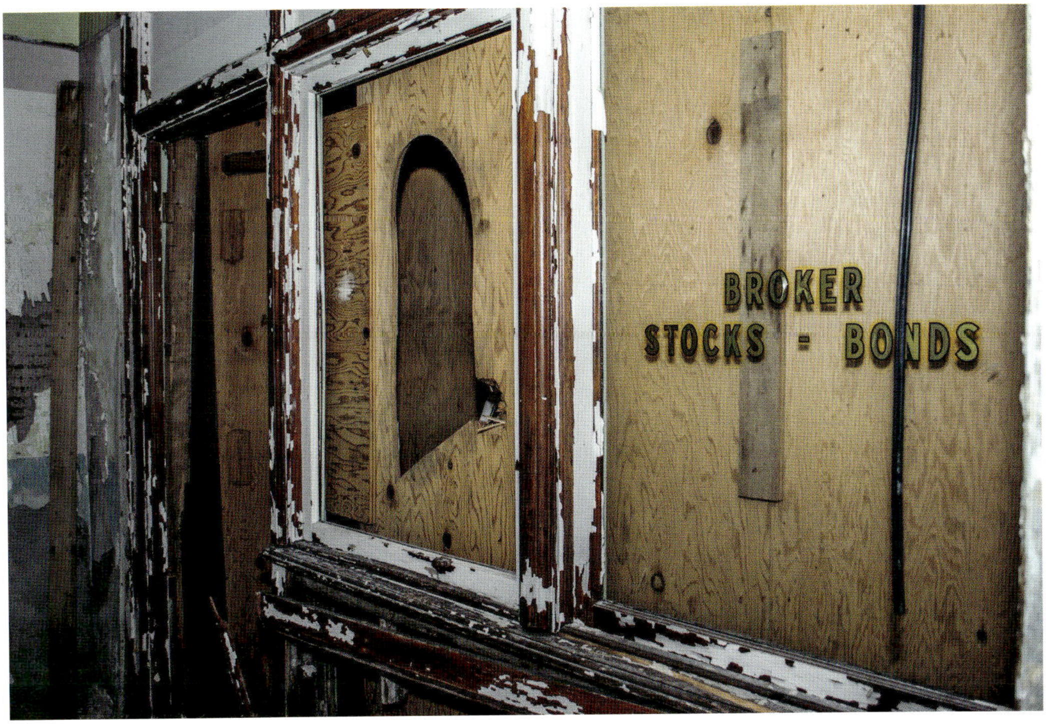

This appears to have been a full-service department store.

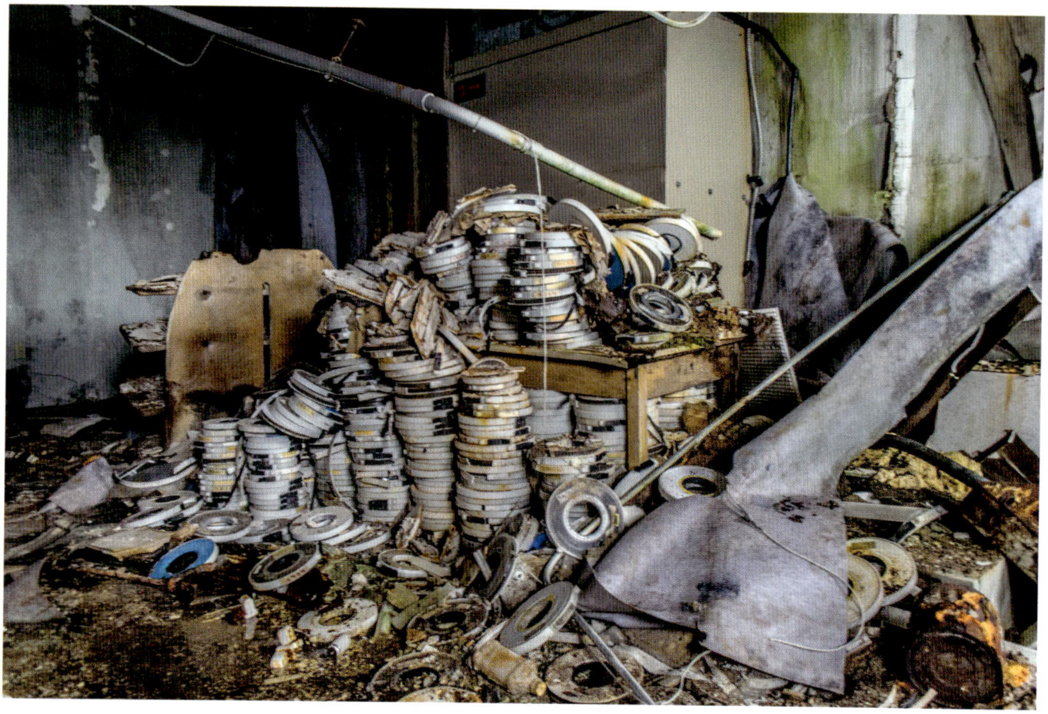

I'm positive that none of the data on any of these reels is even remotely salvageable, but it would have been interesting to see the dates of use.

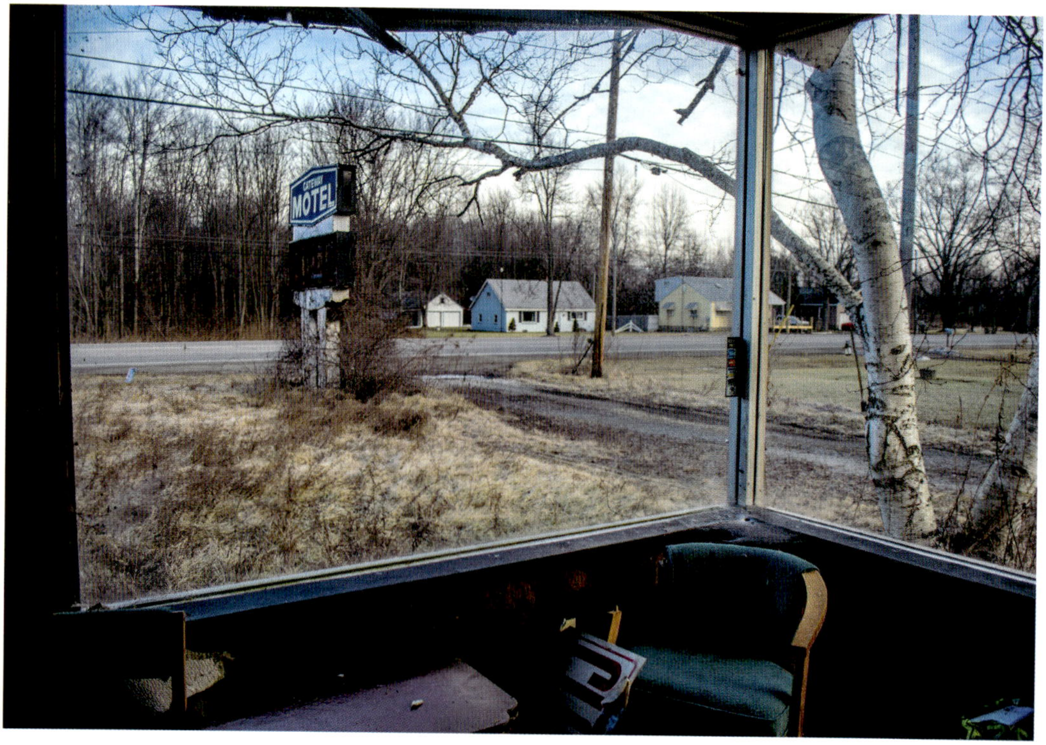

Front office of a small motel. This place probably had a certain charm to it when it was operational.

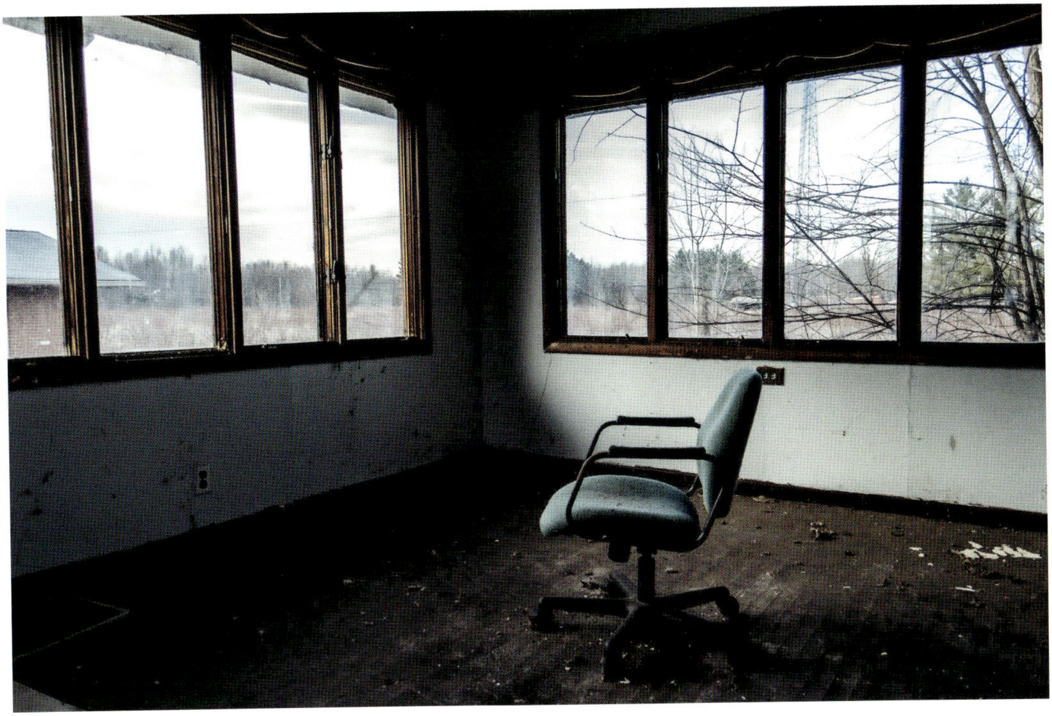

The motel office was connected to a small residence, also abandoned, and this was the back room. It was probably a serene place to sit at one time.

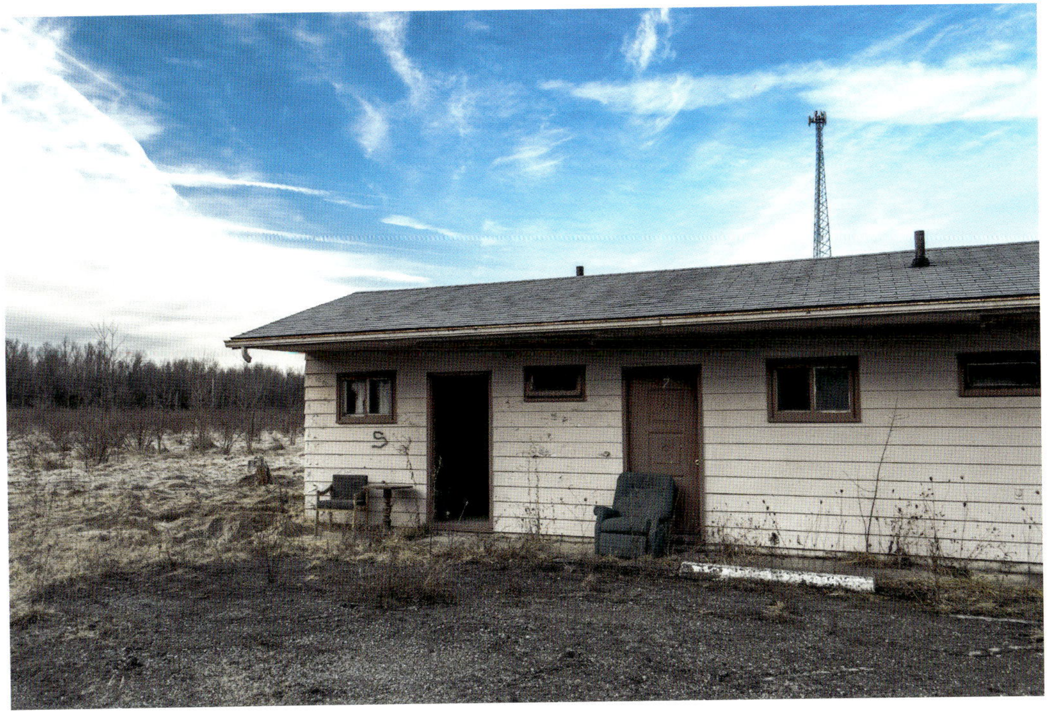

The rooms here were standard cheap motel fare. They were in much worse shape than it looked like they would be from the outside.

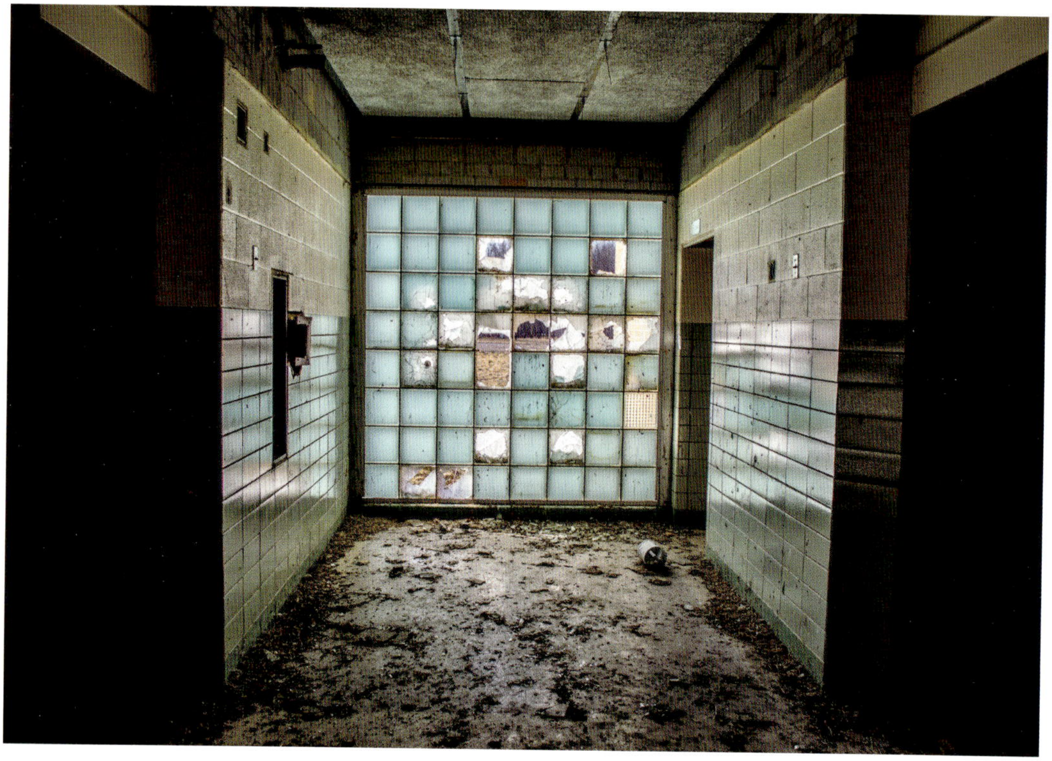

I think this might have been the only set of student bathrooms in the whole school.

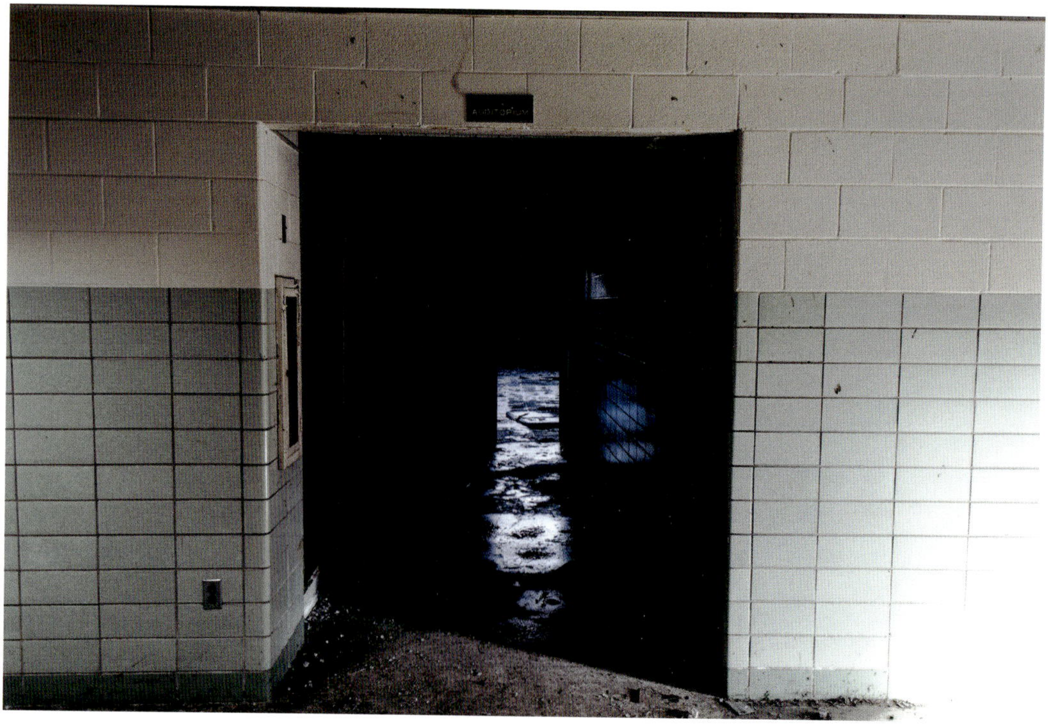

The auditorium in this school was also the gym and was only about 1.5 times the size of the classrooms.

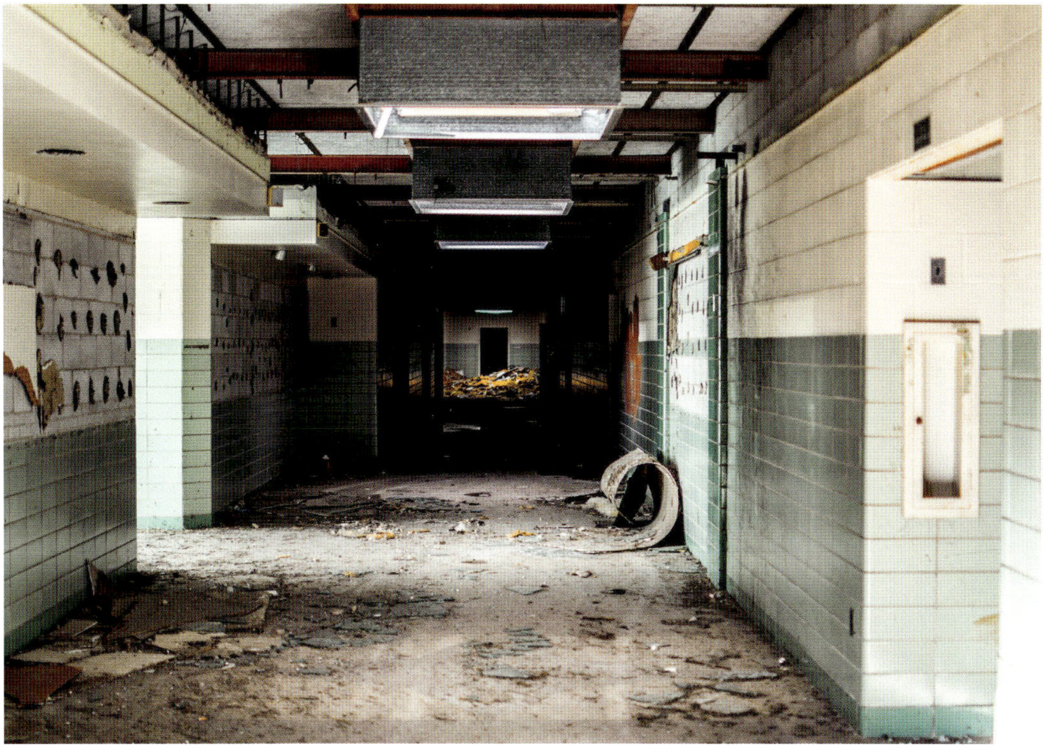

This was a difficult place to photograph in many spots. Everything was either blindingly bright or pitch black.

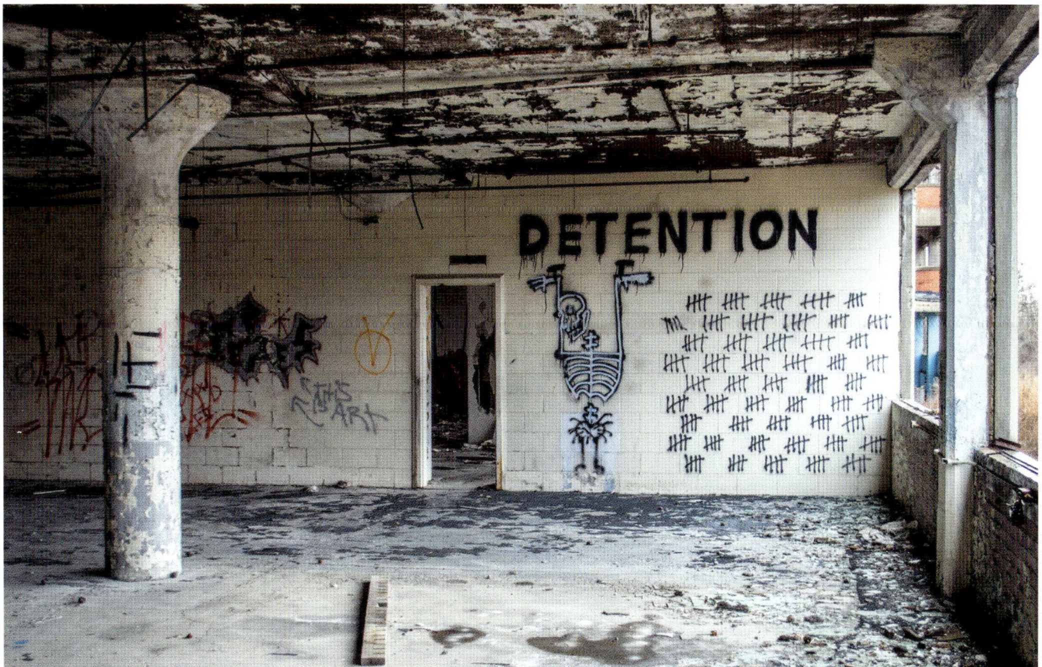

This place was full of graffiti, but for some reason, this was the only piece I felt compelled to photograph.

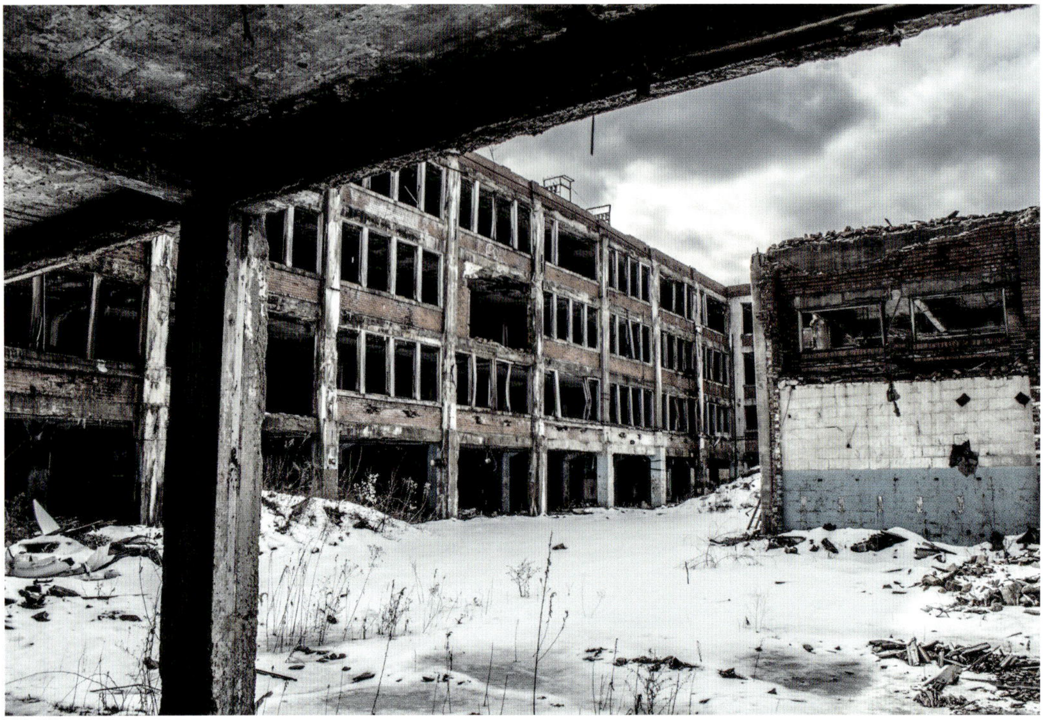

It is probably not going to come as a huge surprise that the basement of this place was completely inaccessible due to flooding.

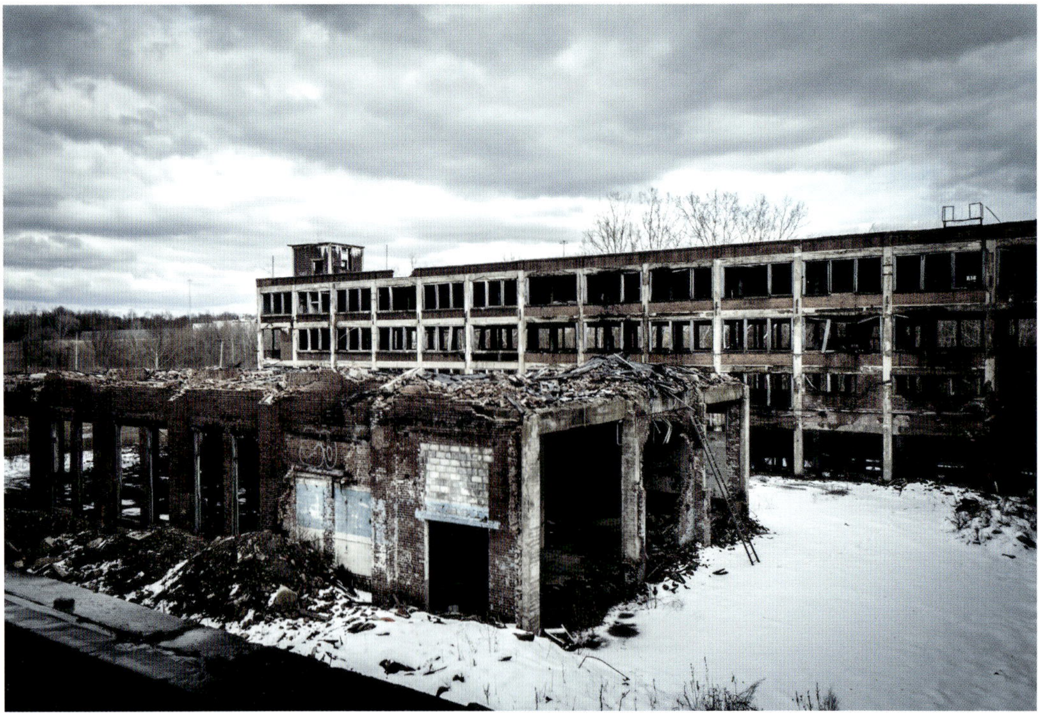

Pretty high on my list of "ways to be safe while exploring": Do not even attempt to climb that ladder.

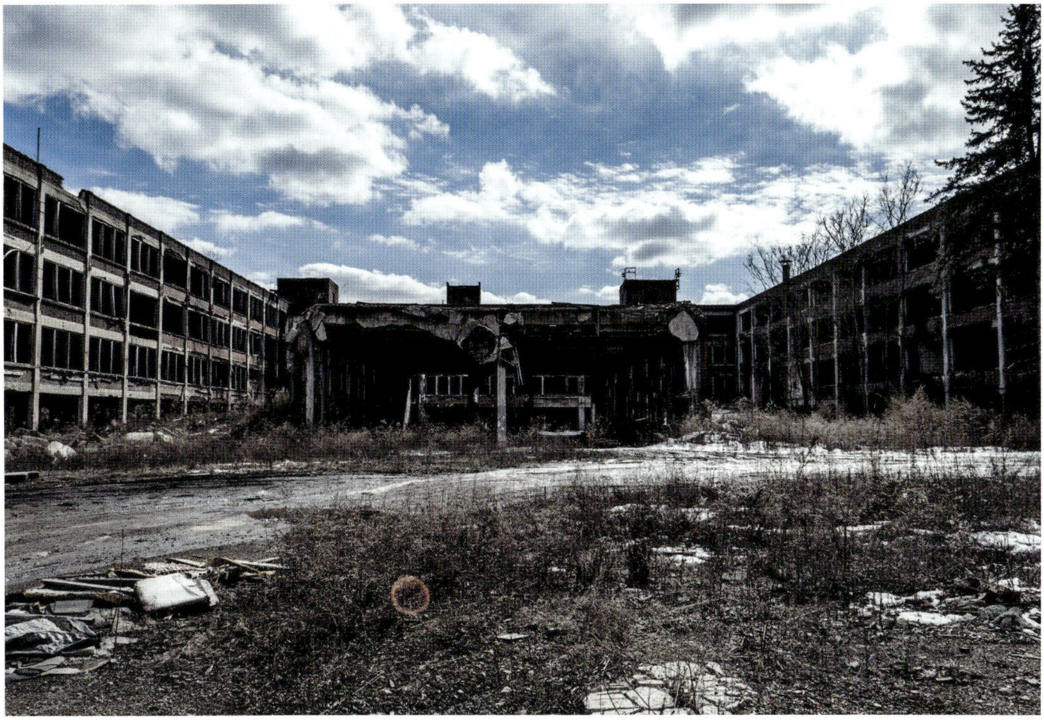

This was one of a couple of spots in the area of Youngstown that was just so far gone that it was barely more than a shell of a building.

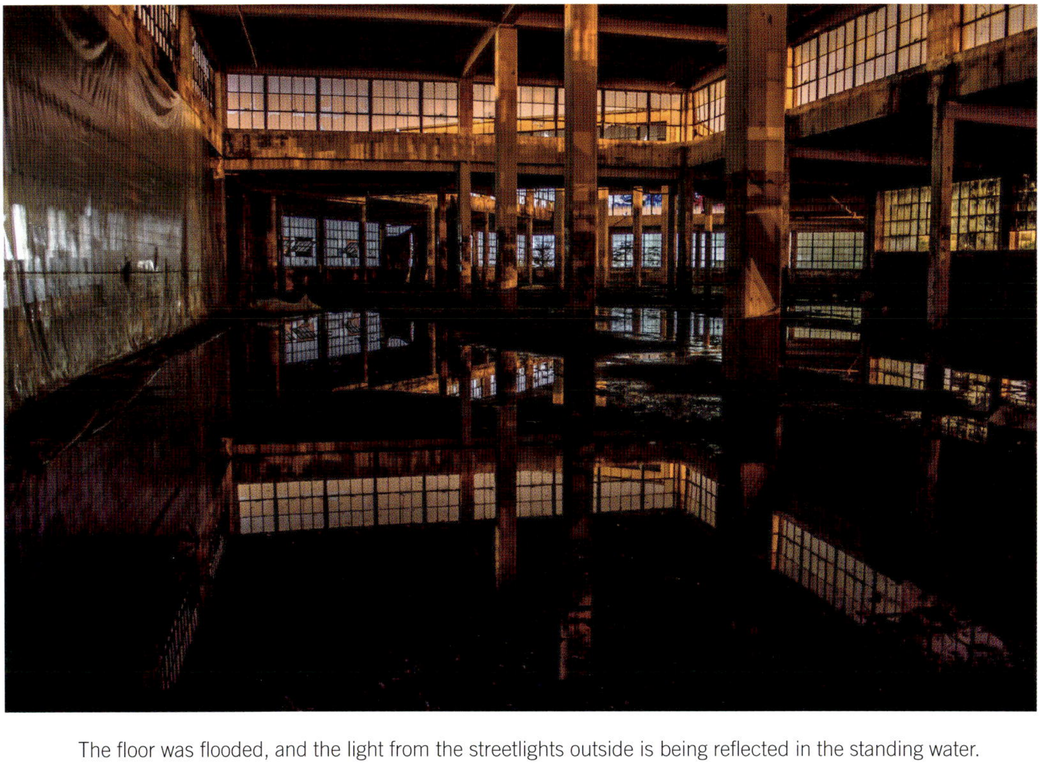

The floor was flooded, and the light from the streetlights outside is being reflected in the standing water.

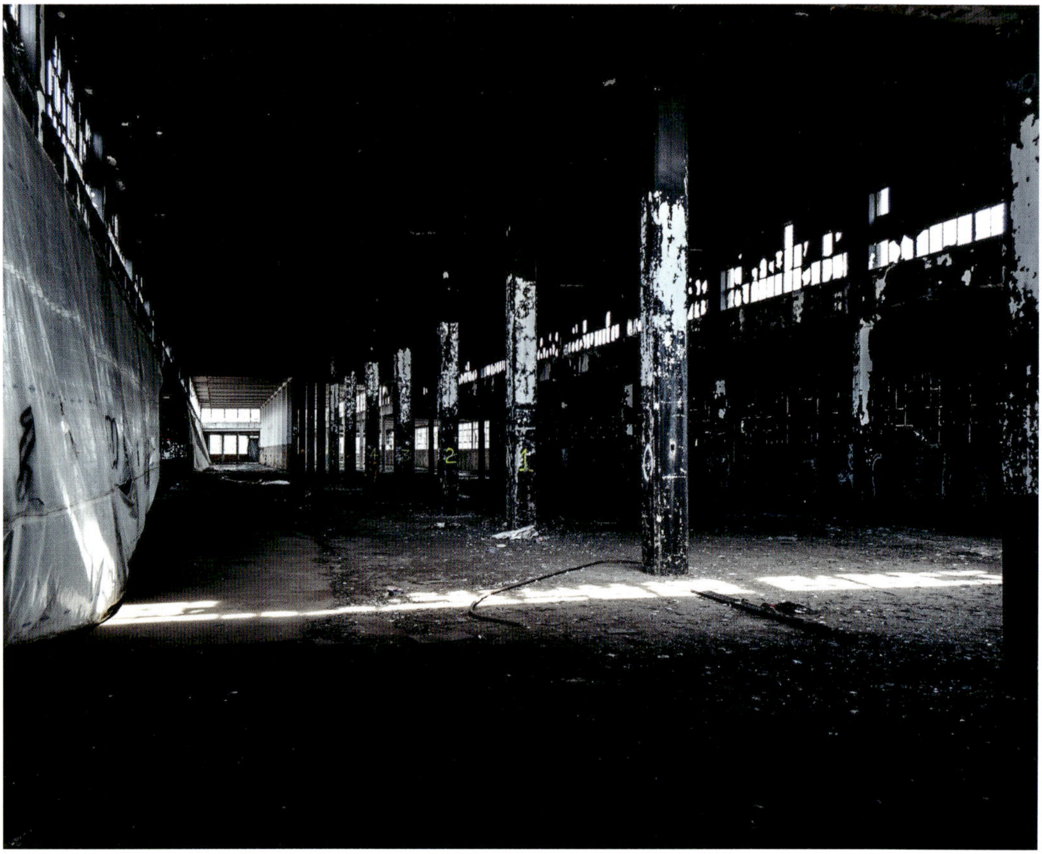

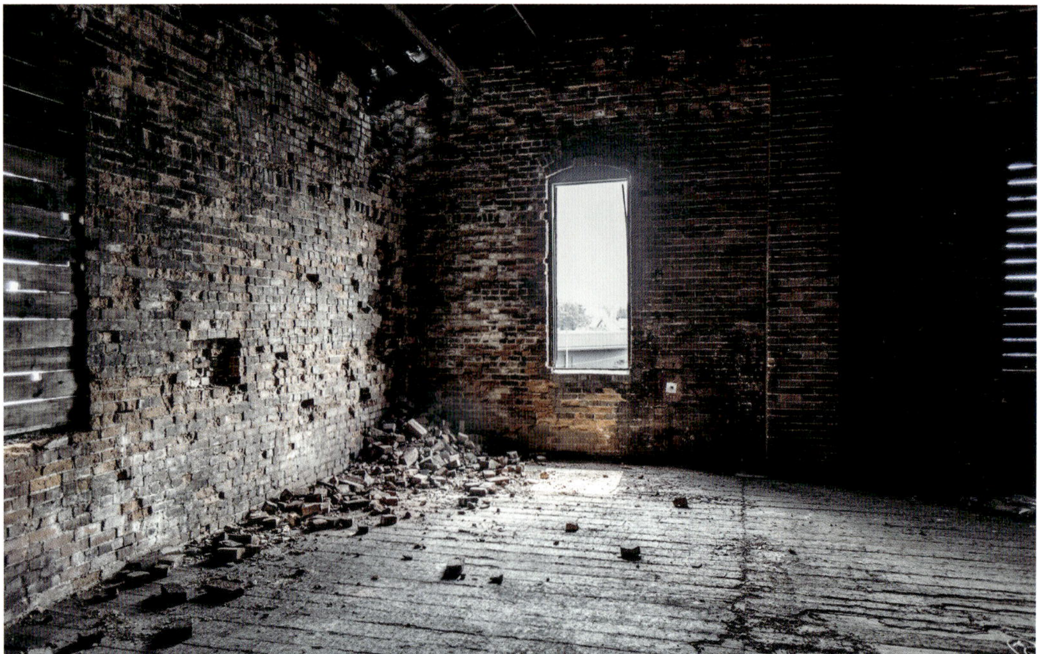

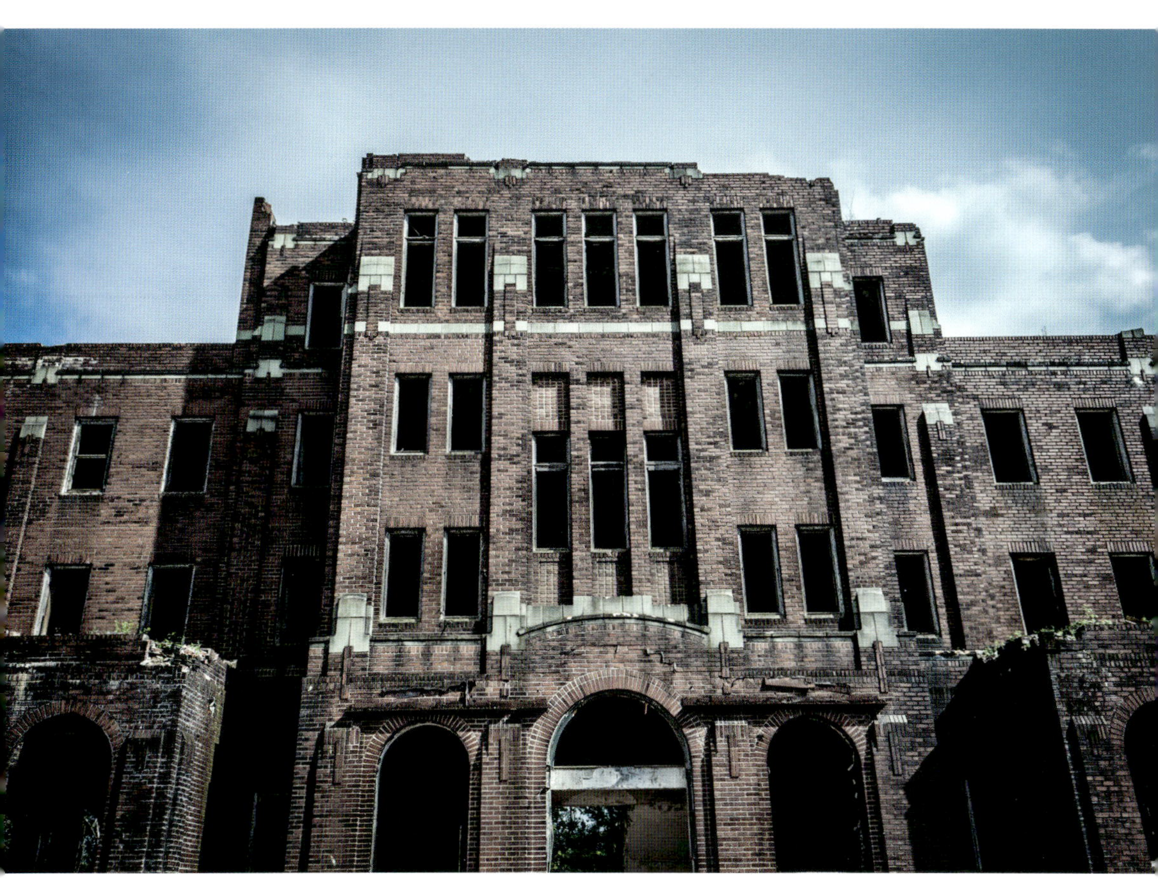

I took this picture at this specific angle to crop out the fencing around the building. But I ended up liking the building against the sky more than I think I would have if I had taken it straight on.

Opposite above: We didn't know about the haunted house our first time visiting this building and could not fathom why it was painted black.

Opposite below: I don't know how much of this older part of the complex survived the conversion to condos, but I hope they salvaged as much as possible. It had real character.

4

FAMOUS DERELICTS

The locations in this chapter are all well-known locations around Cleveland, although several aren't around anymore. They're places local explorers know by name.

The pictures from the YMCA are clearly from a YMCA. For all of the graffiti, the building wasn't in terrible shape when we went. But from what I heard from other explorers, the condition declined rapidly shortly thereafter, and it was torn down just a few years after this photo was taken. The dates that we found on commemorative plaques inside dated back to the early sixties, and from the looks of it, that's probably when it was built. People often ask me how I get into these places, so I included the last picture to illustrate just how easy it can be sometimes.

The photos from the Masonic Hall, abandoned since the early nineties, might not be quite as obvious as the Y, but they're still definitely a Masonic Hall. It must have been quite a place once, but Cleveland weather has done a real number on it. The second photo, a long exposure taken with a tripod, was taken at dusk. While the shutter was open, an exploring buddy walked in front of my camera with a flashlight. I considered taking another shot, but I liked the ghostly figure in front of the big broken windows, and I decided to keep it the way it is. There is a story behind the rubber ducks, although even I can't totally explain it. There was once an abandoned warehouse in Cleveland's Little Italy neighborhood that was absolutely covered in rubber ducks. Thousands of them, all over the place. That warehouse burned down a few years ago, but somehow several dozen of these ducks made their way to the Masonic Hall. It made me happy to see that some survived.

The factory is notoriously difficult to get into, and I was thwarted several times before finally making it in. Sometimes that means you're going to find the place well preserved, with a ton of stuff sitting around from whatever the building was used for before it was boarded up. Not this time though. There was a noticeable lack of graffiti for a place that had been abandoned for so long, but it was otherwise almost entirely empty. The pinball machines were the only interesting things we found, but the sheer size of the place was something to behold. It was pouring rain on the day we finally got in, and I had to change as soon as I got home.

There are a couple of big blocks of abandoned apartments, which are actually in entirely different parts of the city. But both are in areas that have seen big declines in population over the past several decades. This is especially true of the area in the first picture, which shows only a small part of an area where three blocks of apartment buildings, totaling dozens of buildings in all, are entirely abandoned. It is a genuinely eerie place to be, looking like the set from a post-apocalyptic movie.

Possibly the weirdest photos here are from a warehouse that had belonged to a company that sold decorations of all different kinds. It had been abandoned for a long enough time that we found a few boxes that were marked "made in West Germany." It was kind of amusing seeing all these festive decorations in a gloomy abandoned warehouse, and someone who had been there before us had really gone all out with the Christmas decorations. A small part of the front of the building had caught fire a couple of times, which really added to the ambiance of the super creepy clown photo.

The hotel had been abandoned since 1993, according to the phone books we found there. It had once been quite a place, ten stories, with a seriously nice penthouse on the top floor. It was built next to what had been the biggest mall in America at the time, although that title didn't last long. The hotel, and the area around it, began a long and slow decline over the next couple of decades, and the hotel was pretty run down by the time it closed. The owners had tried to sell off some of the furnishings before boarding the place up, but as you can tell from the room full of lamps and the artwork in the lobby, a lot was still left. Almost everything was well stripped, except the one room in the second to last photo. Tucked way off in a corner of the top floor, this is the only real hint you get of what the place had looked like. The photo of the lobby was taken on a later visit at night. The light is coming entirely from the streetlights outside. The hotel was recently razed, and a huge Amazon distribution center sits where the mall used to be.

The decrepit factory had manufactured Geiger counters, and other radiation monitoring equipment. The company is still in business, but this facility hasn't been used for decades. This was another day spent exploring in the pouring rain, and the pictures don't do it justice. A section of the roof had collapsed, and trees were starting to grow out of the rubble. It's always interesting to see something living and thriving in these places that have been abandoned by humans.

I still sometimes fret over what might have happened to the stained glass in this church since I was last there. This was just a small neighborhood church that had been largely undisturbed when I went the first time. There was no graffiti, and nothing appeared to be intentionally broken. Everything was still there, too—all of the bibles, hymnals, and everything in the pastor's office. It was a rewarding find, and I hope it doesn't get trashed too quickly.

The building with the green tint had just been bought by a local brewery and was going to be converted for their use. We received permission from the crew that was moving their equipment in to come in and take a few pictures while it still looked abandoned. It was a standard looking industrial space, but the green plastic that had been nailed up over the windows gave the whole place a very weird look. I haven't altered the color of these photos in any way—it really was that green.

There is also a bigger church here, which I understand might be slightly confusing, but they don't look very similar. Attached to the big church is also a school, which was run by the church. It was interesting to see how much further gone the school was than the church. I expect that the school must have closed quite a while before the church finally threw in the towel as well. The church was an interesting place, with some great artwork on the ceiling. I loved the skylights in the school most of all.

The photo of the office was from a factory. By the time I got around to exploring this place, I had gotten pretty used to big, empty, industrial buildings. The offices set this one apart. They were in far better condition than I was used to seeing. The corner office was huge, much bigger than any that I can recall seeing in any of the other buildings I've been in. It was an oddly tranquil place to be, a unique feature of abandoned buildings. Something about the quiet and the lack of clutter can sometimes make you stop and soak it in.

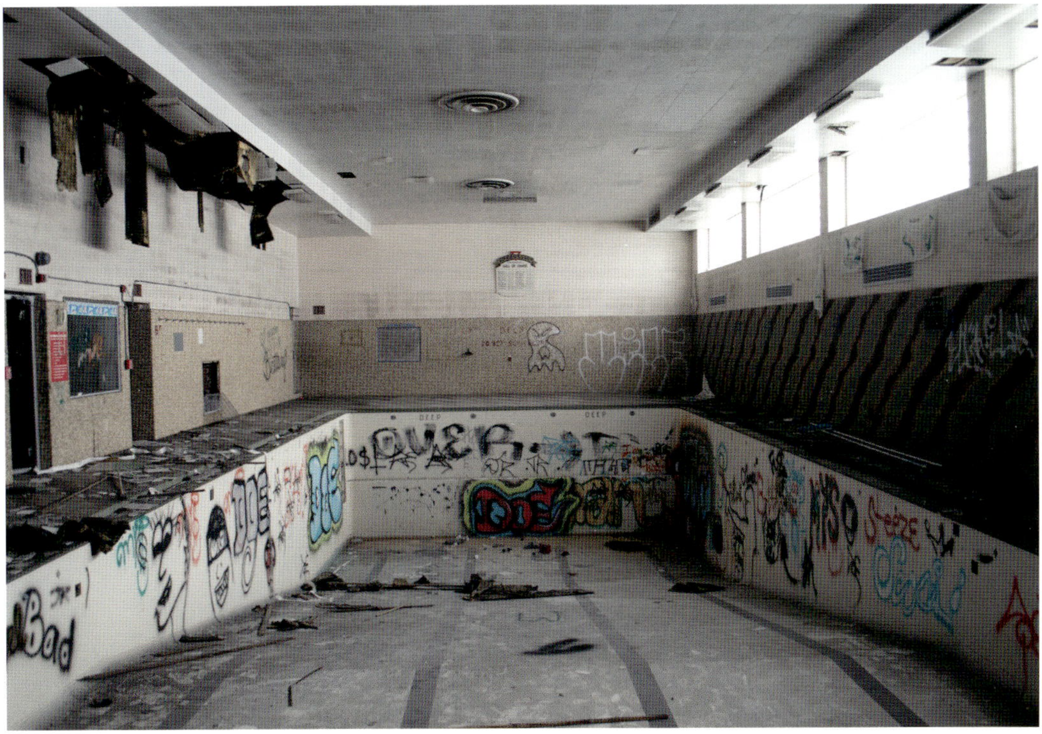

On the far wall is a "Swimmer's Hall of Fame" sign with a list of names. All of them are from the 60s and 70s. I guess they ran out of space and just gave up on the whole idea rather than get a second sign.

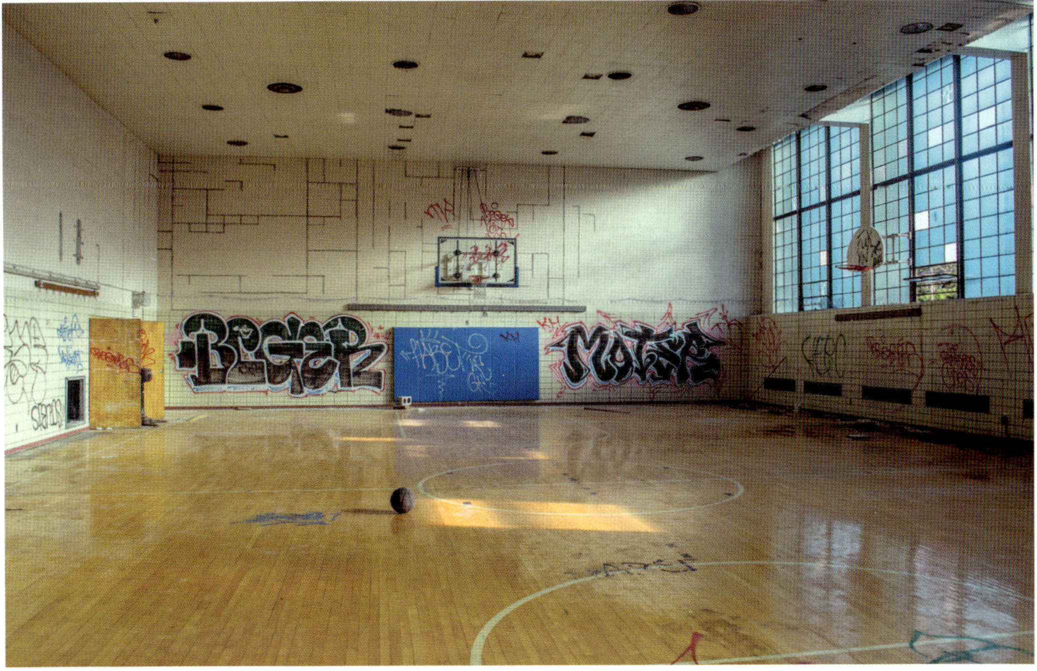

The gym itself was in decent enough shape, you could have still played basketball there. Although all the basketballs we found were really low on air.

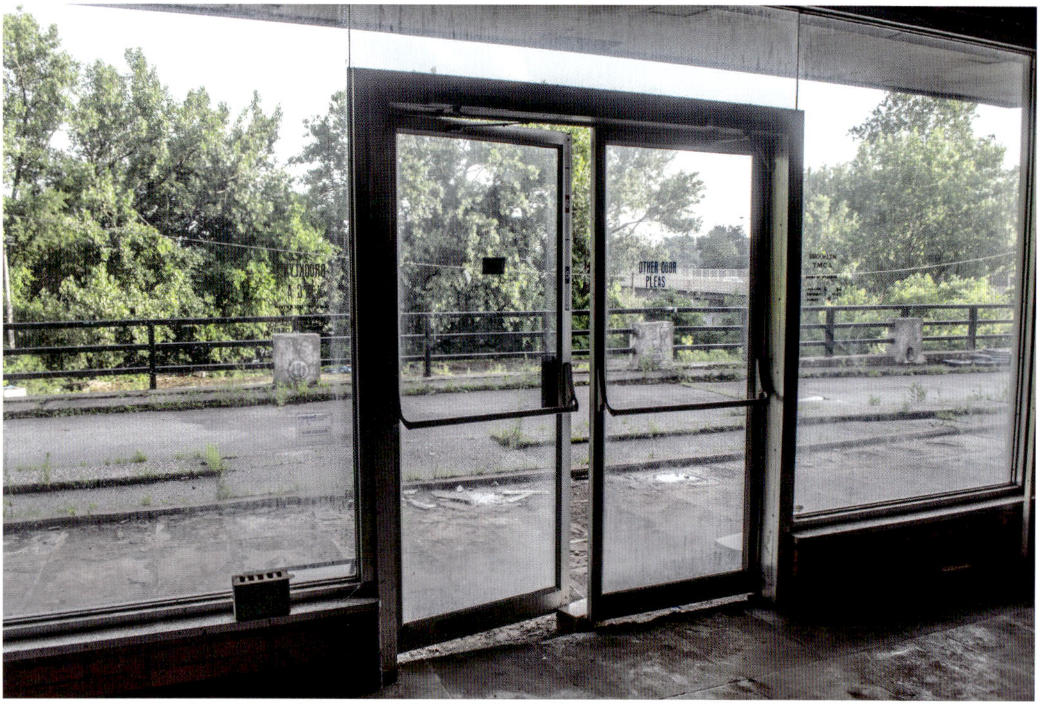

We didn't expect there to be an entrance facing the ravine, and we went to a good deal of trouble to get in. This was one of many times we found the easy entrance once we were already inside.

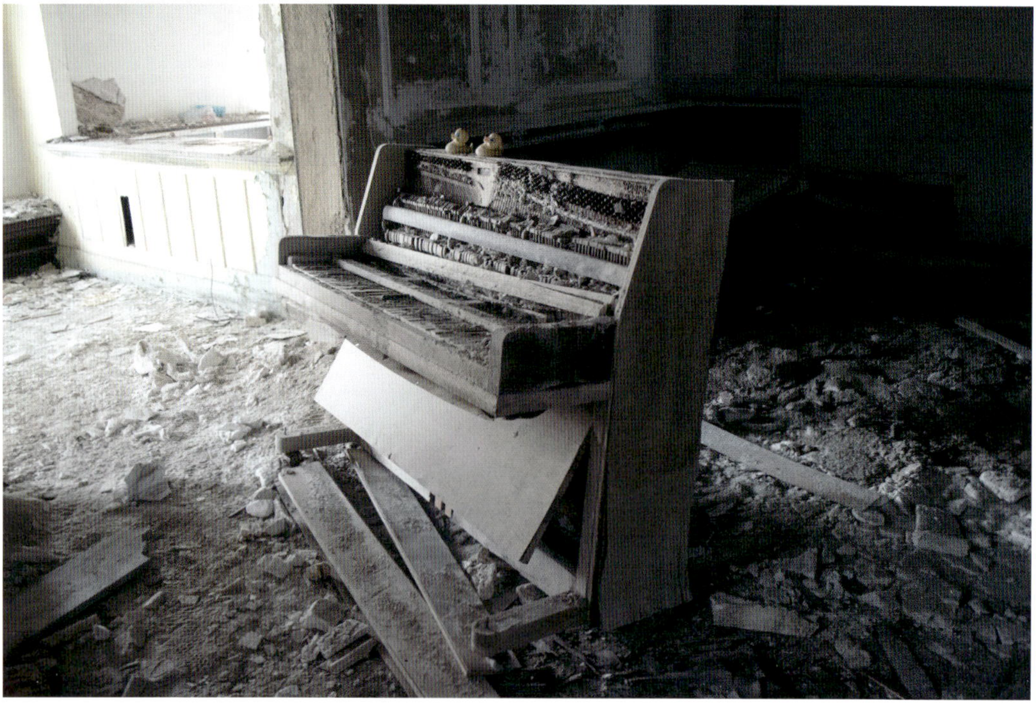

This piano was already not in the best shape. But if you were to go back today, you won't find it. It has essentially disintegrated.

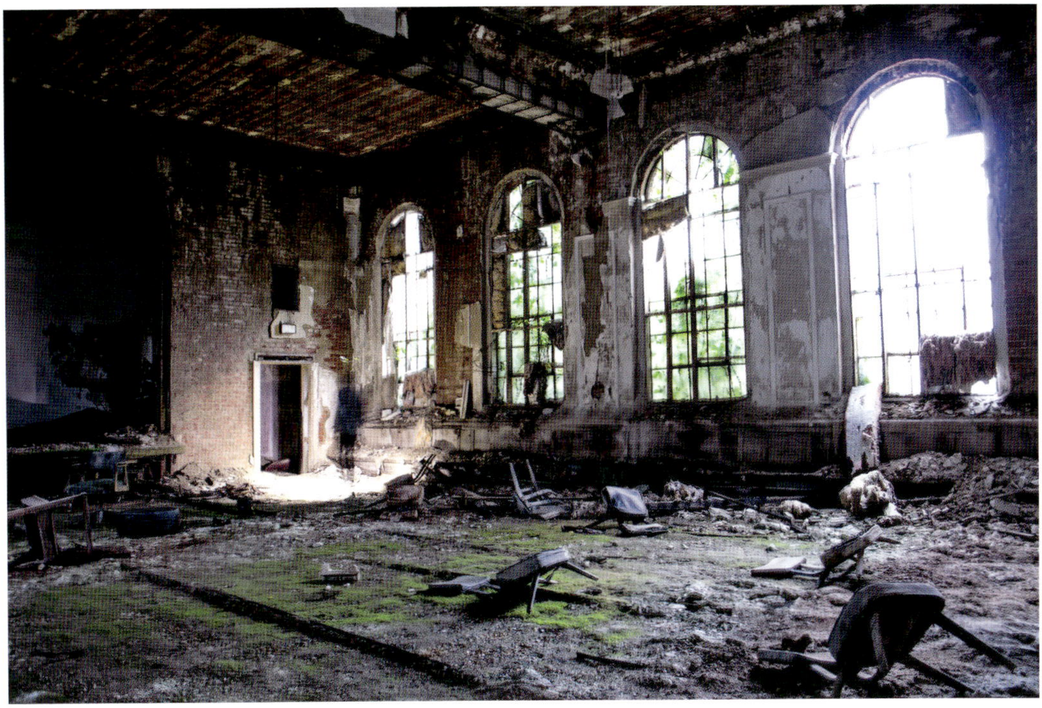

I would never do this kind of photograph on purpose—it would look too contrived. But sometimes you accidentally take a photo that you end up liking more than the one you were trying to take.

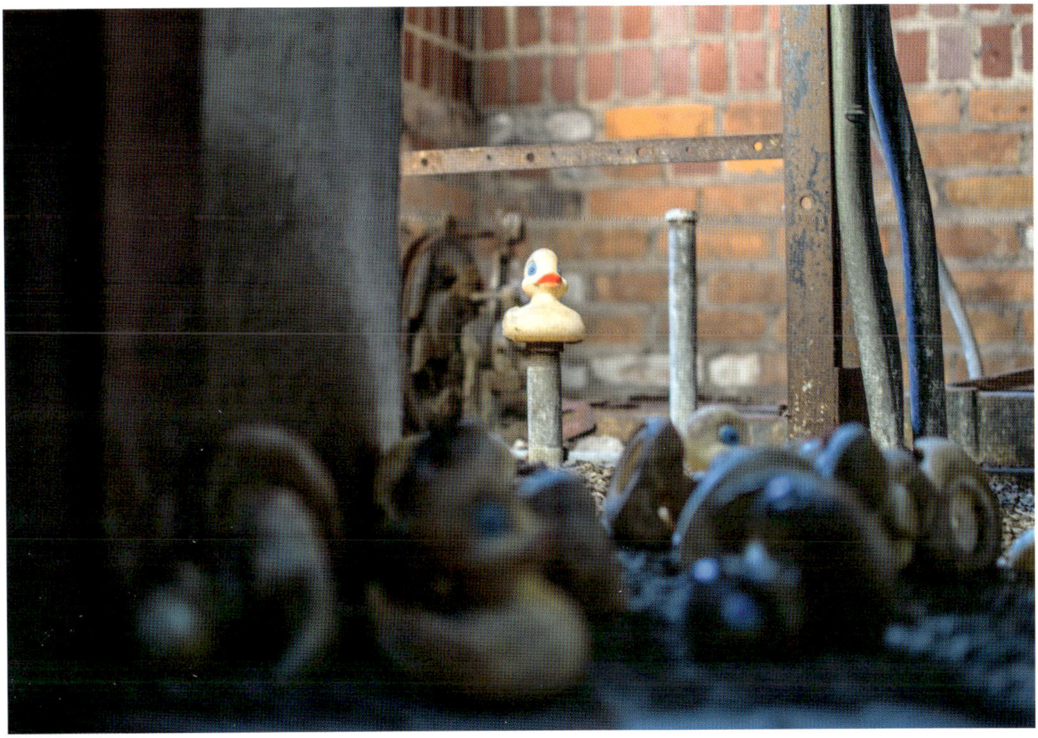

I didn't put the duck up there on its perch. I just walked up, and it was there to greet me.

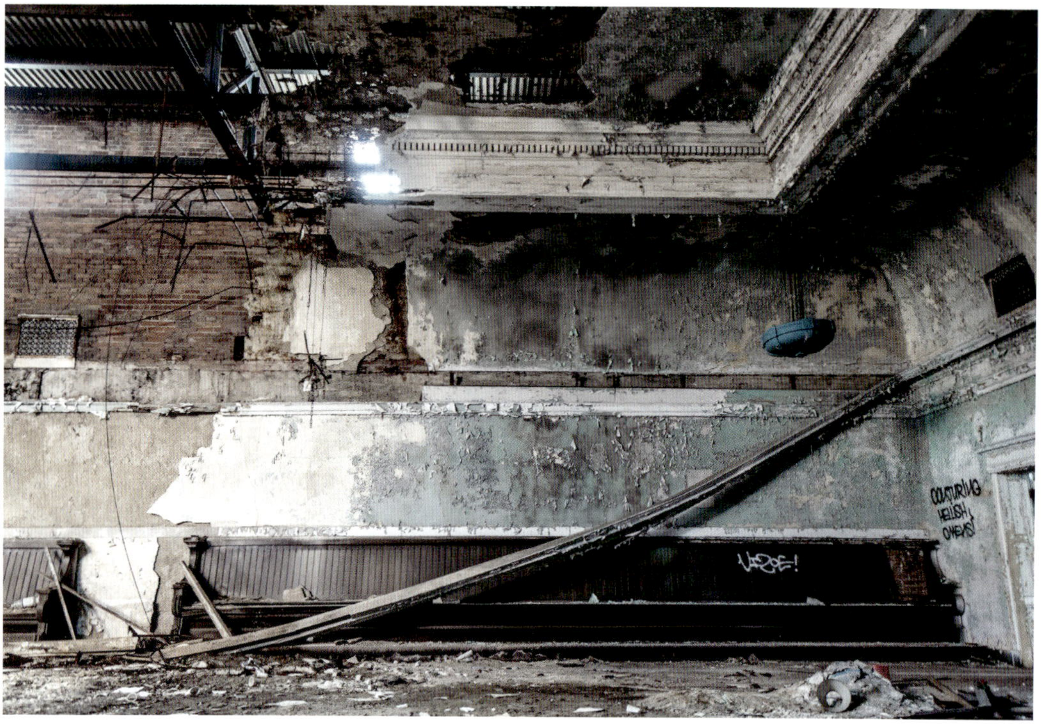

This was probably an impressive room back when the building was first built. But some of that grandeur fades away when the plaster facade falls off and you can see the pedestrian brick wall behind it.

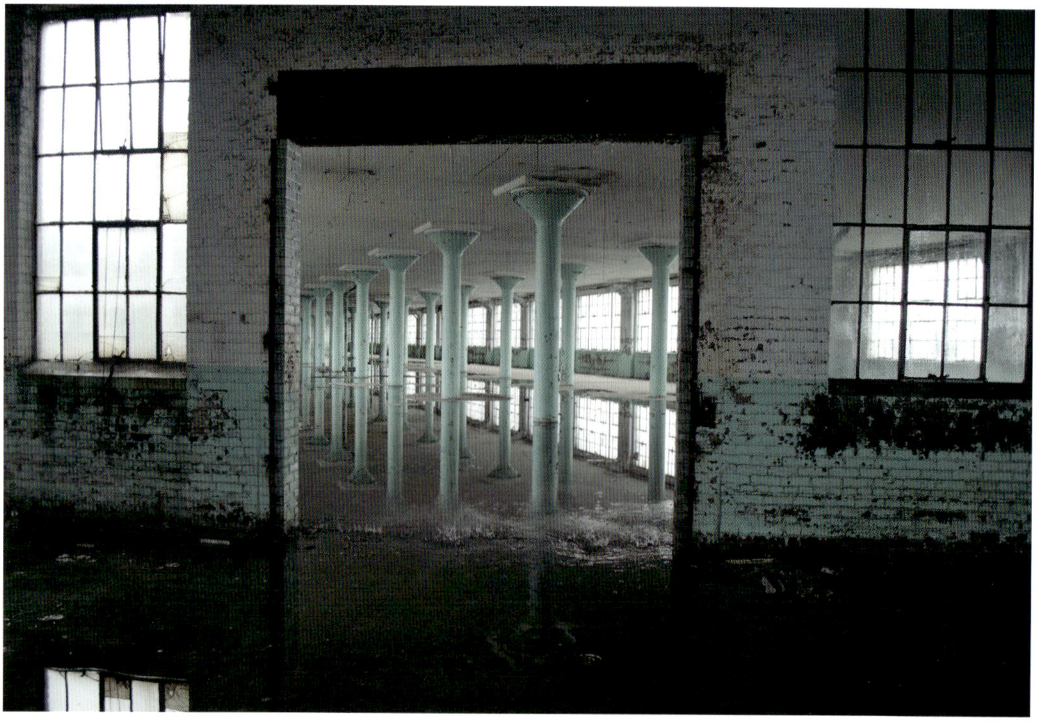

The sheer volume of water leaking from the roof of this building was something to behold.

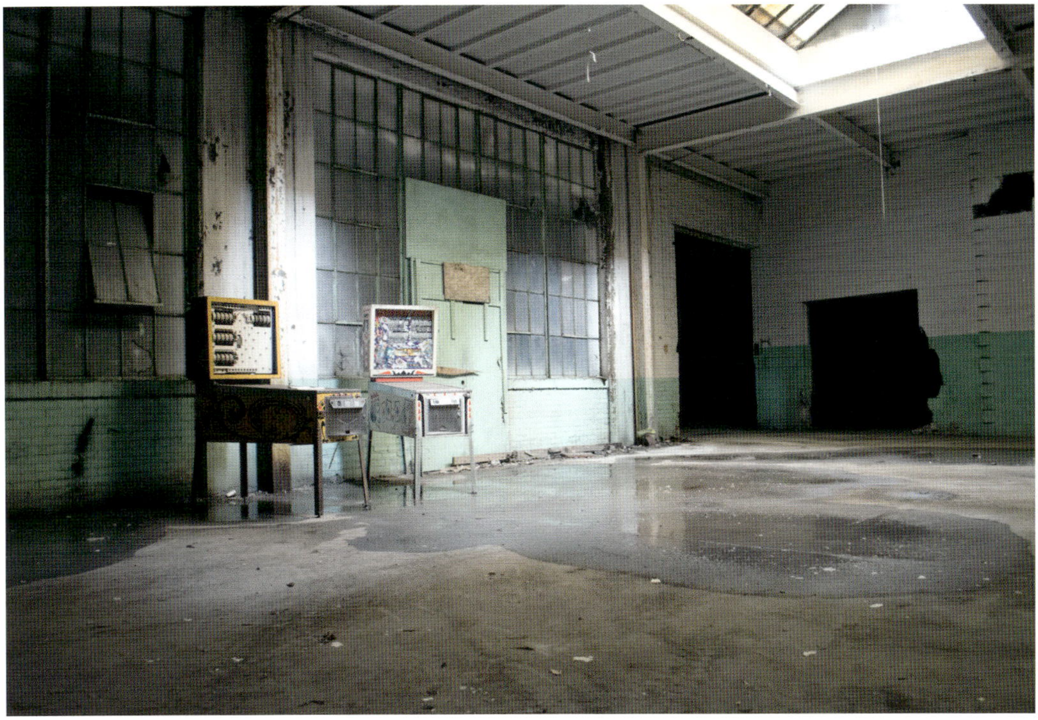

I've heard this was a cool company to work for—a 70s precursor to the tech companies that have ping-pong tables in their staff lounges. That could explain the pinball machines.

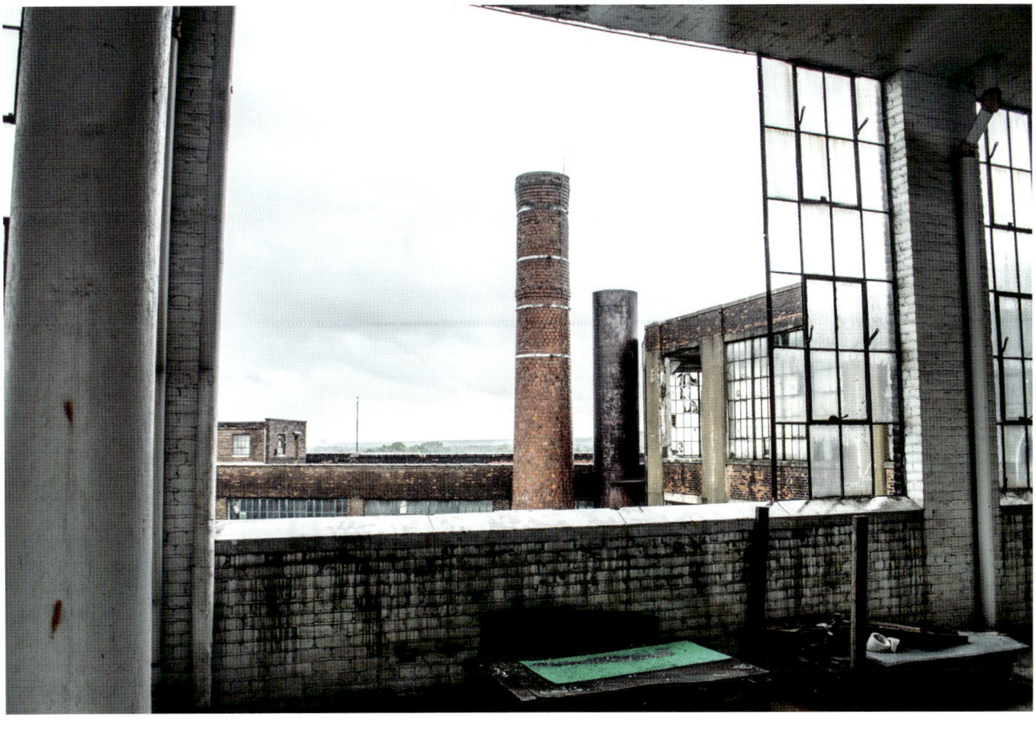

This was the tallest building in the area, which gave us a good view of the storm clouds dumping rain on us.

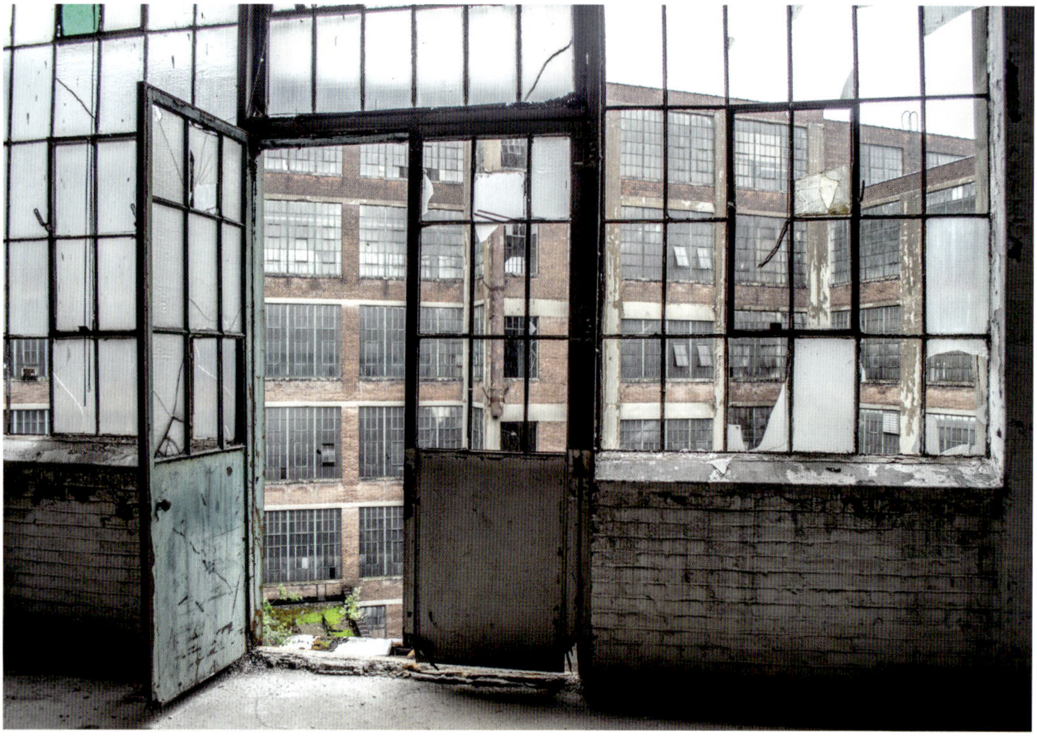

There was just a sheer drop outside this door, and absolutely no evidence that it had ever led to anything.

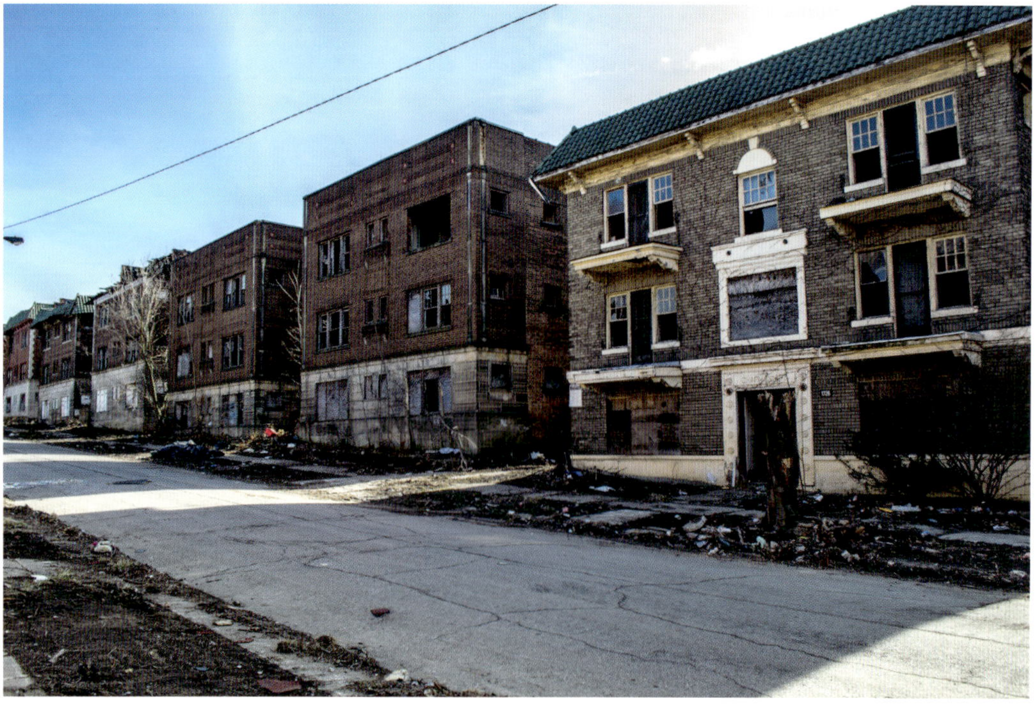

There is an unsettling feeling that you get in this neighborhood. Something about all the empty windows makes you feel like you're being watched.

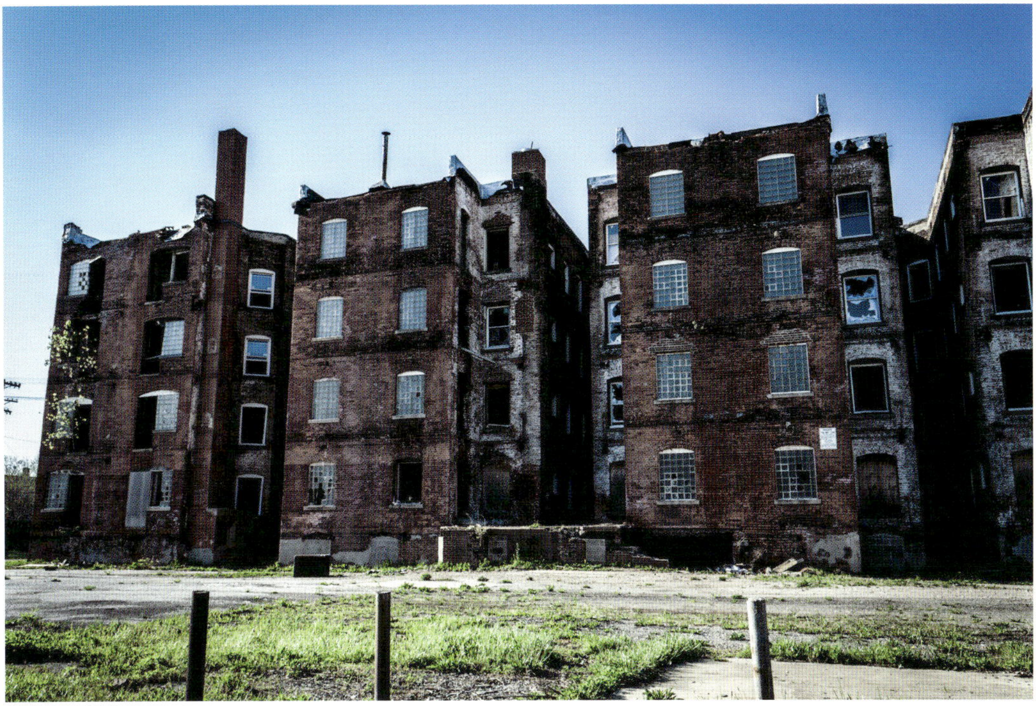

You might be able to see that there are a couple of brand-new windows installed here. I really don't know how that happens in a building where clearly nothing else is being done, but it's not the only time I've seen it.

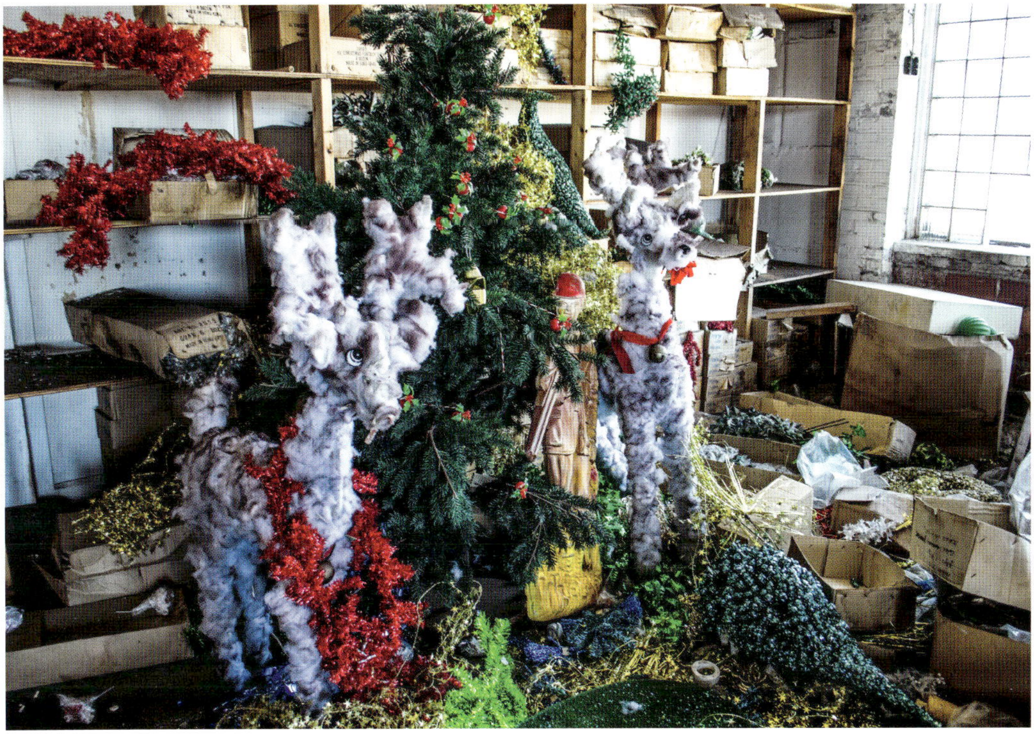

I laughed out loud when I saw this. It was the filthy reindeer that did it for me.

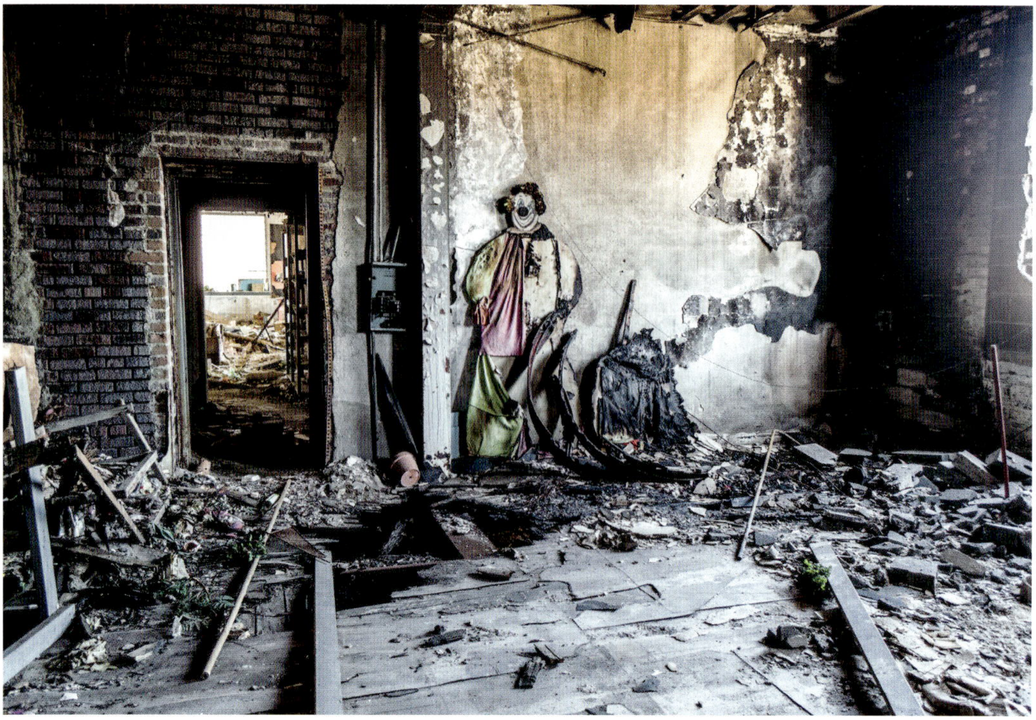

If I learned this clown started the fire, I would accept it as truth.

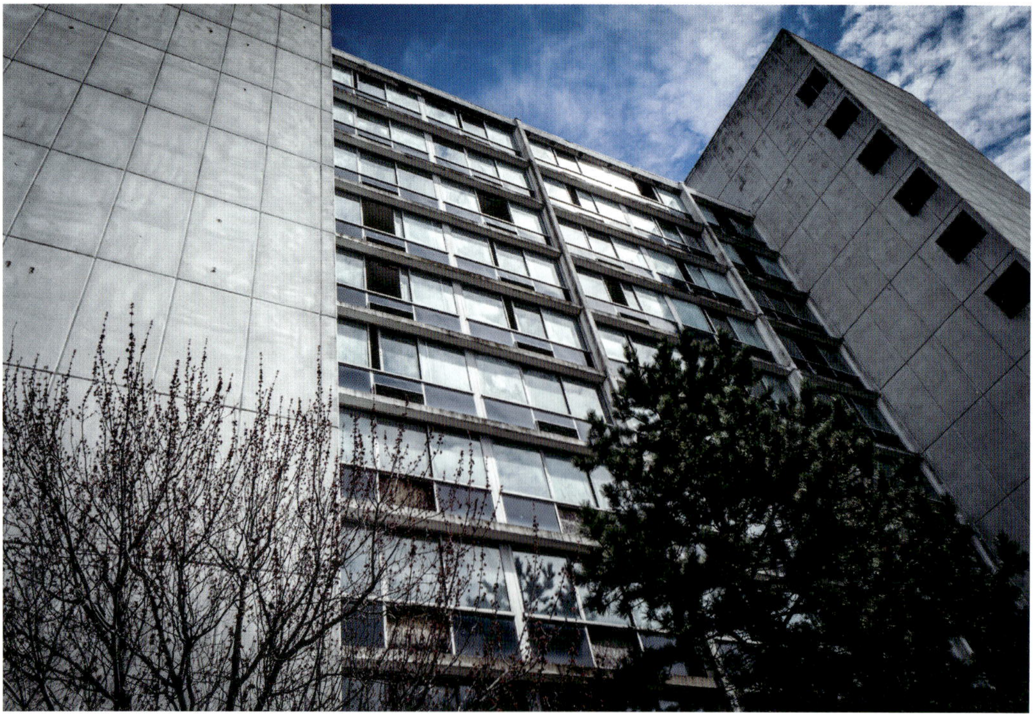

Some geese had taken up residence in the pool area on the ground floor of this hotel, and one charged us right after I took this picture.

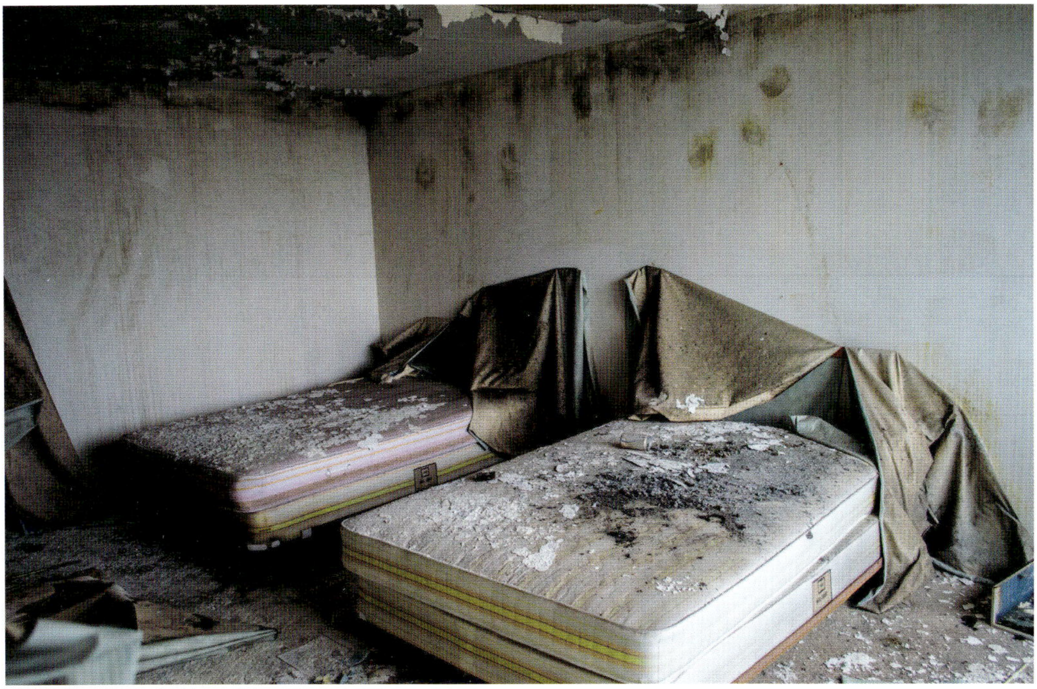

The beds had been removed from the lower floors, but whoever was doing that had given up by about halfway up the building. The smaller furniture was still taken in many cases, but the beds were clearly too much hassle.

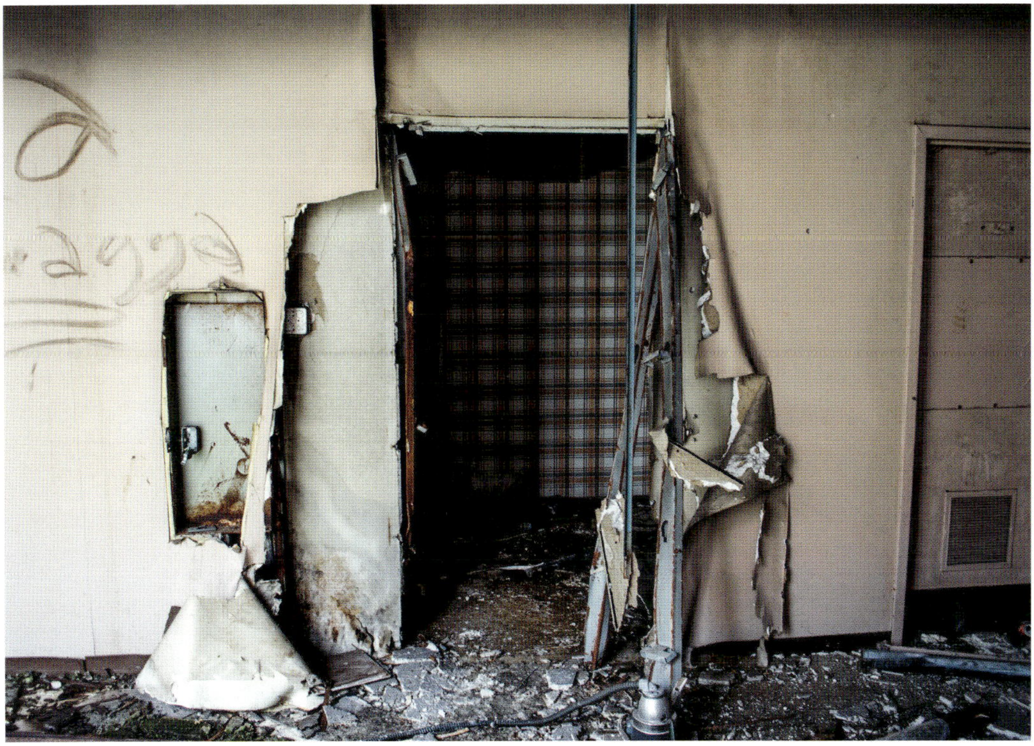

I don't know what this had been used for, but the wallpaper choice was great.

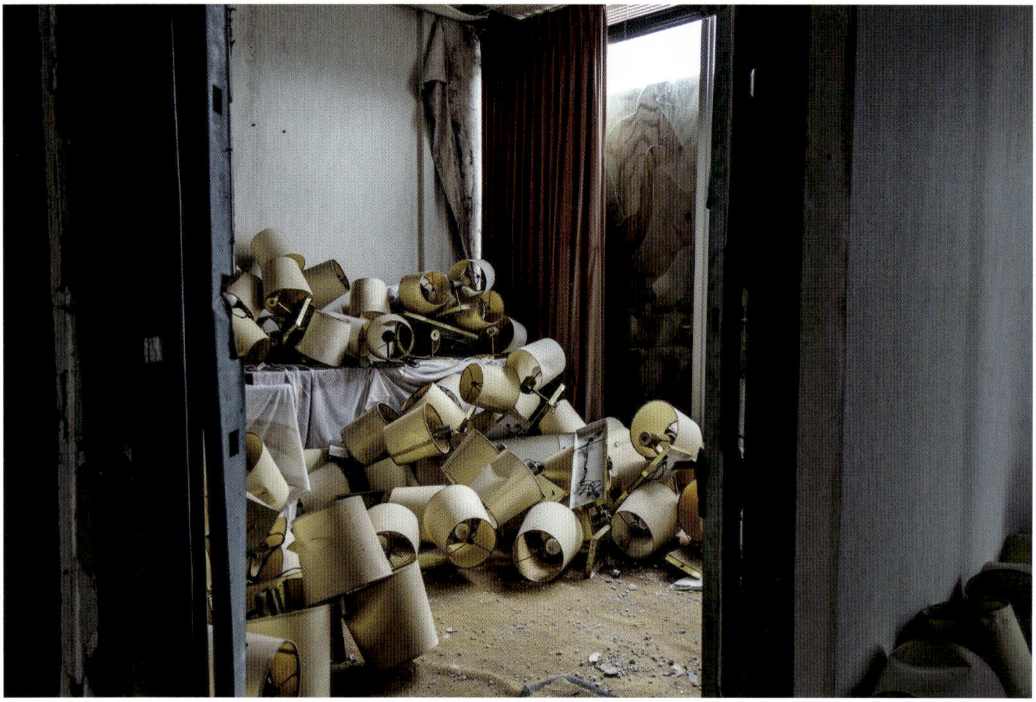

This was one of a couple of rooms packed full of lamps and sconces. They had clearly had some difficulty getting rid of them. I guess brass fixtures aren't as popular as they used to be.

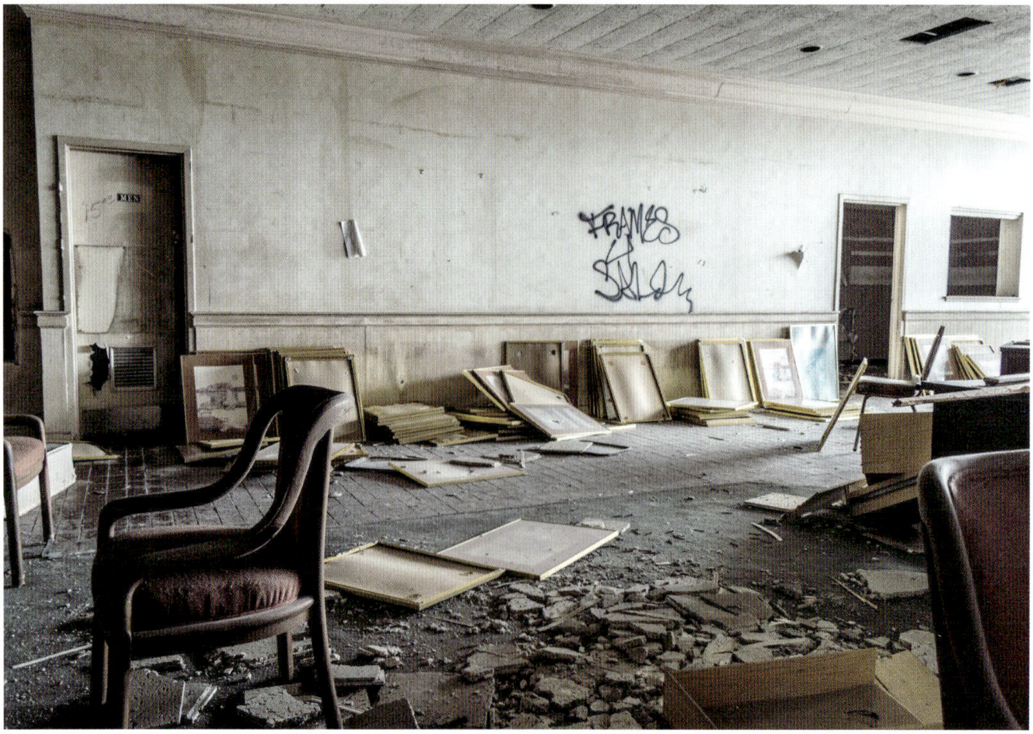

Frames and bad hotel art for sale. It also appears someone was trying to sell the men's room door for $15.

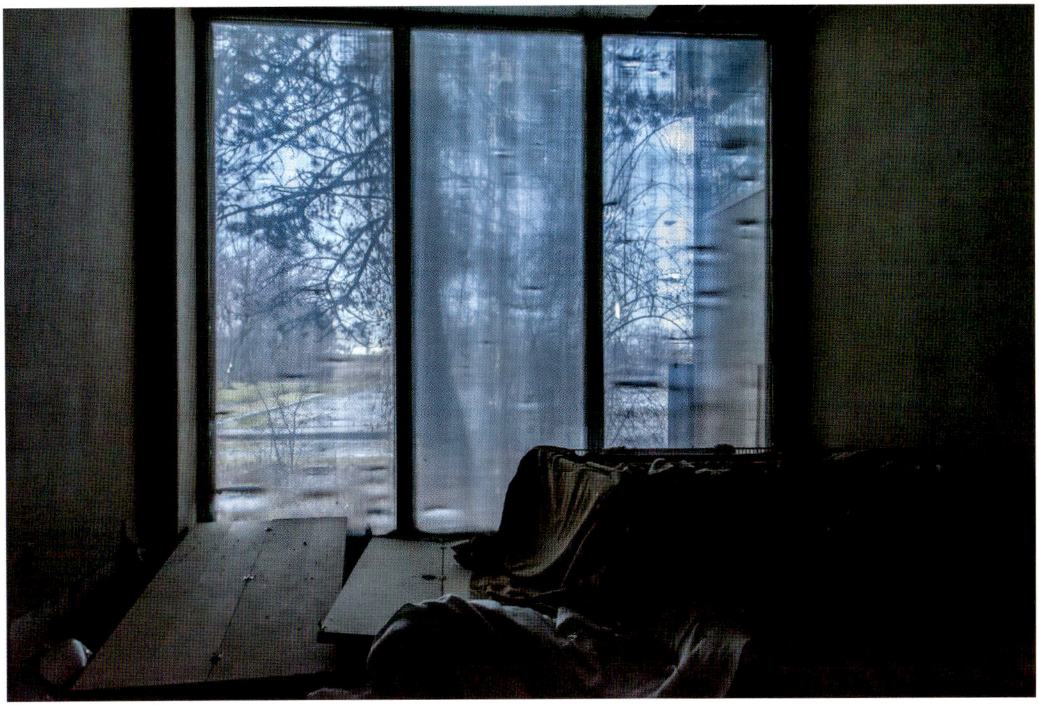

I could not tell you what had done this to the windows in this room, but it was such a strange effect that I had to get a photo.

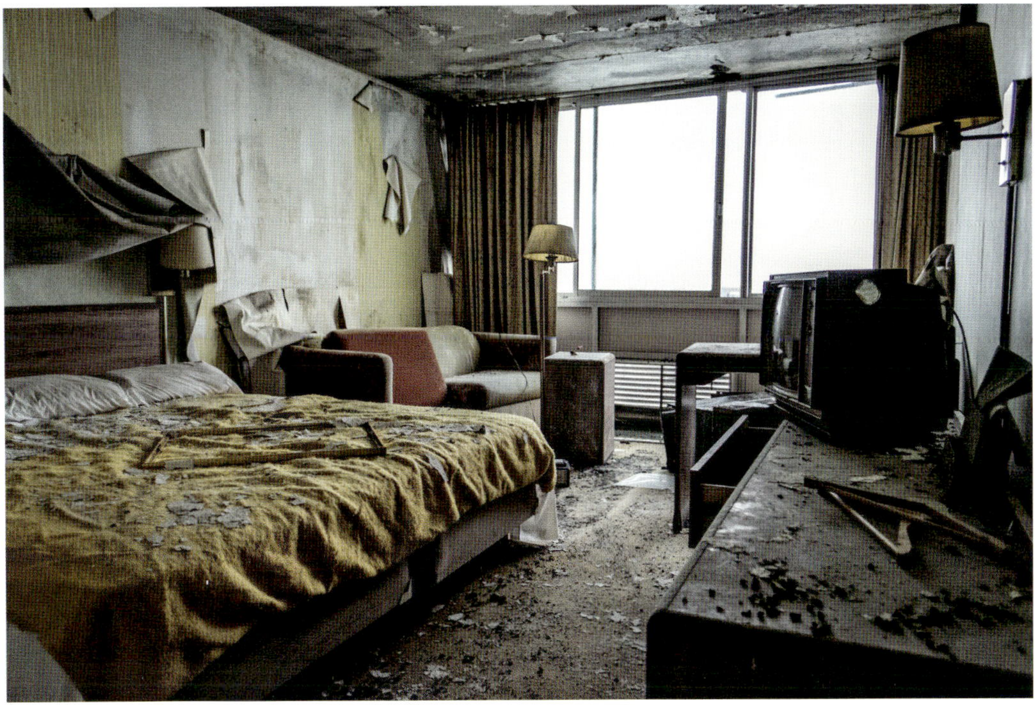

The closest thing there was to an intact room, on the top floor. The TV and clock radio were bolted down. Maybe this wasn't the nicest hotel.

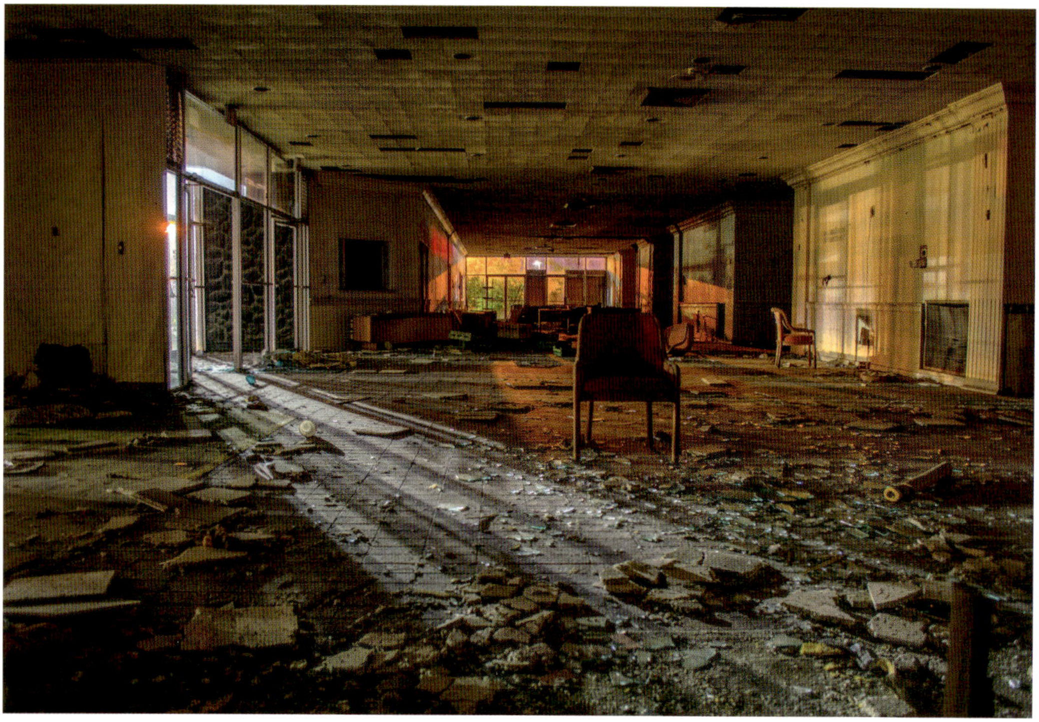

I wonder whether the light looked like this when the hotel was still operating. Nighttime check-in would have been a pleasant experience.

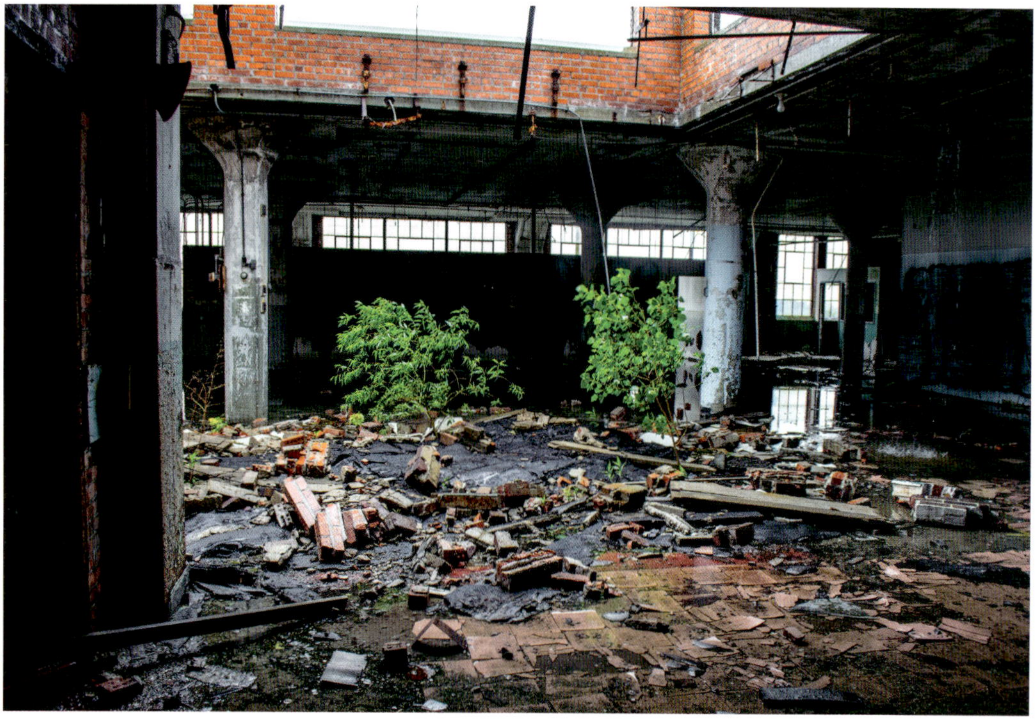

It rained so hard this whole day. This was possibly the most soaked I ever got exploring.

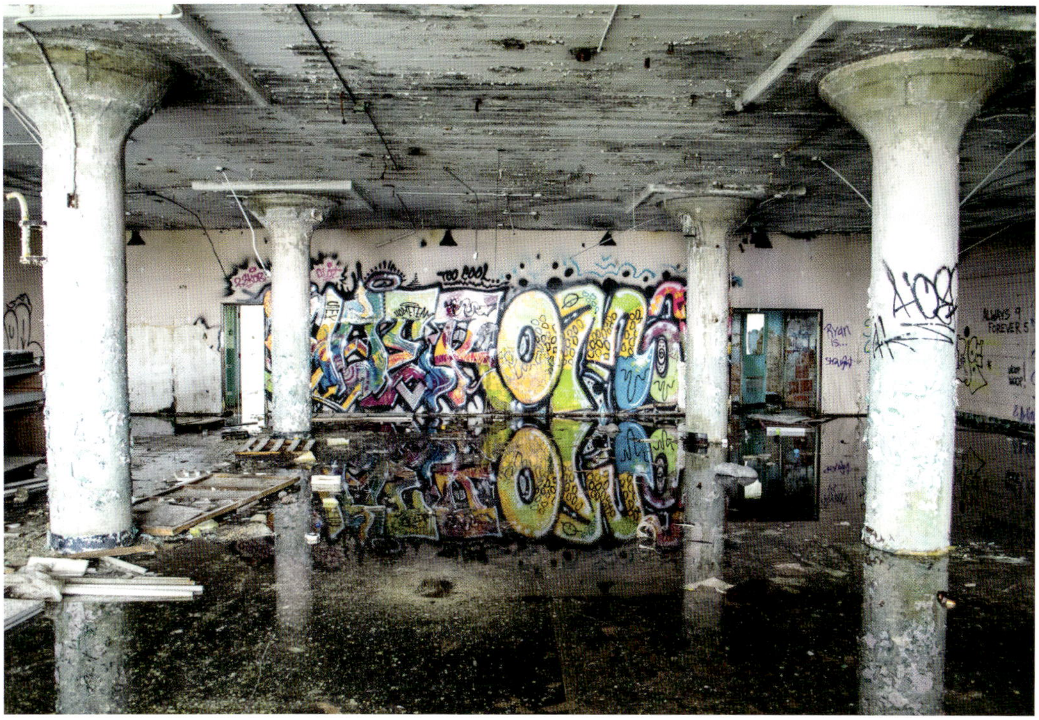

I usually don't take many photos of graffiti, but I really liked the vibrant colors of this one, especially reflected in the water.

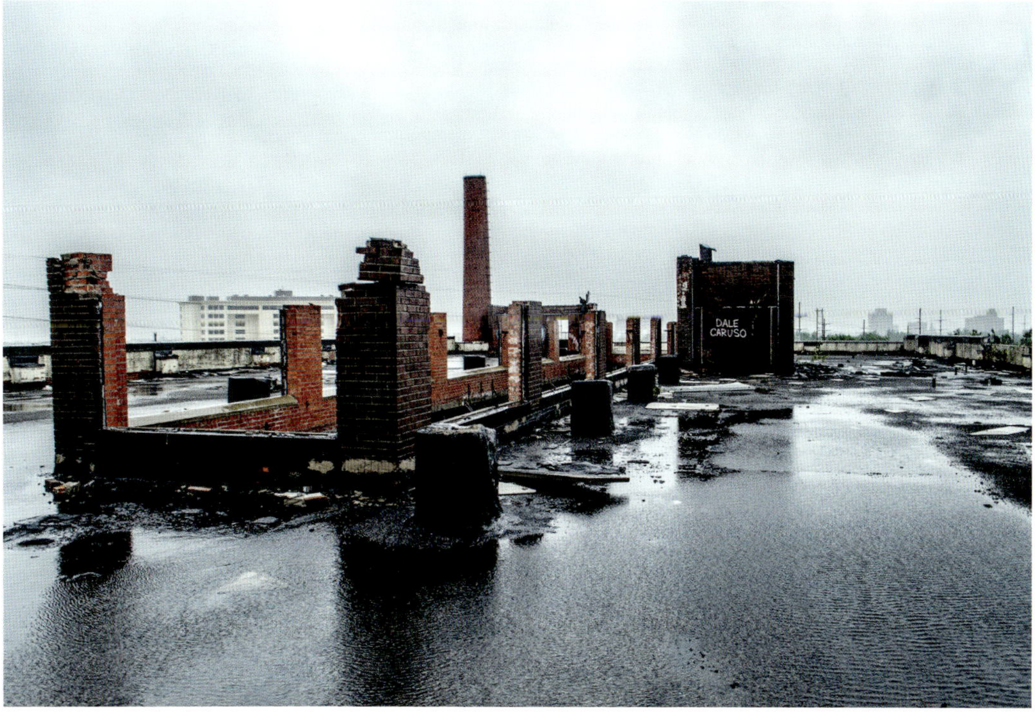

I still have no idea who Dale Caruso is, but his name was tagged all over every part of this building.

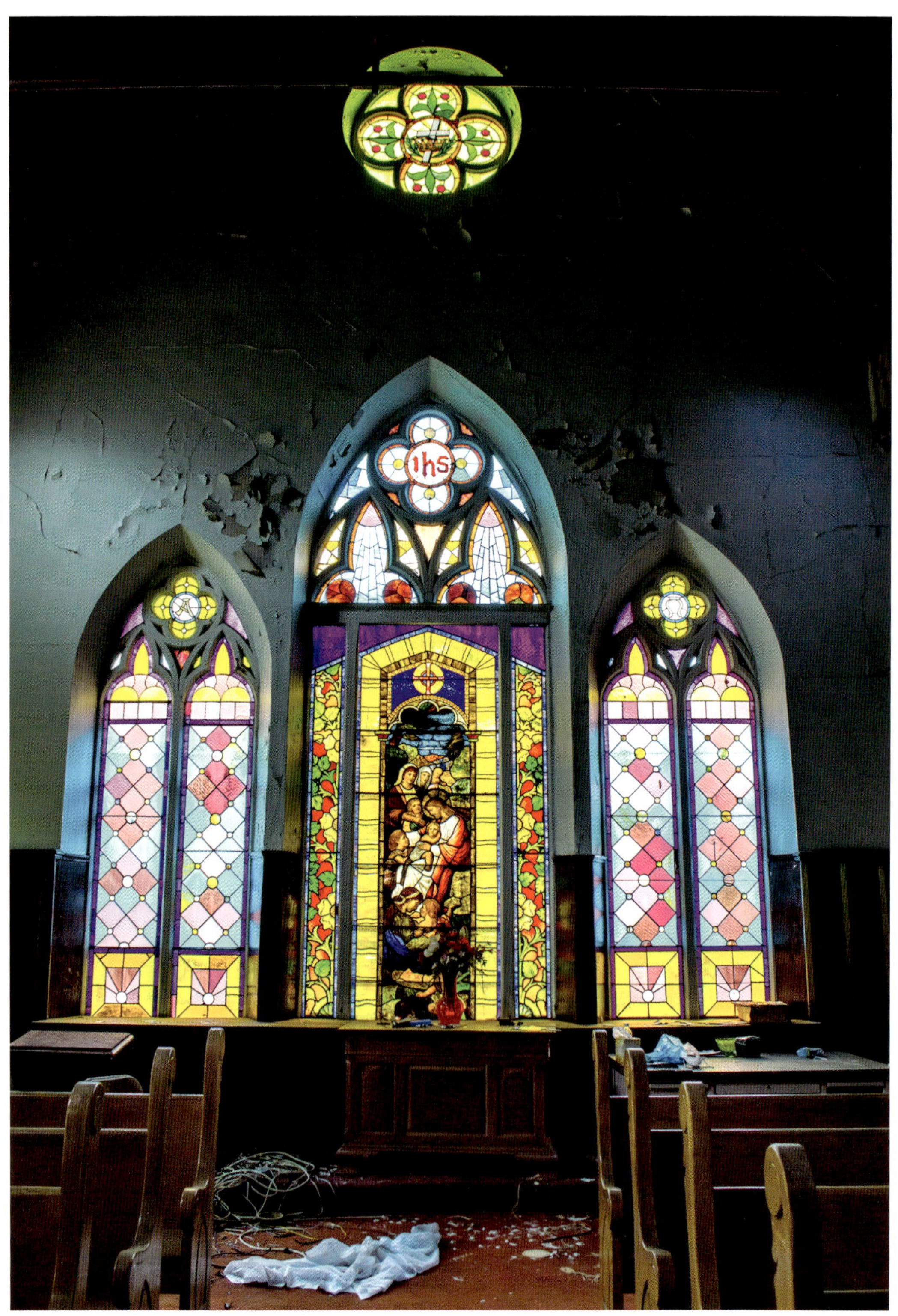

Several regular windows in this church were broken or missing, but the stained glass was entirely intact. I don't know if it was respectful vandals, or just luck, but I got a photo out of it.

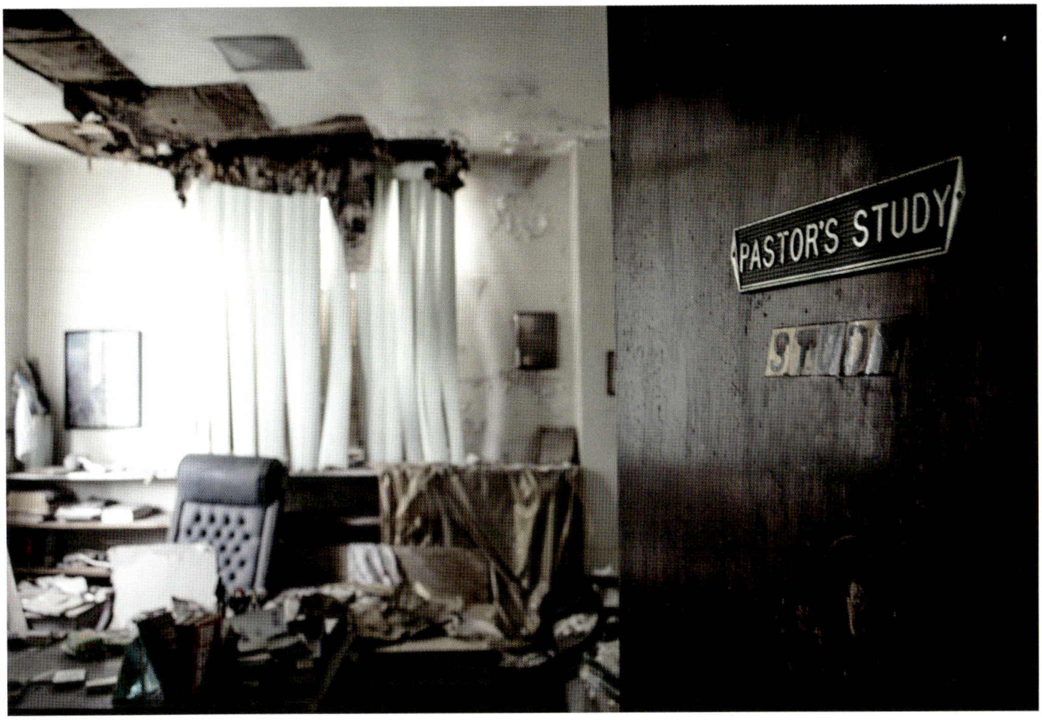

With the obvious exception of what had happened to the ceiling, the study here looked like it was just as it had been left. Although it is hard to ignore the ceiling.

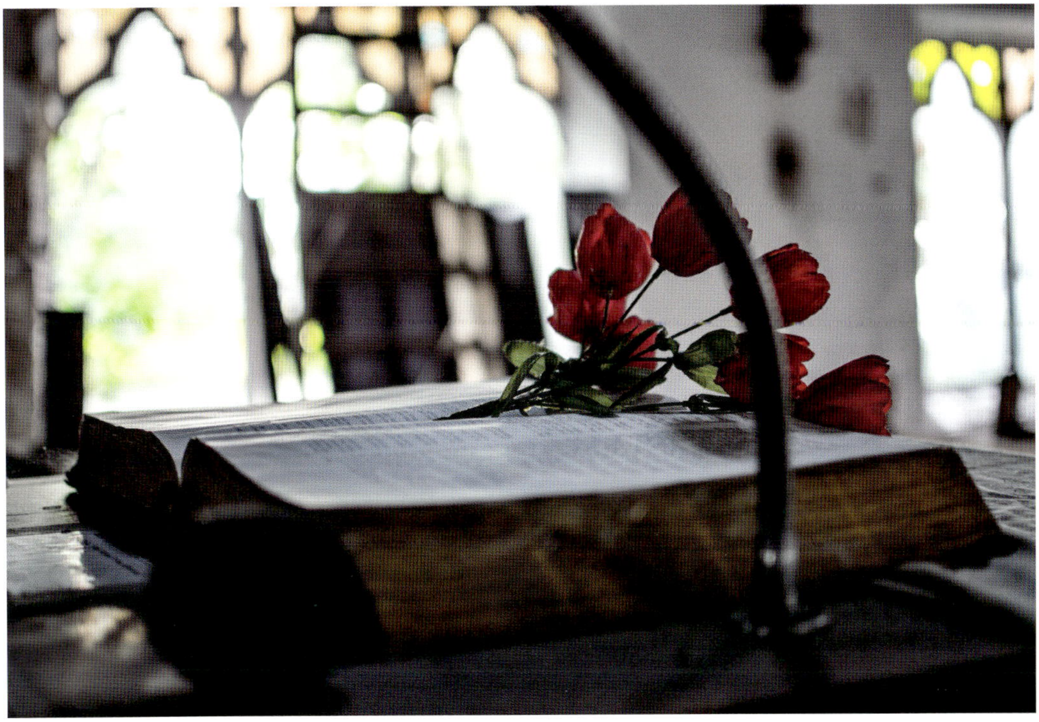

I'm sure you won't be too surprised to learn that these flowers were fake.

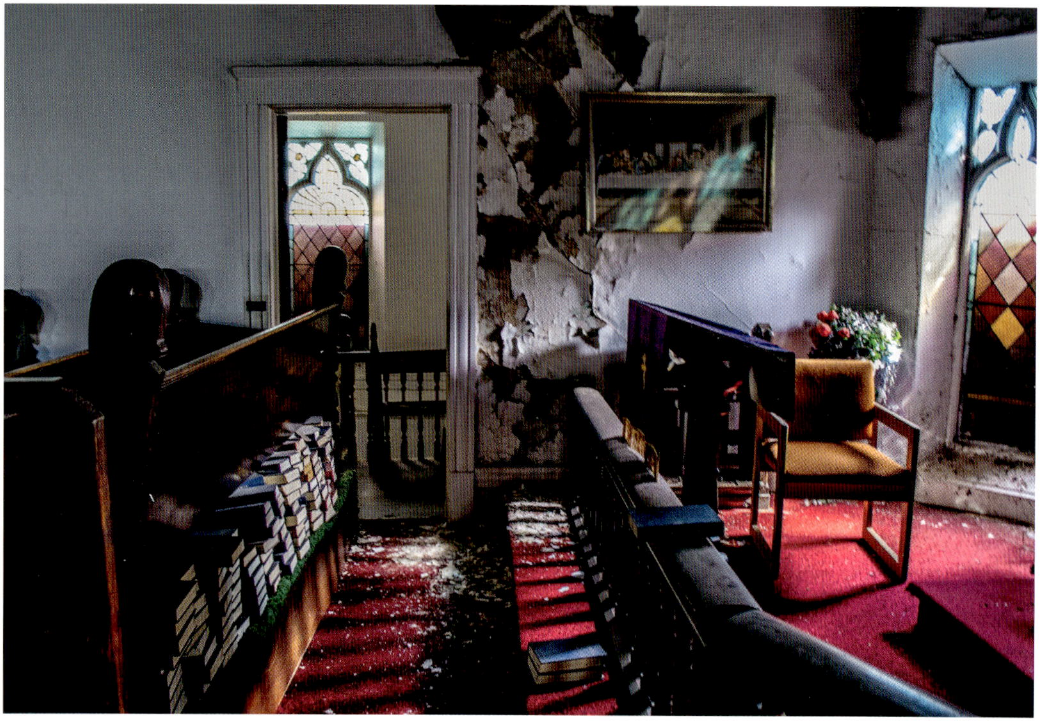

It's unusual to see something that has been left alone by humans for so long still fall apart like this. Vandals and scrappers usually do the bulk of the damage to a building in the early period of its abandonment.

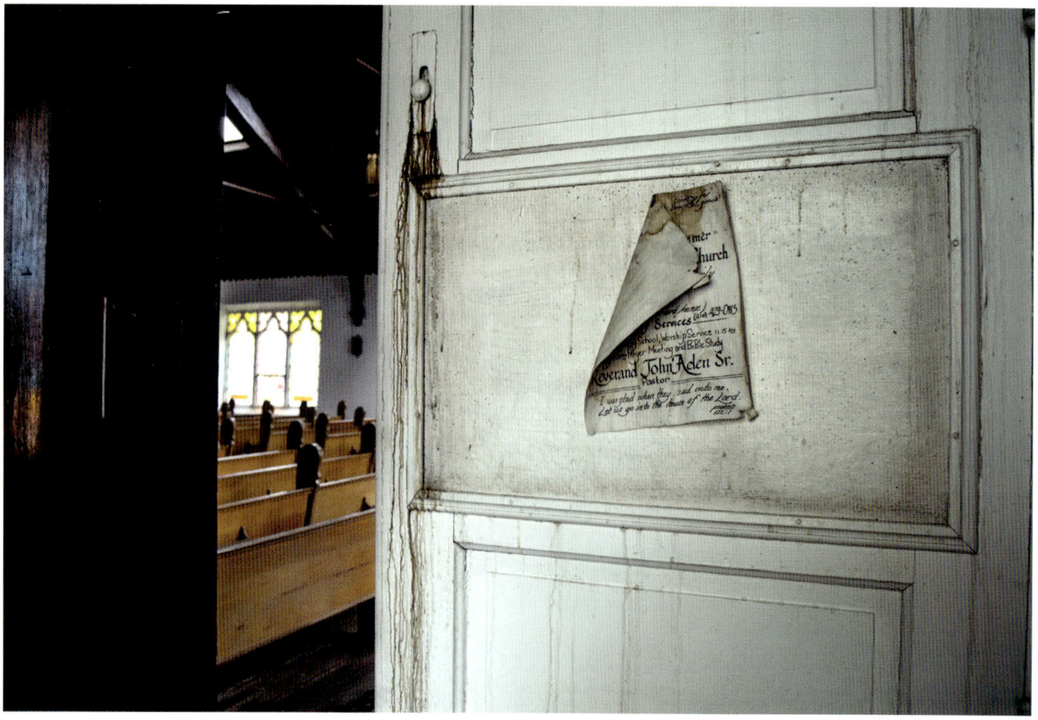

I didn't take this photo just because I was impressed with the penmanship on the flier, but I was impressed.

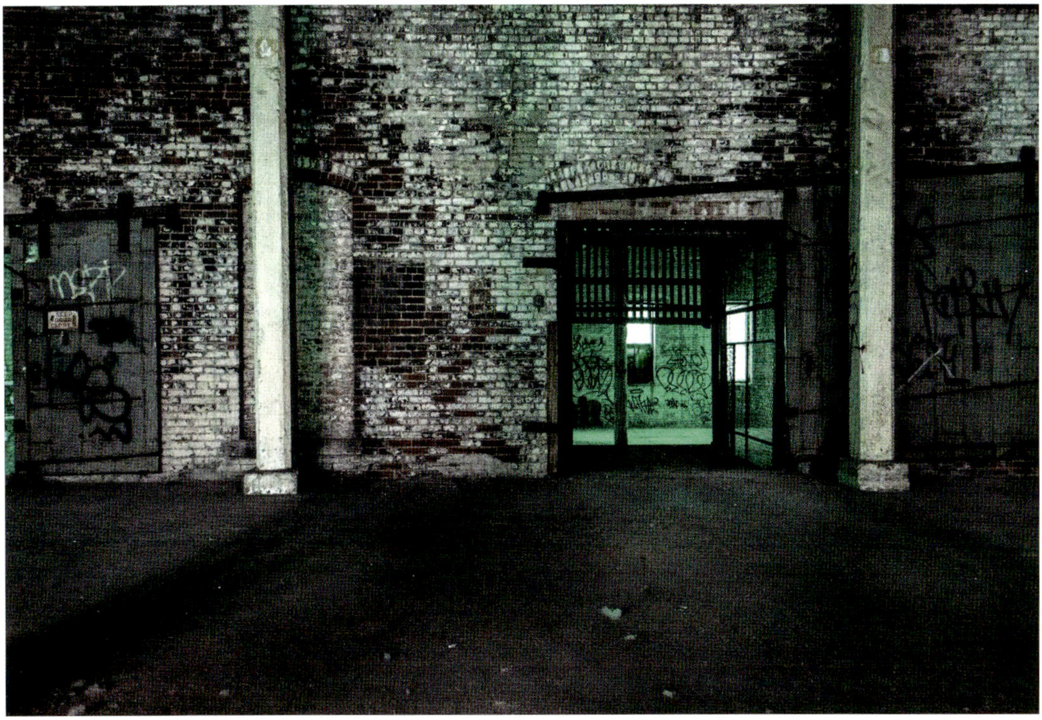

This really is the kind of spot that has exactly the right kind of look for a craft brewery to take over. I haven't been in since it was converted, but I bet they kept a lot of it the same.

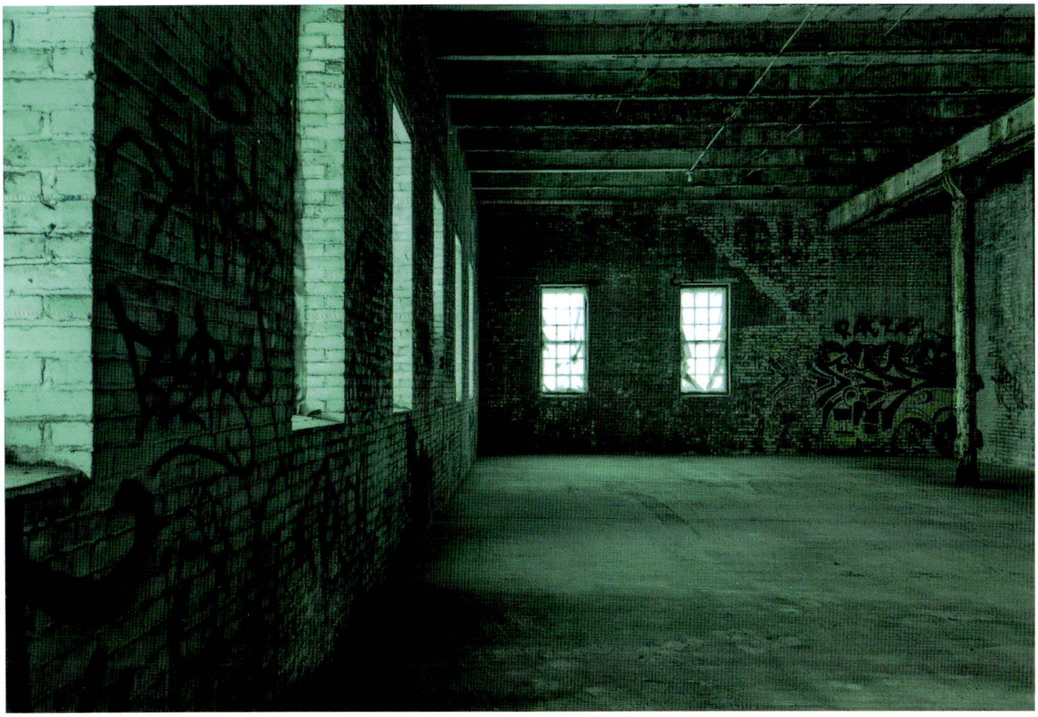

When I saw the plastic over the windows, I was expecting it to be a lot darker in this place. Instead, it was just green.

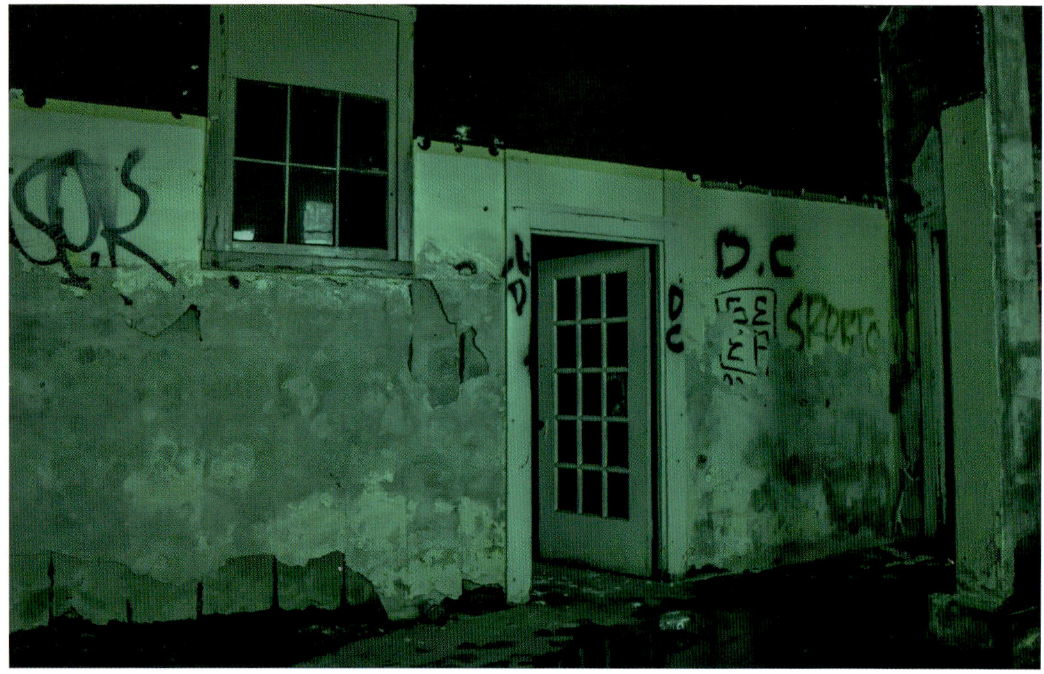

This place had been abandoned for a long time before we got in, and there was no trace left to give us a hint as to what it had been. Offices like these are usually where you can find documents or something that will give you some kind of clue, but we found nothing this time.

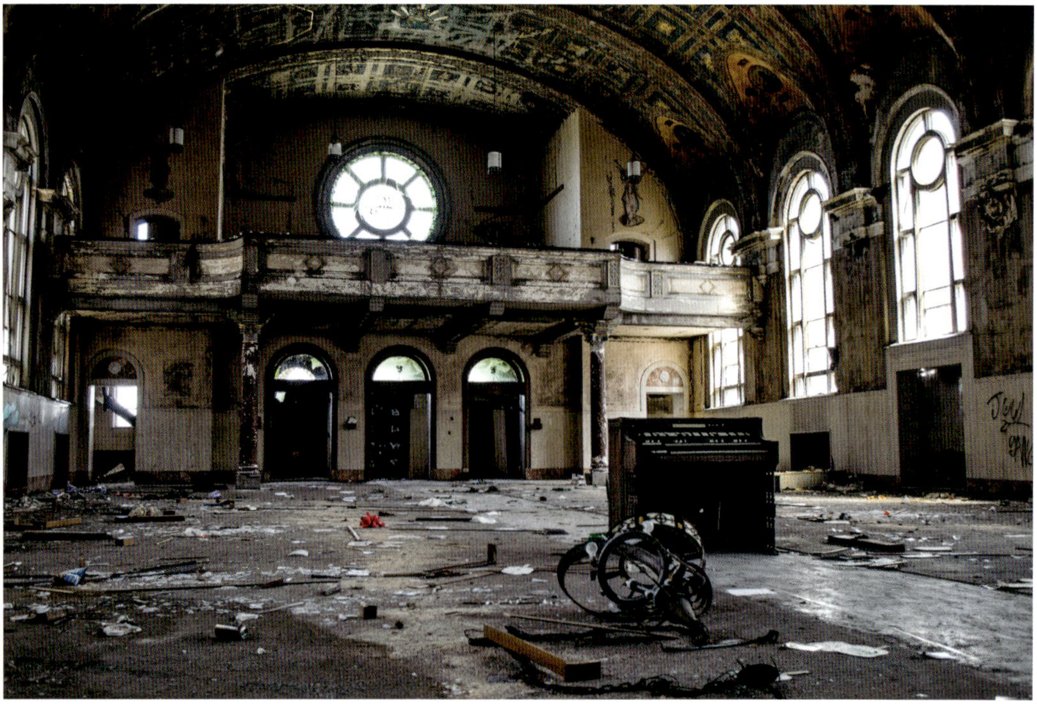

On my first visit to this church, all the pews were still in place. I took this photo on my second visit, and I haven't been back since. I can only imagine what else has been looted at this point.

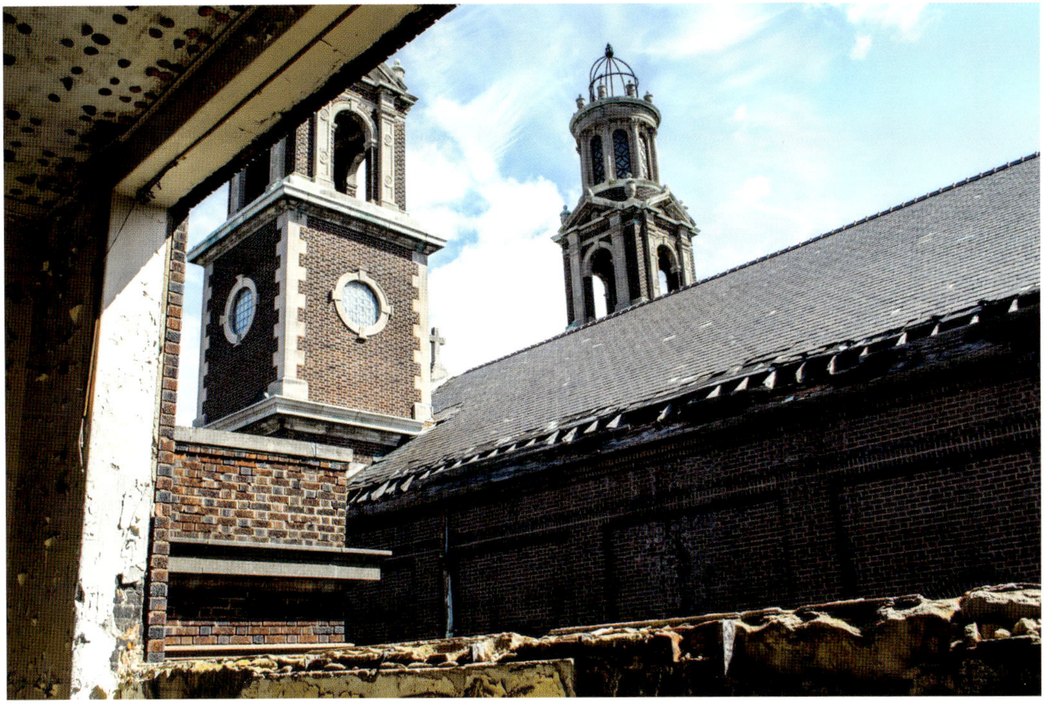

The church as seen from the school. A large number of birds made their homes in these towers. There was a truly impressive quantity of droppings at the bottom.

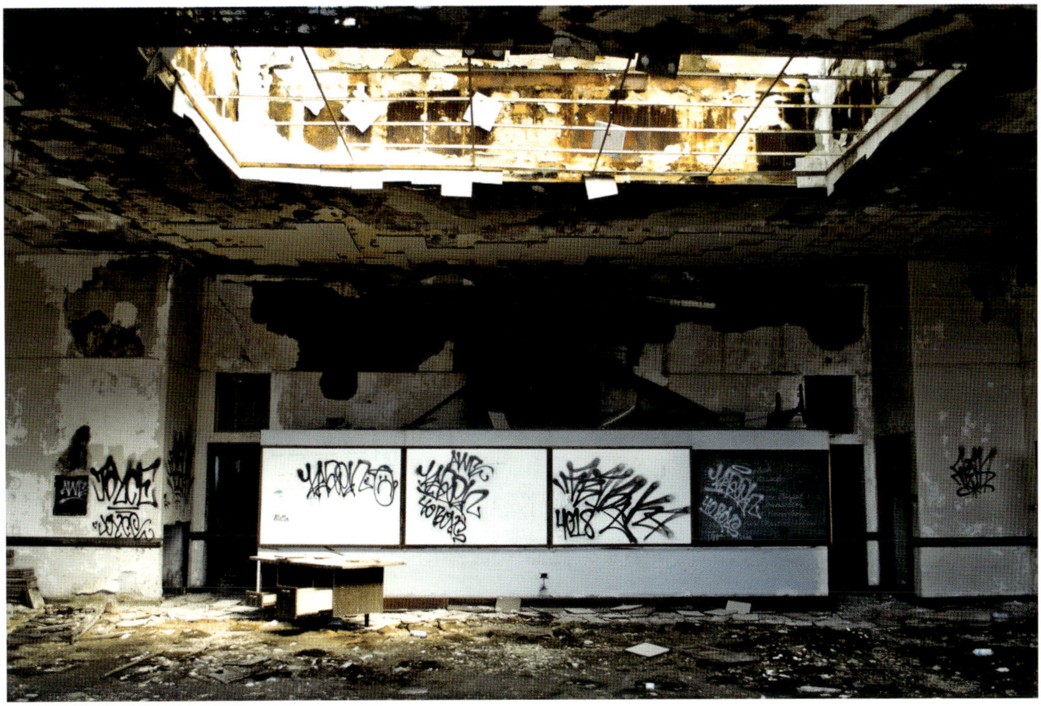

There was not a whole lot left in this place, but there was enough to suggest that this had been the science classroom. This was a very small school, so it's likely this was the only one.

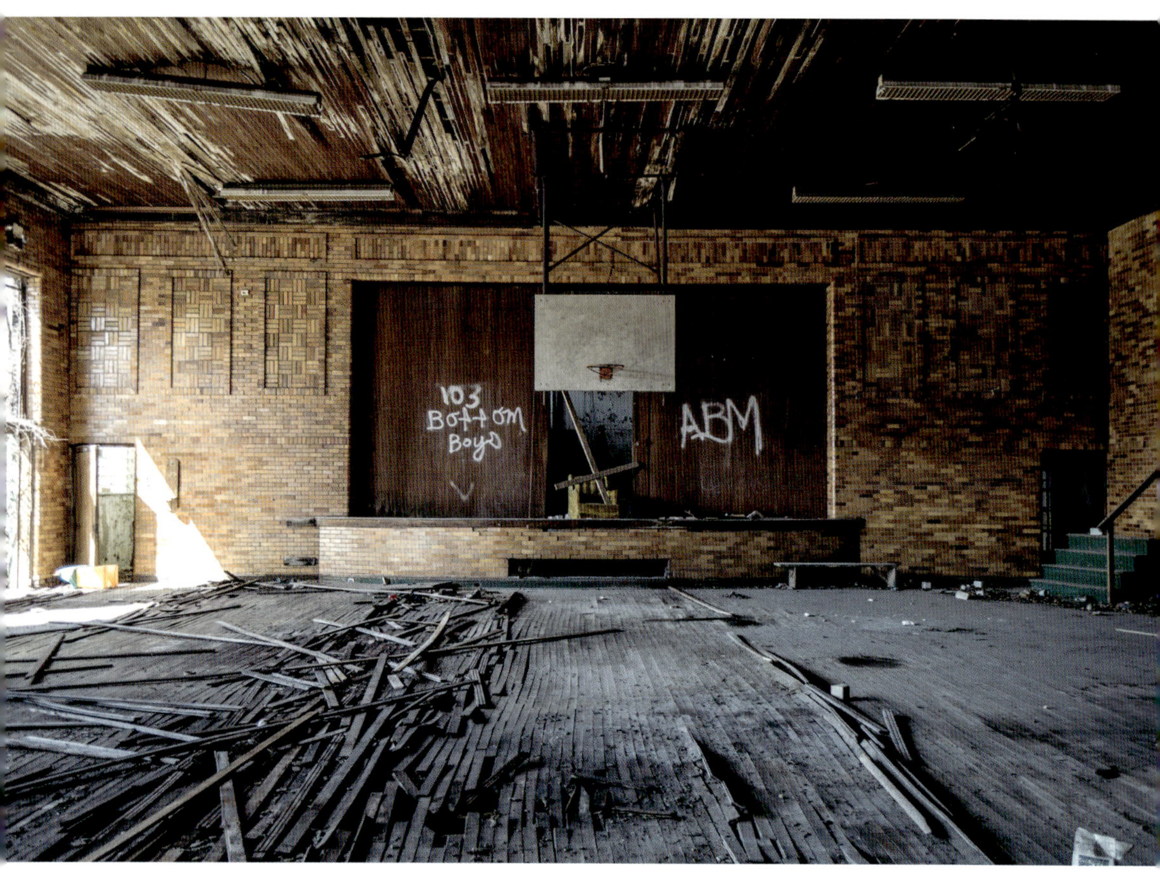

Abandoned gym floors always end up looking like this. Once the windows go, moisture gets in and the wood swells and buckles. Only the best preserved (or newest) spots haven't had this happen yet.

Opposite: Skylights are just so helpful when photographing abandoned buildings. It's a way to actually get some natural light.

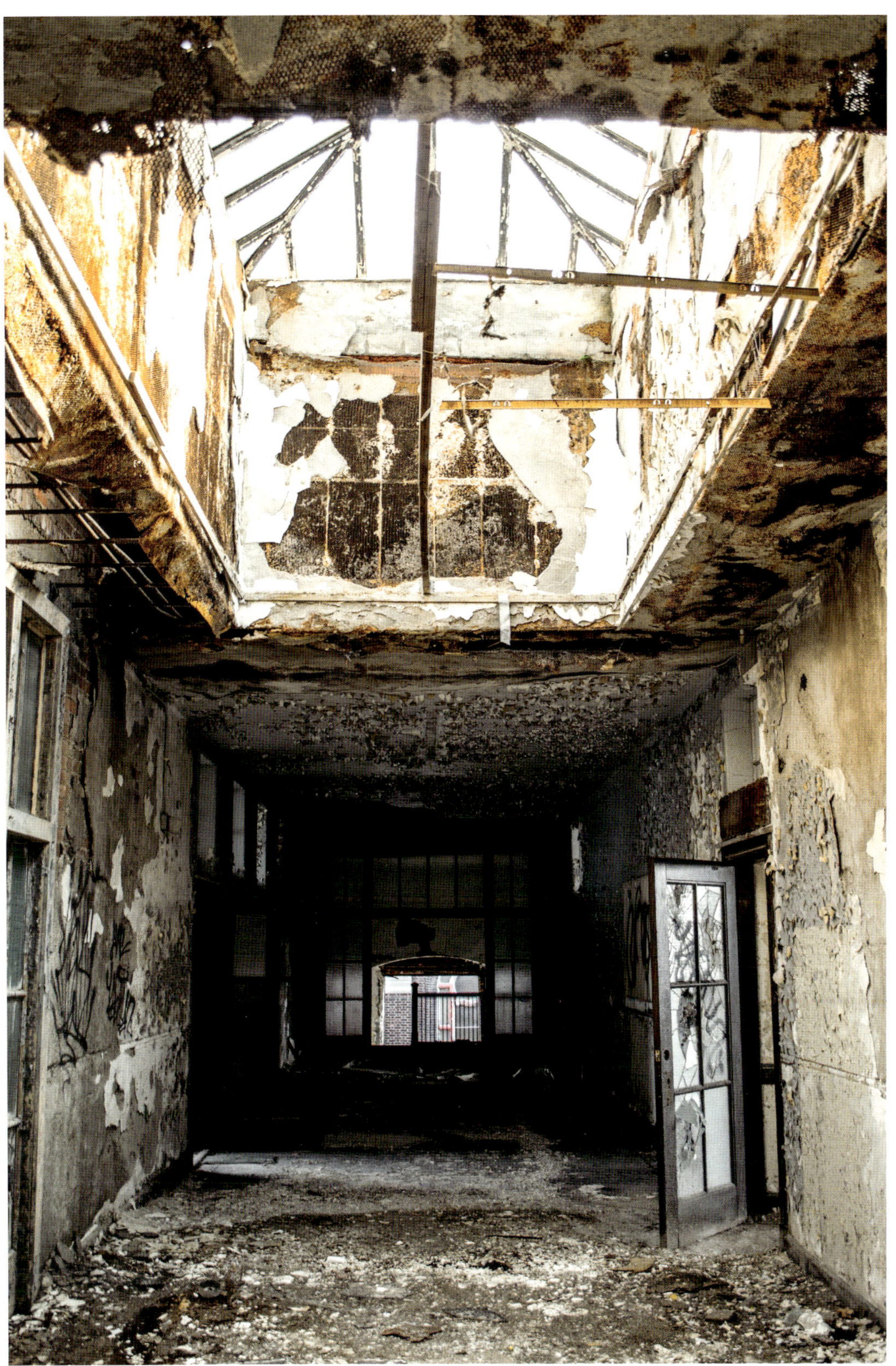

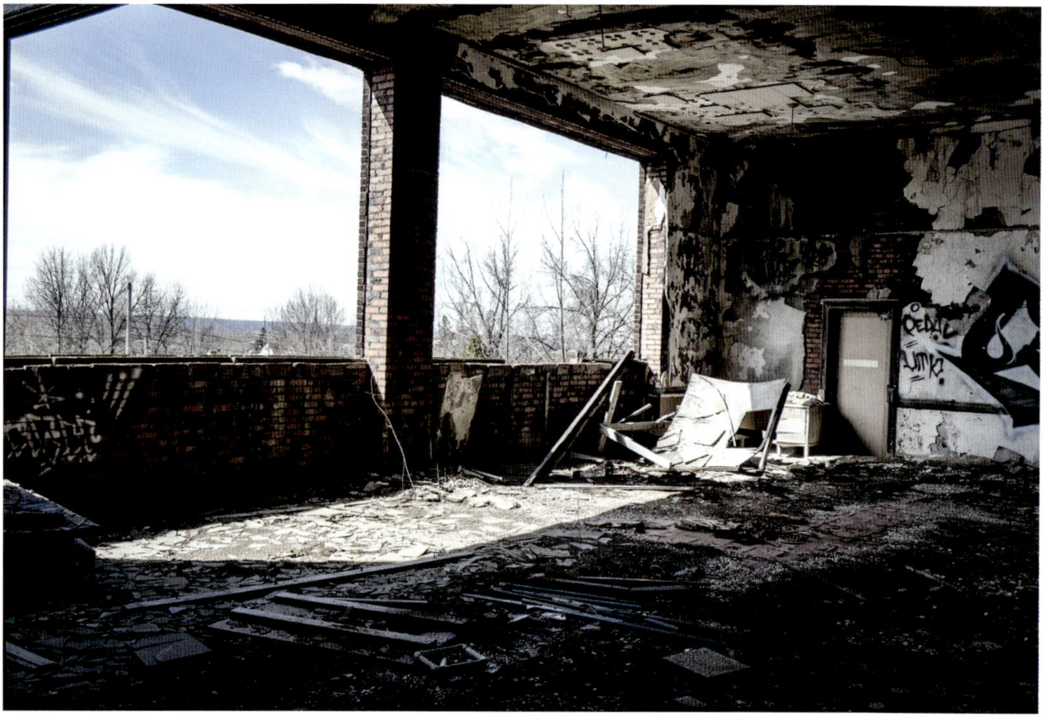

All of the exterior windows were like this—completely gone. We ended up only sticking our heads into the front rooms, since the windows there faced the street and were way too obvious.

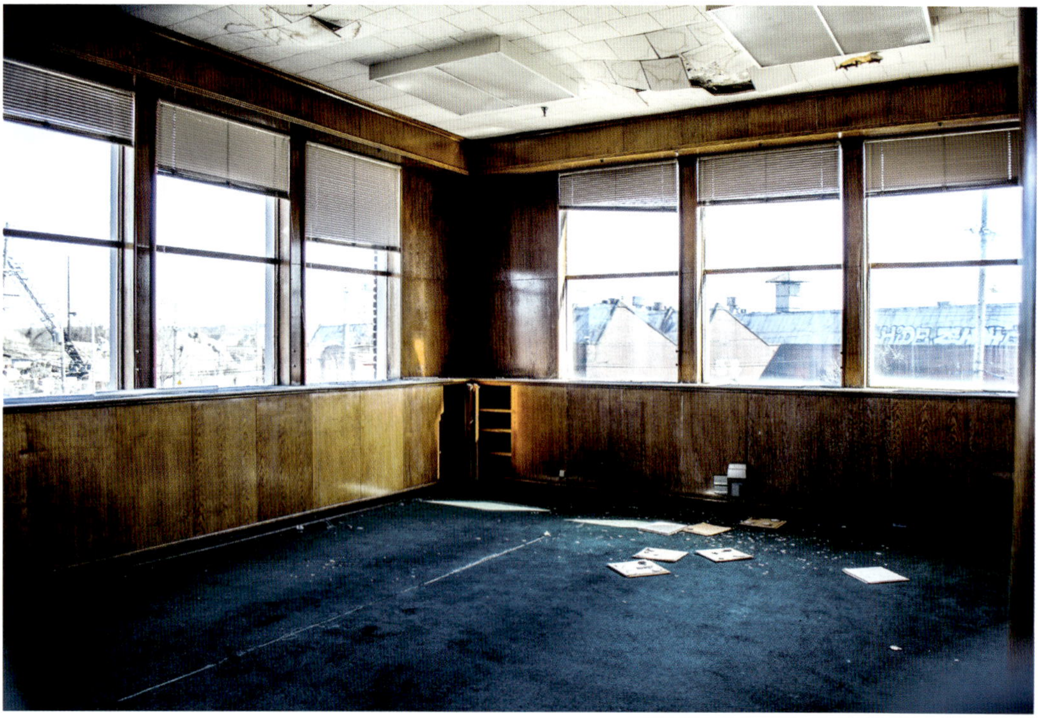

Actual wood paneling is always much nicer than the fake stuff.

5

ROAD TRIPS

None of these locations are in Cleveland. They are all in Ohio but scattered all over the state. I met up with other explorers who knew where to go, sometimes even meeting them for the first time. The social aspect of this hobby can be a lot of fun.

We didn't expect to get into the old Eagles Club building. It was still well sealed off, but we were in the area looking at somewhere else, so we decided to stop and try. We were lucky enough to find a way in, although it took some effort. It was mostly empty, but the bar in the basement showed evidence of being popular in its day. I took the second picture from a walkway that had once been a small balcony before the installation of a drop ceiling. The main hall of the club must have been a lot more grandiose.

The old military buildings took a lot of map studying to find. It's an old Air Force radar station from the height of the Cold War, way off in the middle of nowhere, Ohio. Some of the buildings obviously used to be barracks, but the place has been abandonod for so long that it's hard to say what purpose the rest of the buildings served. As a veteran, it was interesting to see what the old post looked like, even if the floors were so rotten that we could do little more than just peek into the doors.

The stadium once belonged to the Zips, the University of Akron's football team. It wasn't especially big, but it was unique. That's me in the picture for scale. If nothing else, these photos really show just how durable artificial turf can be.

The hospital is more of a complex of buildings than a single location, with the main building comprised of an older and newer portion. It was one of the better hospitals for explorers to visit, relatively secluded, and intact enough to still be identifiable. We initially climbed in through a low (but not low enough to be easy to climb through) window, Then, after exploring a while, we found an open door on the other side of the building—something of a theme for a lot my outings. There were even some buildings on the property which looked to have been short-term living facilities. There were maybe a dozen of these, as well as a handful of other builds with less obvious functions.

There wasn't a whole lot to the abandoned ballpark. Even when it was operational, it wasn't a major league park or anything. But what amused me so much about it was that there was no trace of the field itself, and all those seats were now just facing a big empty field. This was one of the most exposed places I've ever been. We had to just walk in and hope nobody minded.

It's not often that I hear explorers discussing the most disgusting building they've ever been in, but when I do hear it discussed, it's almost always in connection to the second hospital here. Soggy, moldy carpet in every room, and a smell throughout that made me strip off and throw my clothes in the wash the instant I got home. Still, sometimes you see an abandoned building and you've just got to know what it looks like inside.

Featured next is a ski lodge. When the lodge closed, many years ago at this point, the roads leading up to it were ripped up too. It's now just the lodge building itself, sitting in an open field. But to get to that field, you must hike through some woods, and there's no trail. A good sense of direction is required. Getting there isn't difficult, but this was by far the most complicated building to get into that I've ever explored. It did make it rewarding though, and it was a very unique location.

I'm not entirely sure what grades attended the school featured next, but my guess has always been K-8. There was water damage in one part, but the place was mostly in good condition. There wasn't any vandalism, and there were still a lot of supplies left. In fact, the boxes you see in the hallway in the last picture are all full of books. Getting in took a little bit of looking around, but it wasn't really that hard, so it was surprising to find the place in such decent shape. The neighborhood it's in is largely abandoned these days—at least two-thirds of it is empty lots—but even in places like that, there's still someone who will come along and trash the place, either for scrap or just for fun.

Next, the brick church had crews clearing out rubble for a while before we got around to going in. We just picked a weekend when they weren't there and got in easily. As you can see, there are holes in the roof and the floor, and even being as sturdily built as it is, it's not going to last a lot longer. I'm assuming those crews have been getting it ready to be torn down, but I don't know any details. I'm hoping that, at the very least, those stained-glass windows get rescued before it comes down.

The factory featured next was partially torn down, and the debris had even been cleared away. Well, most of it had, in the areas of the lot where the building had been completely razed. I don't know why the demo work had stopped before the building was completely removed, but there was no trace of any of the work having been recent. In fact, this building was interesting, because it was overgrown with more plant life than most. The word "ruins" is a tempting one to throw around while doing this kind of thing, but this is one of the only places where I've felt it to be apt.

The photo of the ceiling is from an abandoned retail space that we wouldn't have normally looked at too closely, but it was right next door to another abandoned building that we hadn't managed to get into, so we figured we'd give it a shot. The most interesting part was when we climbed the stairs to the second floor. It was the sort of strange garage sale assortment of items that we were expecting to find, but there was also an impressively ornate tin ceiling, all the more impressive because this wasn't even an area the public would have ever seen. Rotting though it was, it still looked out of place in this dank and otherwise unfinished upstairs storage space.

The large and better-preserved industrial building is much older than it looks in parts of the inside. It had started life as a Packard plant, the luxury brand from Warren, Ohio. But unlike the big—and now famously dangerously decrepit—plant in Detroit, this one continued making parts for other manufacturers after Packard folded. We found a Mitsubishi logo painted on the floor in one part, and there may have been others as well. It's an interesting mix of eras of automotive history.

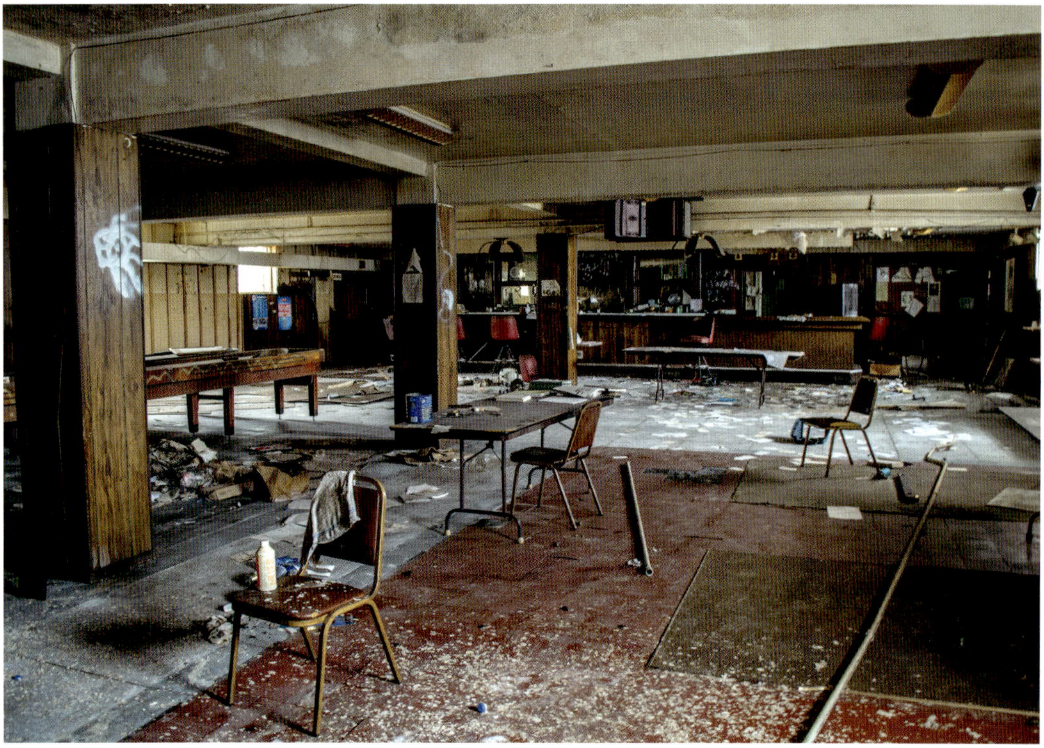

Bars with this much fake wood paneling always have the cheapest beer.

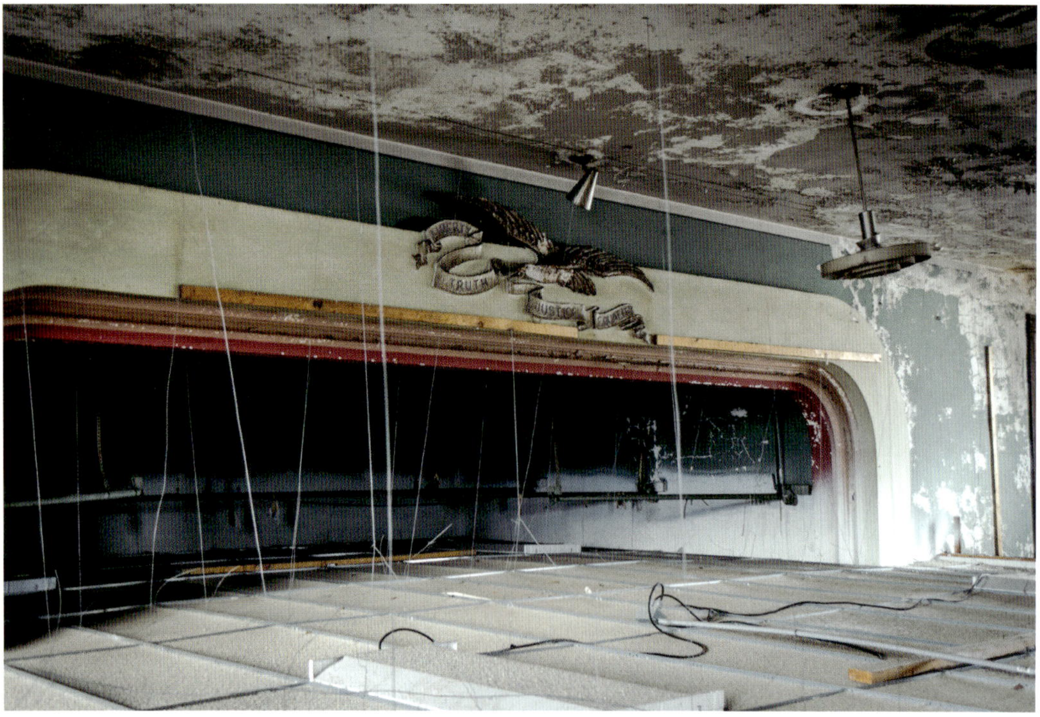

I sometimes wonder how much truly spectacular architectural detail is hidden by drop ceilings.

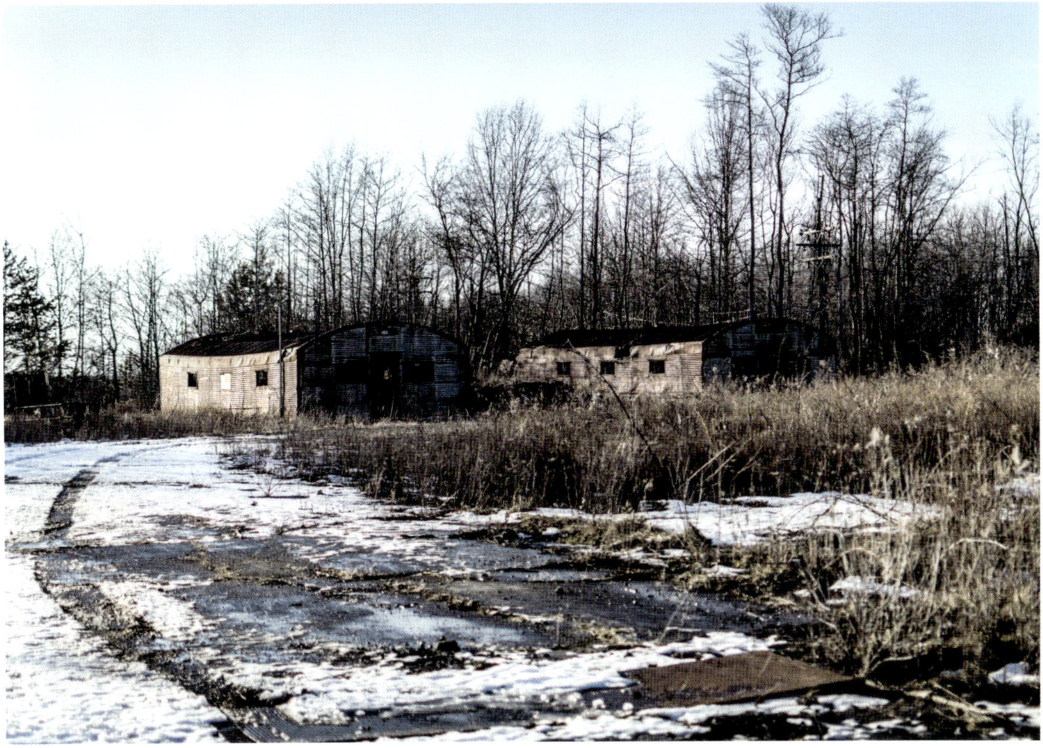

We had a weird feeling of being watched the whole time we explored this spot. It was worse in open areas like this.

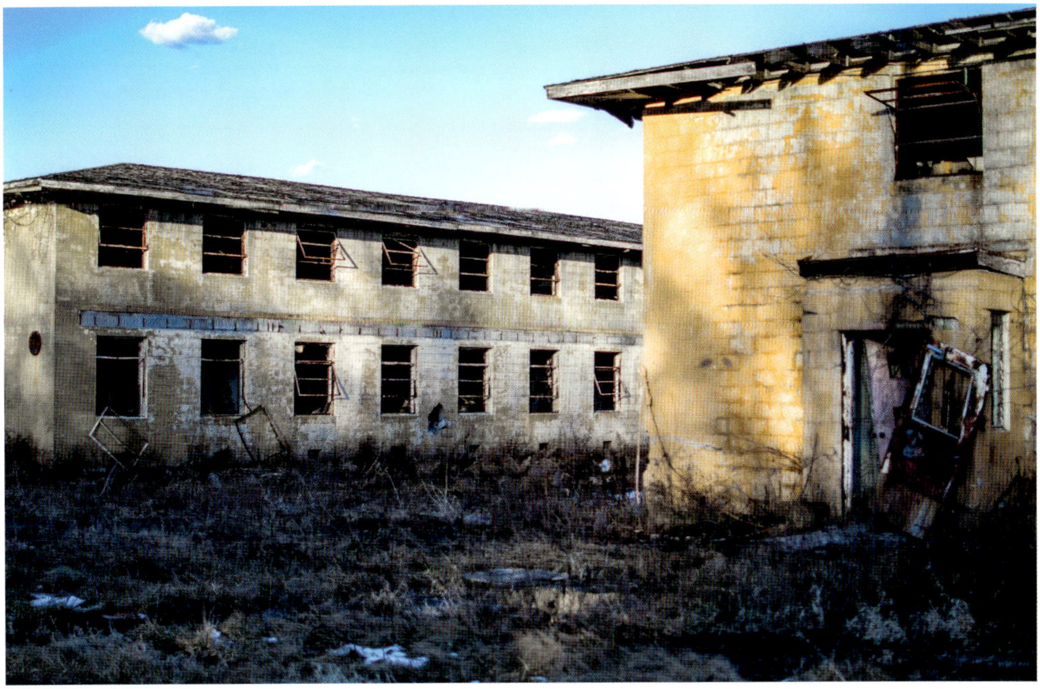

These barracks looked to be all communal areas. It would probably get pretty old living here for any kind of extended period.

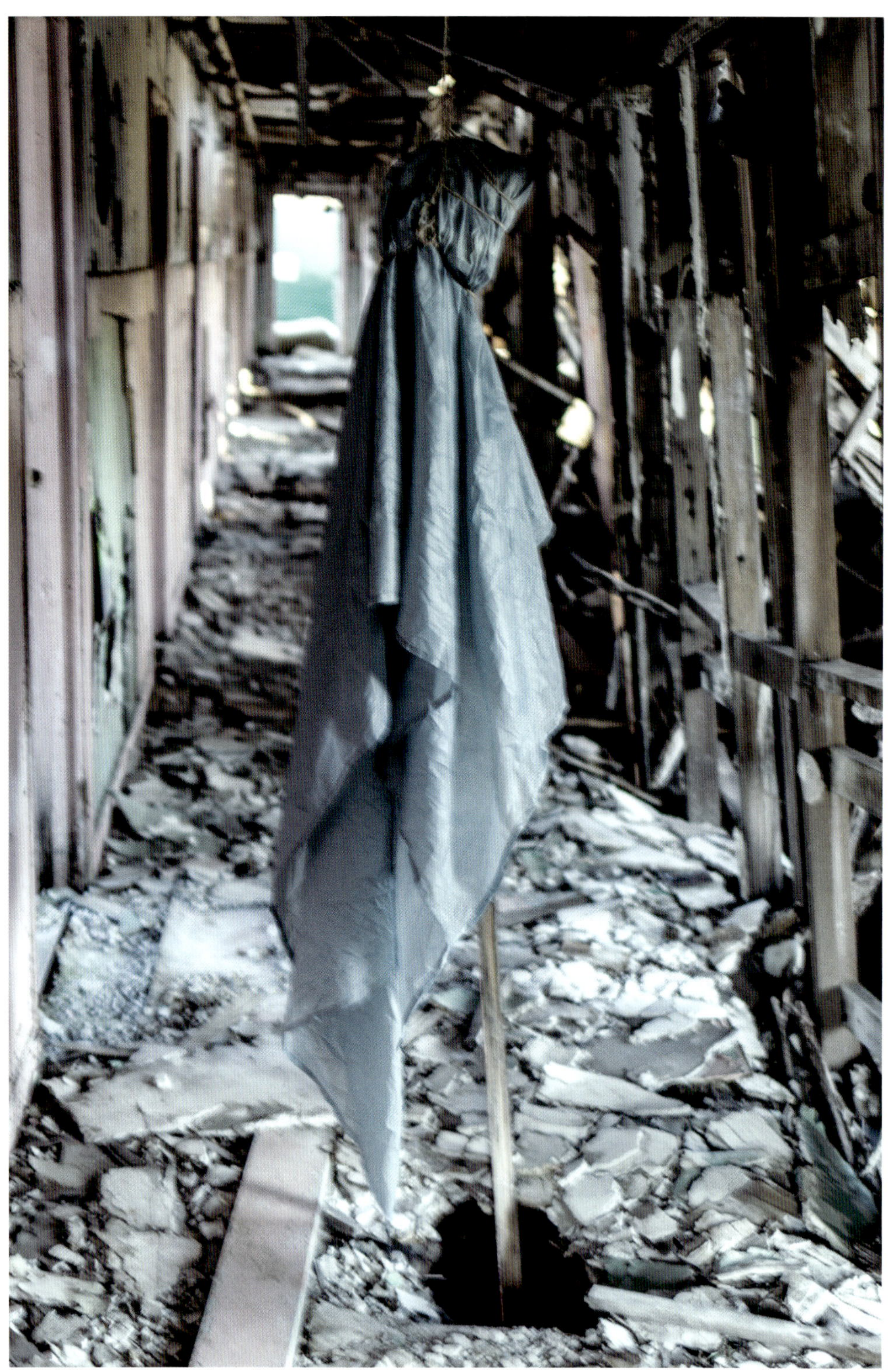

I don't exactly know what this is. It seemed to be some kind of effigy hanging just inside the entrance of one of the barracks buildings. I have no clue why it was there, but it was an unsettling thing to find. I asked some explorers who were there after me if it was still there, and apparently it isn't. I don't know whether that's good or bad.

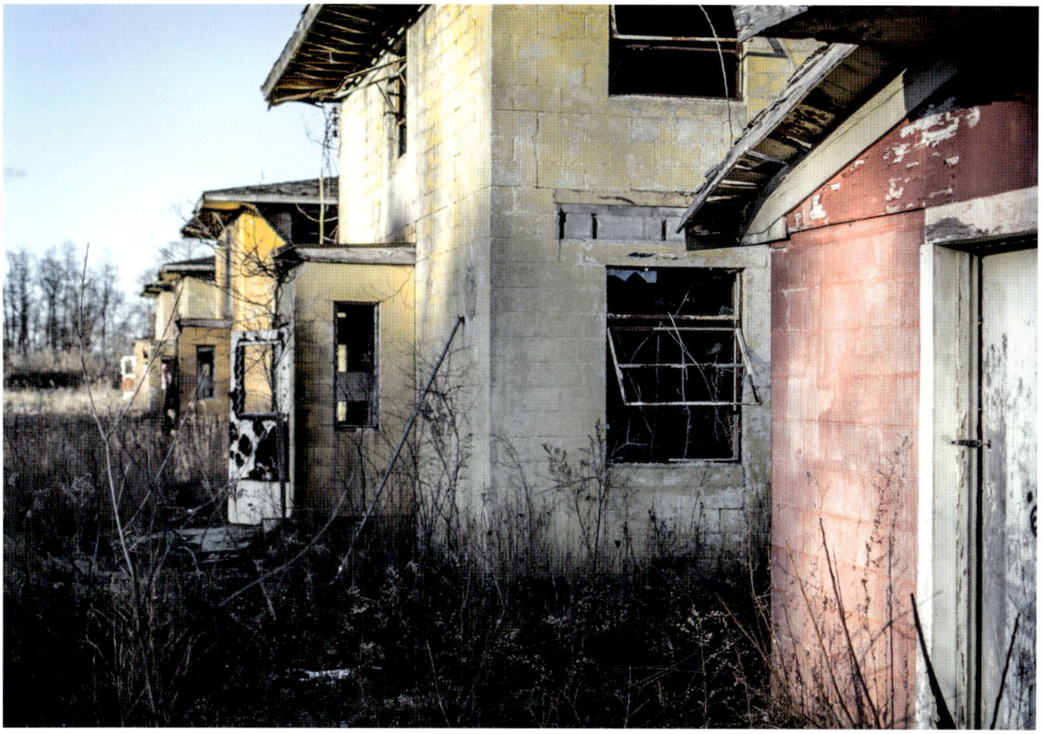

If I was forced to guess, I'd say this facility would have held a maximum of about 200 servicemen in its day.

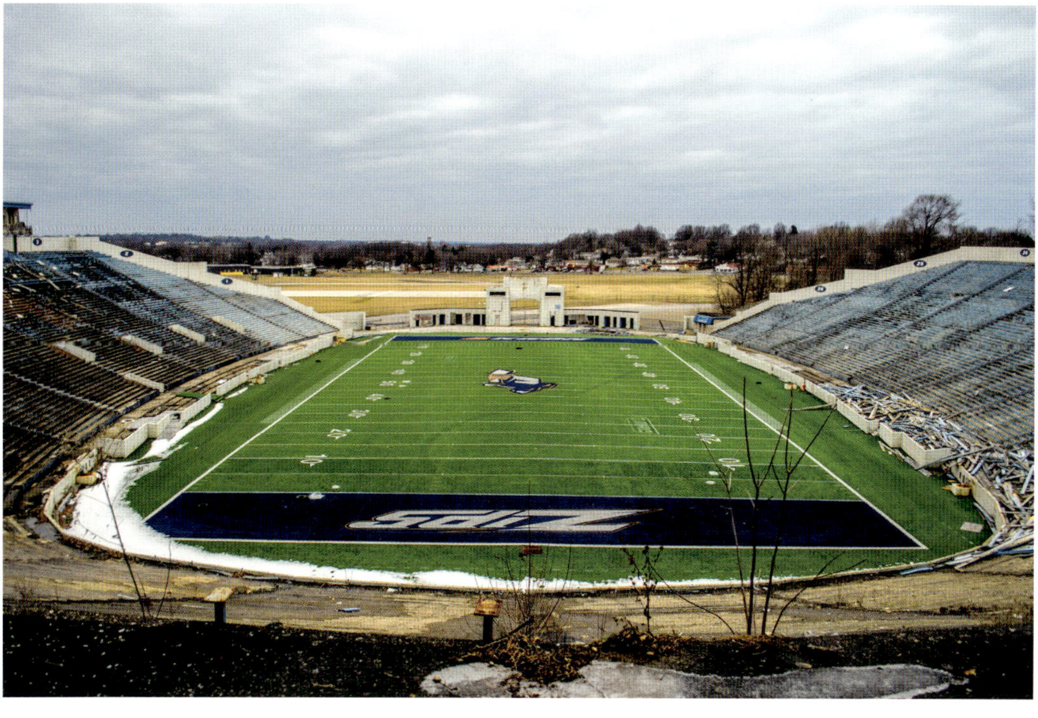

There was a fence around this place, but it simply ended about three-quarters of the way around. Getting in was just a matter of walking a little further.

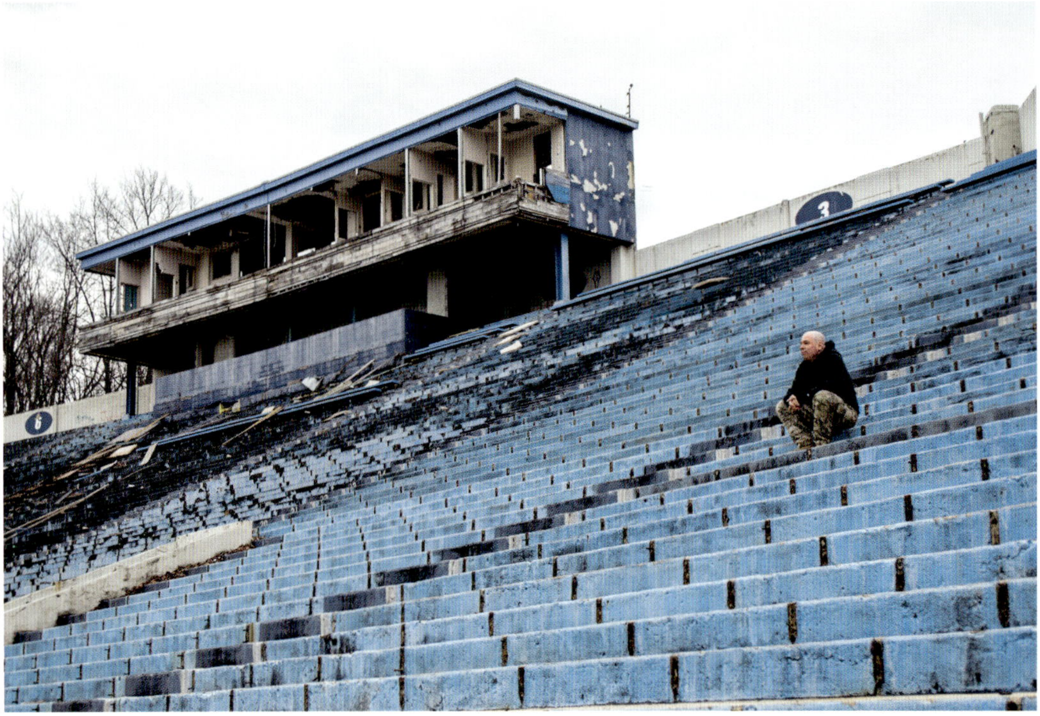

I've never been a big fan of photos of myself, but at this distance I suppose I can stand it.

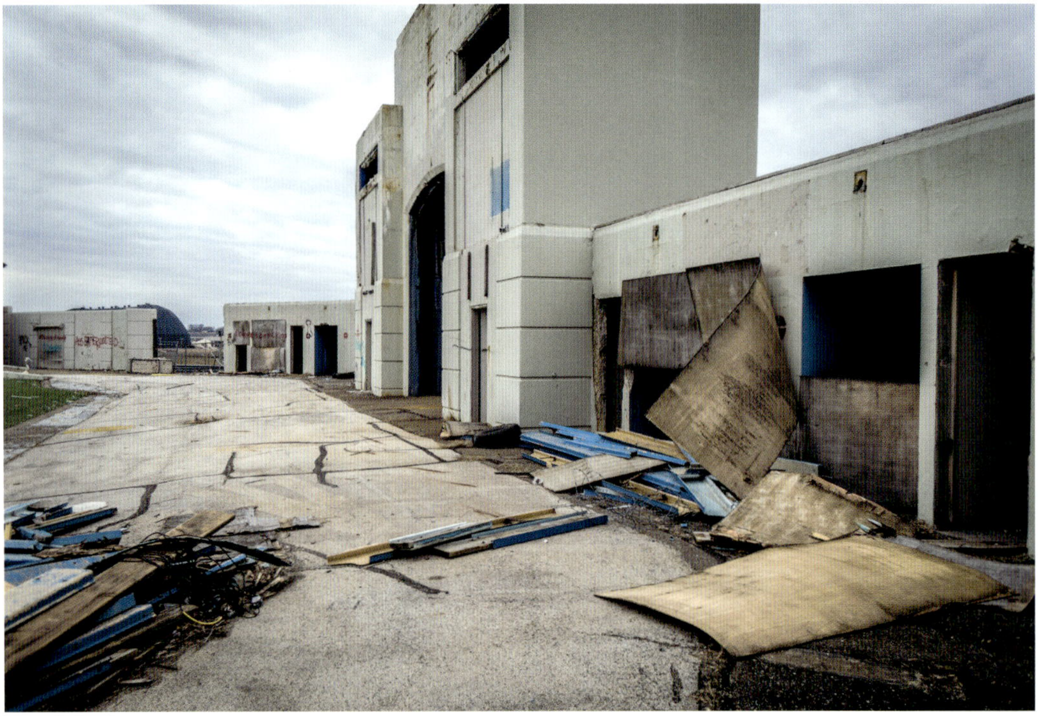

I really don't know what a lot of this part of the stadium was for. In the background, you can see the hangar for the Goodyear blimp.

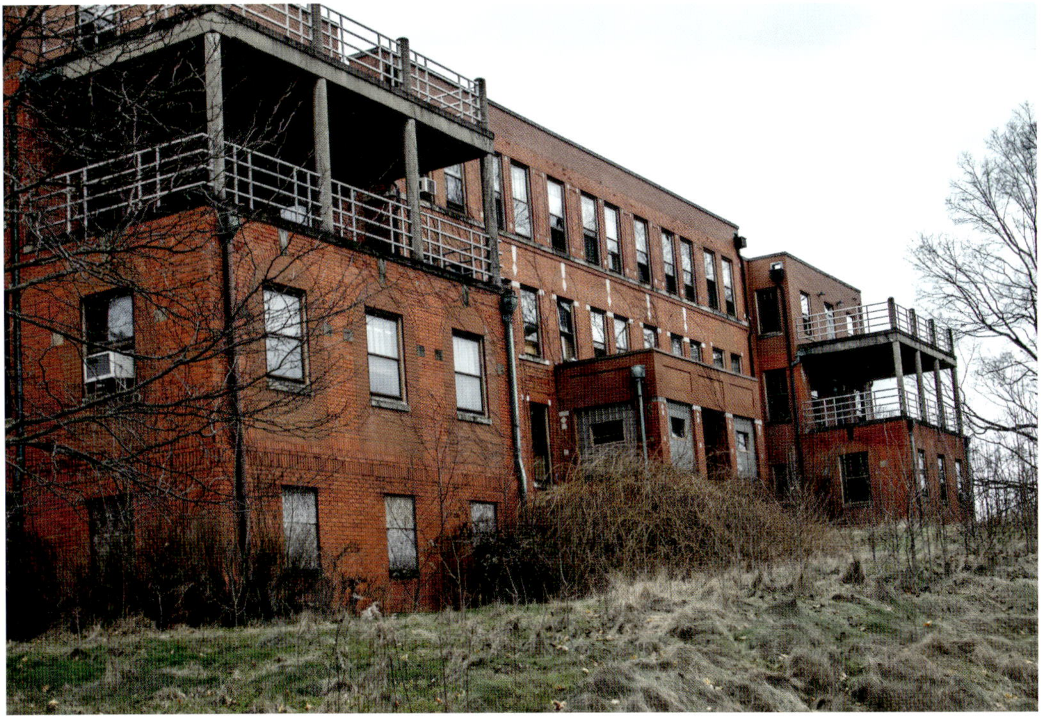

In this photo is the window we climbed through, and it is not one of the ones on the ground floor.

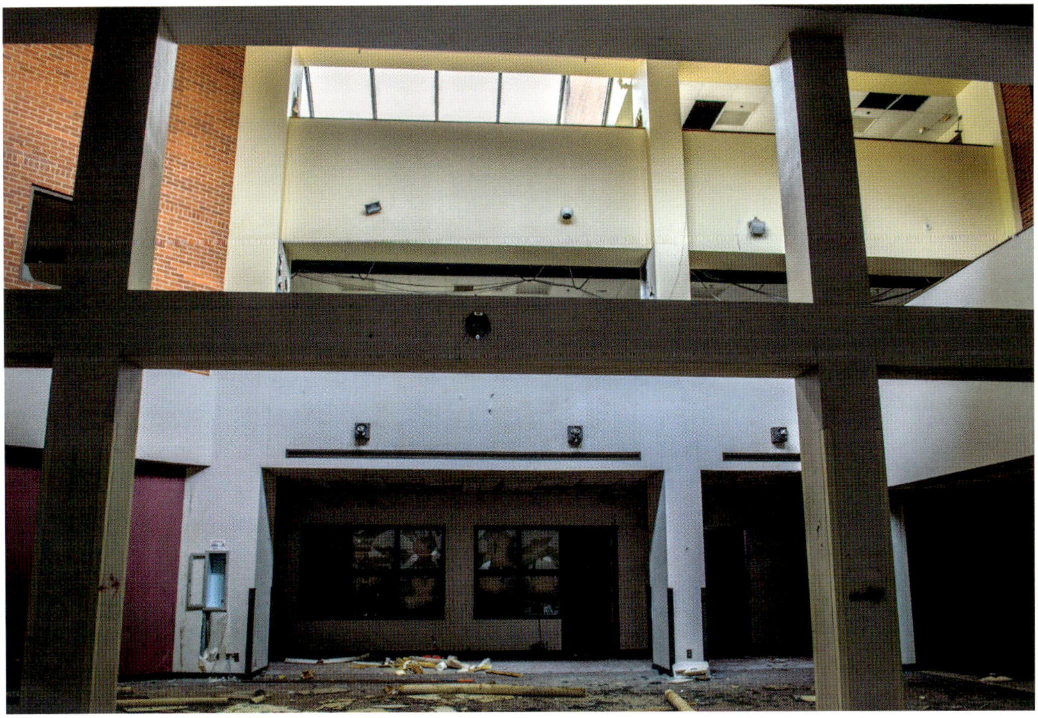

This area was a kind of atrium, but without enough windows to make a convincing one. I'm not sure what they were going for.

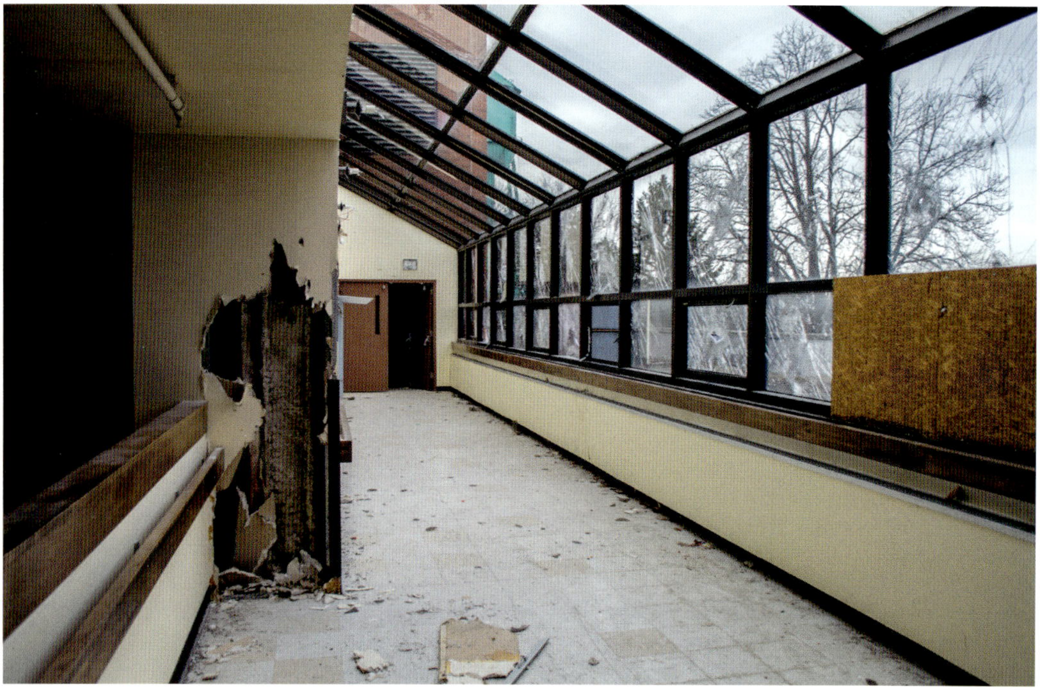

The natural light here must have been nice to have when this was a functioning hospital, but the view was awfully unimpressive—just a whole bunch of roof.

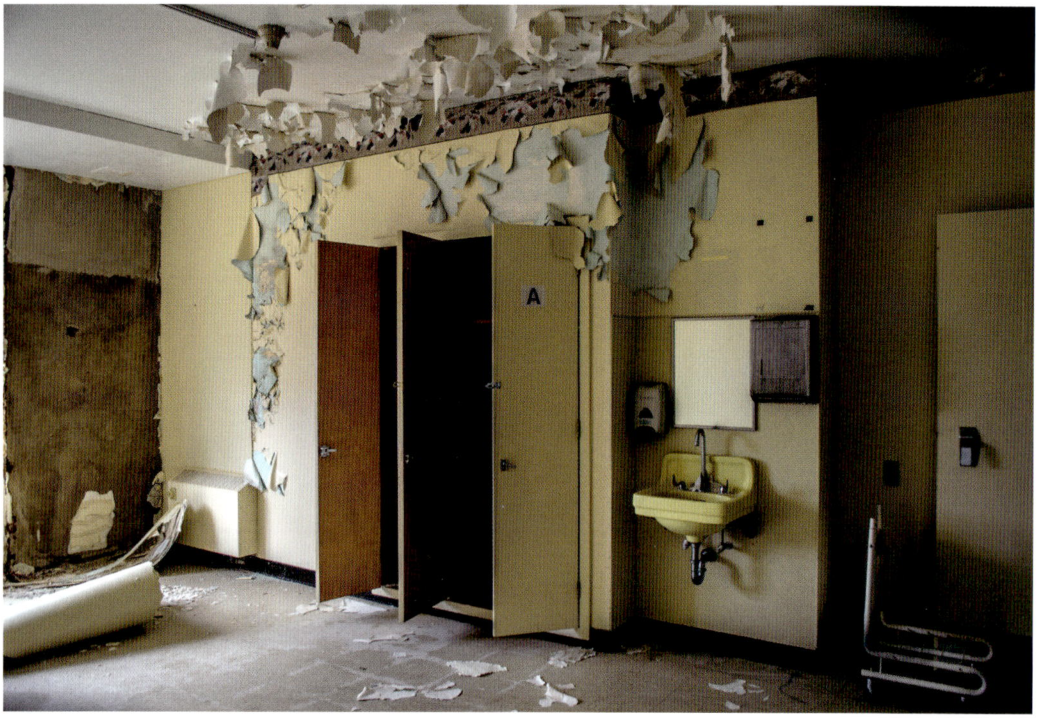

Nearly every bit of salvageable equipment was taken out of this place when it closed, so this was as close to an intact room I was able to find.

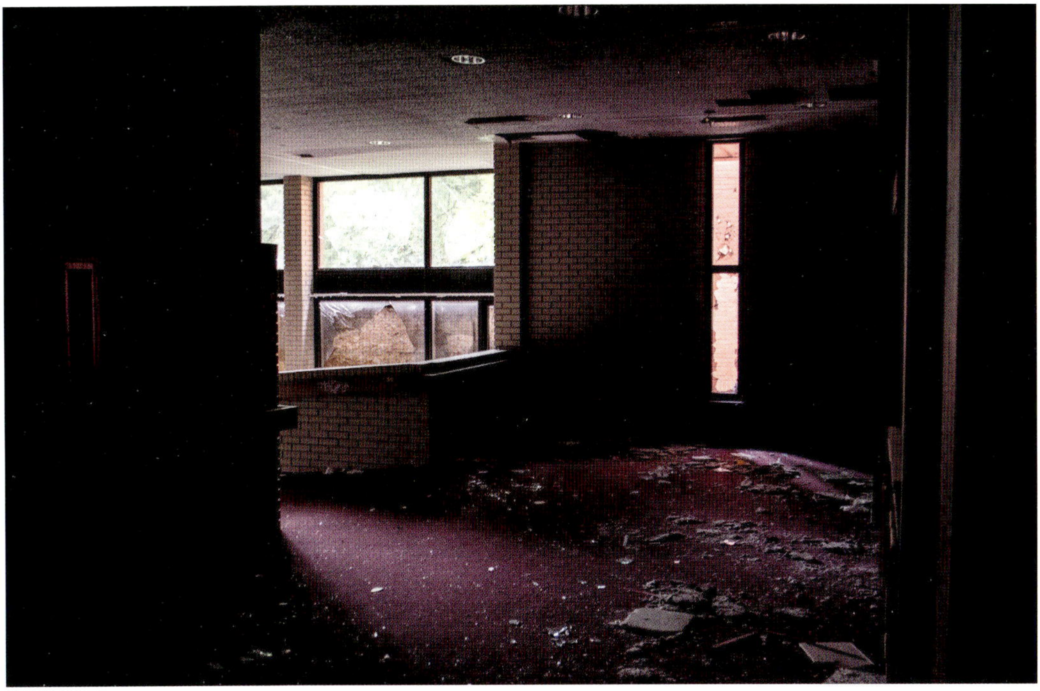

I think this had been the main entrance to the hospital at one point. This was in the older part, and it was much smaller than the newer section, so this may have sufficed as an entrance for such a small facility.

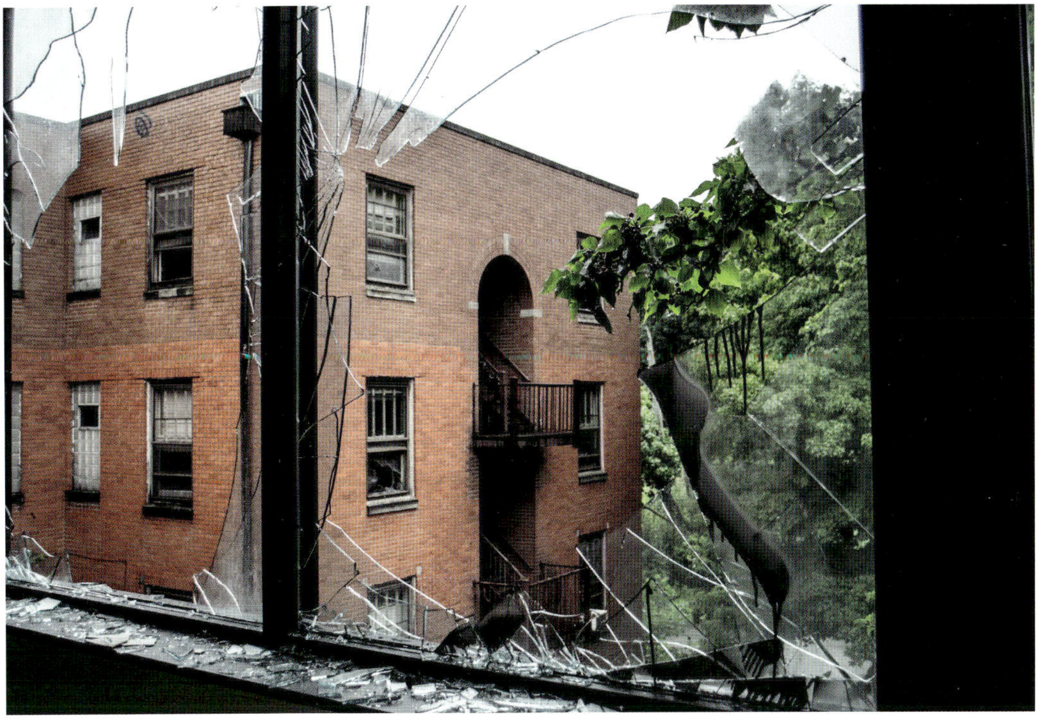

The old building section as viewed from the new section. It looks as though the top floor might have been added after the bottom two, but I don't know for sure.

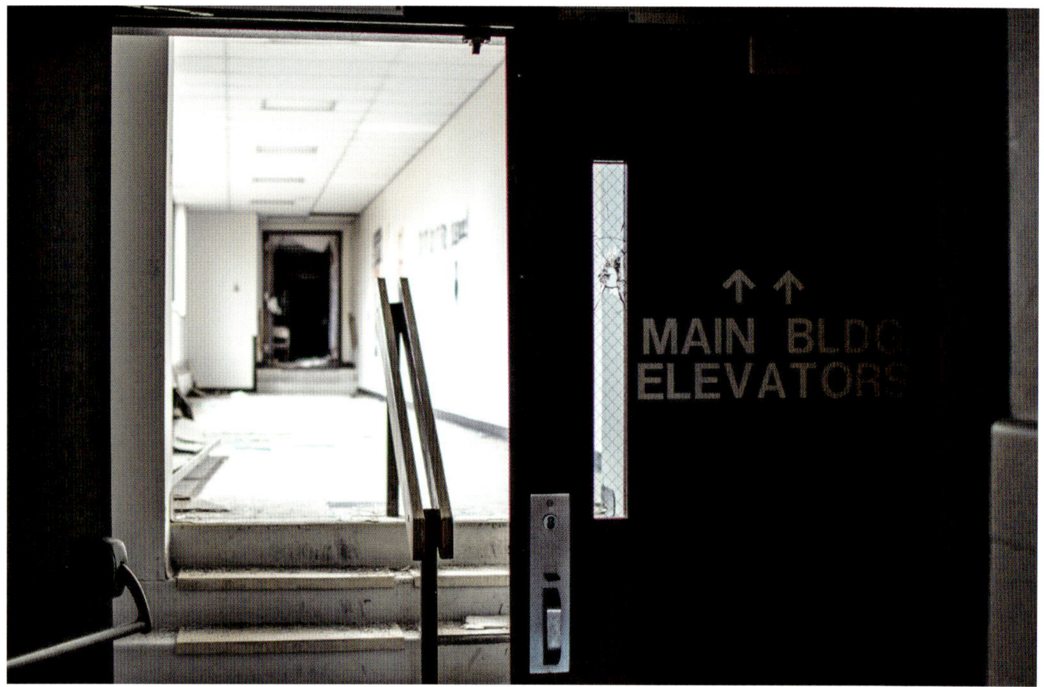

This walkway connected the two sections of the building. All the windows were broken, which isn't unusual, but there was glass all over the floor, suggesting they were broken from the outside. That is unusual, since this was the third floor.

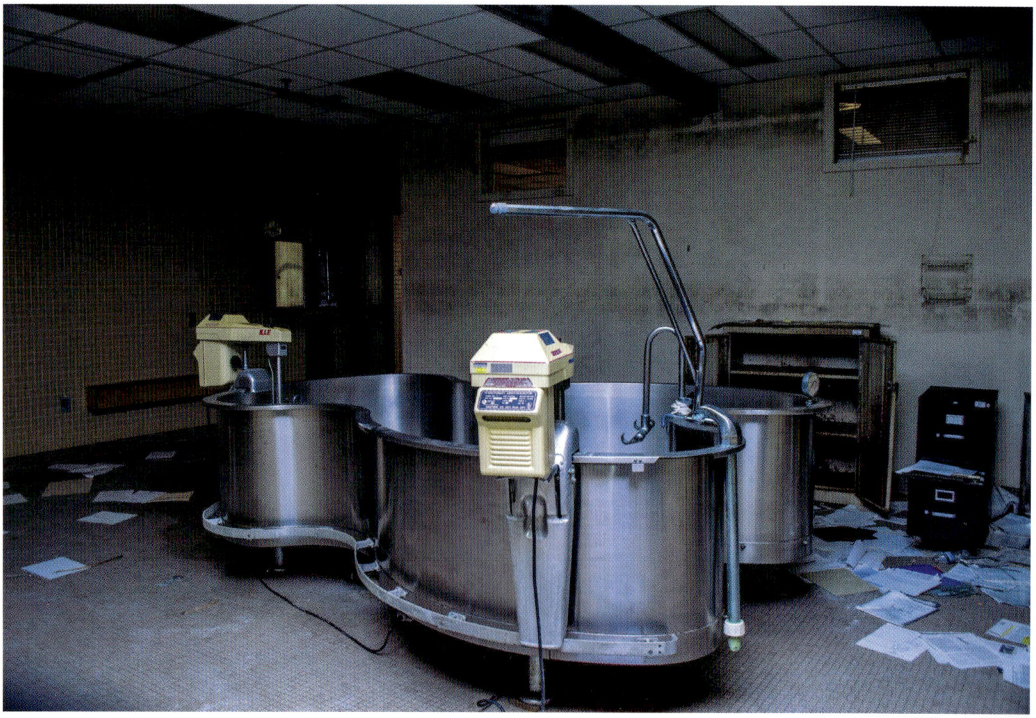

Lacking any kind of medical training, this looks to me like what you would use to make the world's largest milkshake.

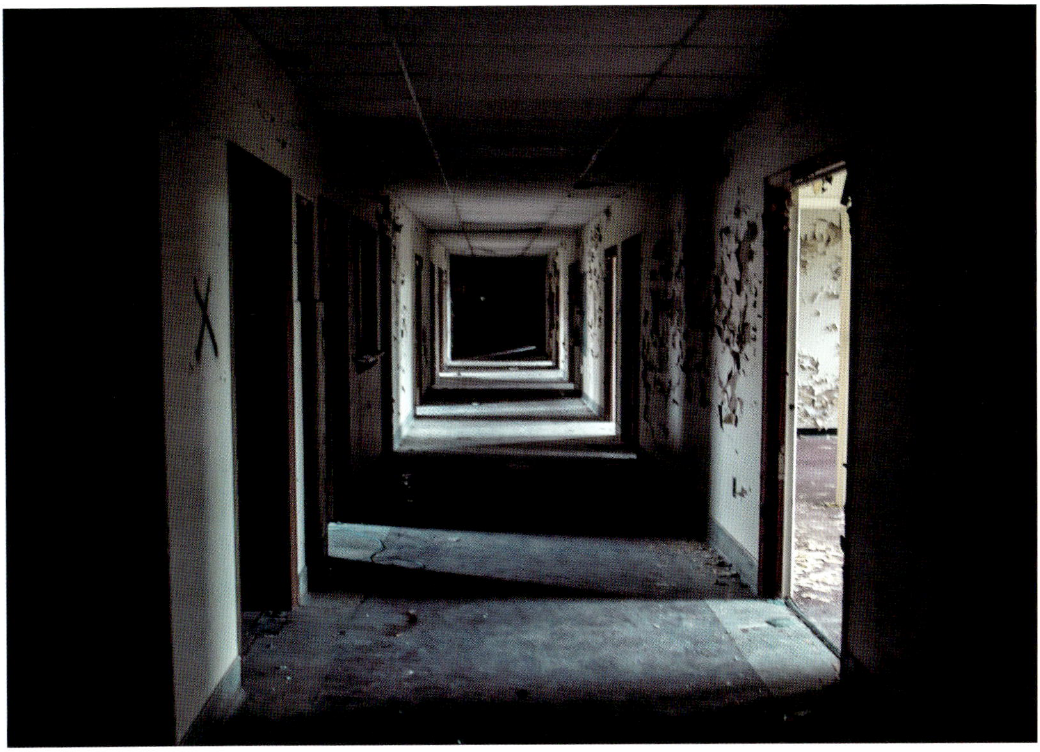

The older section of the building wasn't beat up as much and aged better than the newer section.

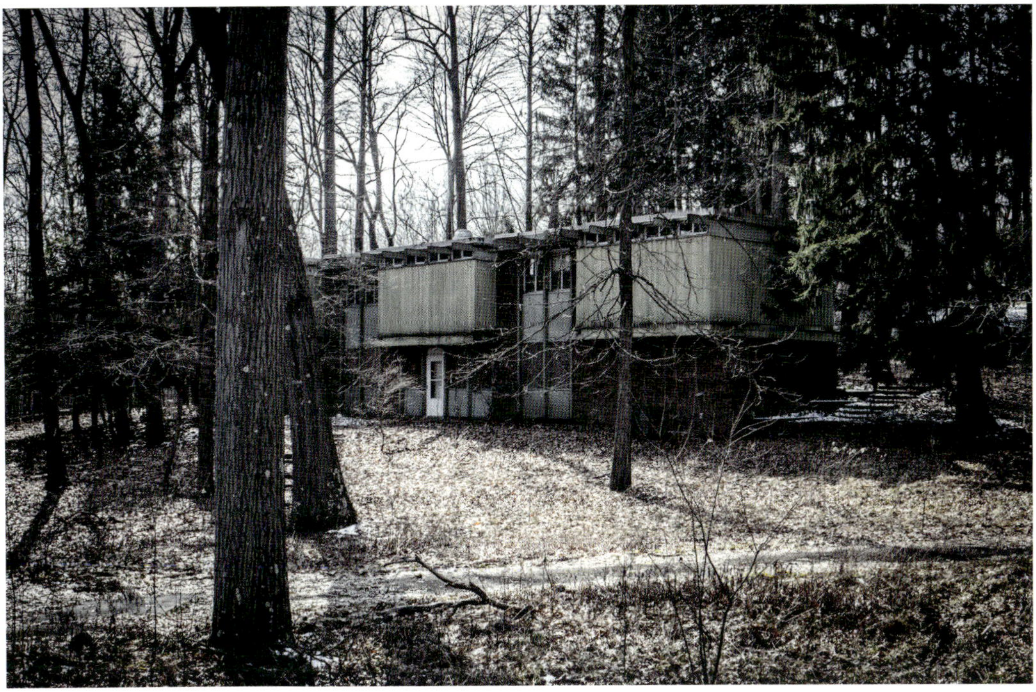

These buildings were being used as some sort of dorms, but there were also rooms in them that clearly served a medical purpose. With all of the equipment removed, we couldn't begin to guess what that specific purpose was.

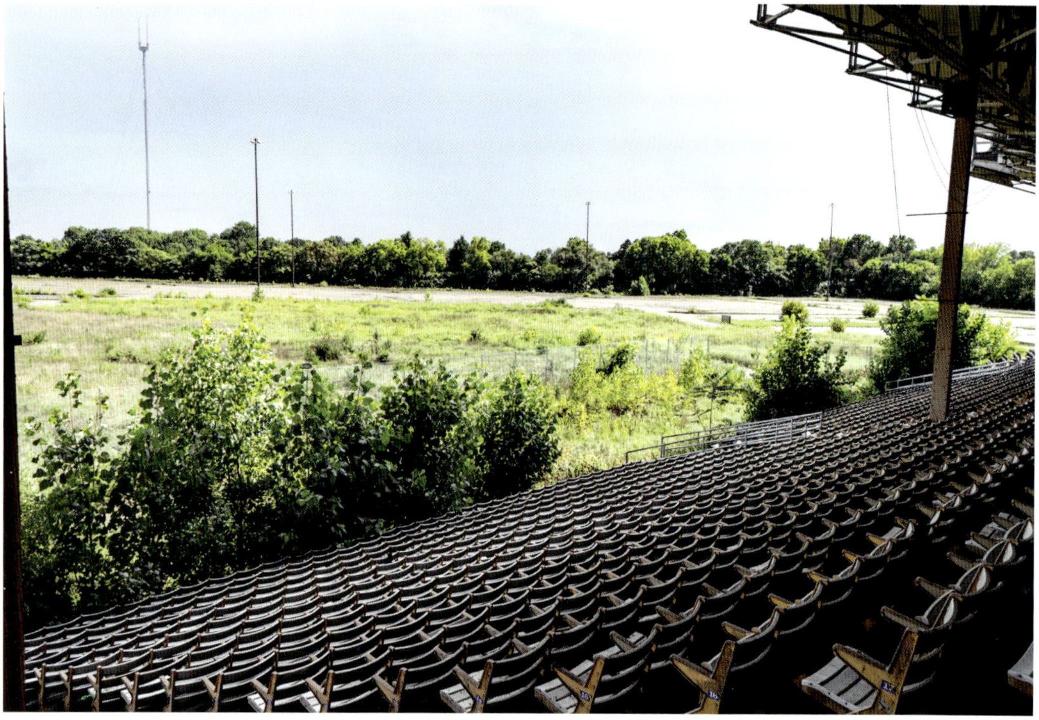

While we were exploring this place, trucks kept driving through the far parking lot for reasons we could not fathom. It made me uneasy, but was also just confusing, as it didn't connect to anything.

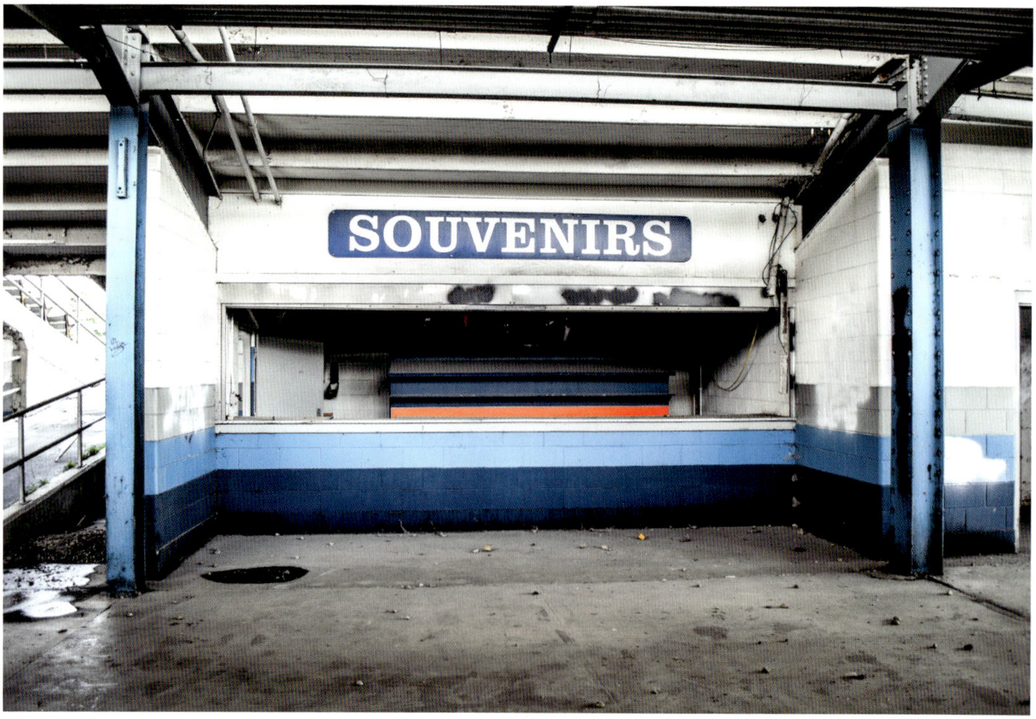

I was really hoping to find some leftover souvenirs somewhere here, but no such luck. It was a long shot.

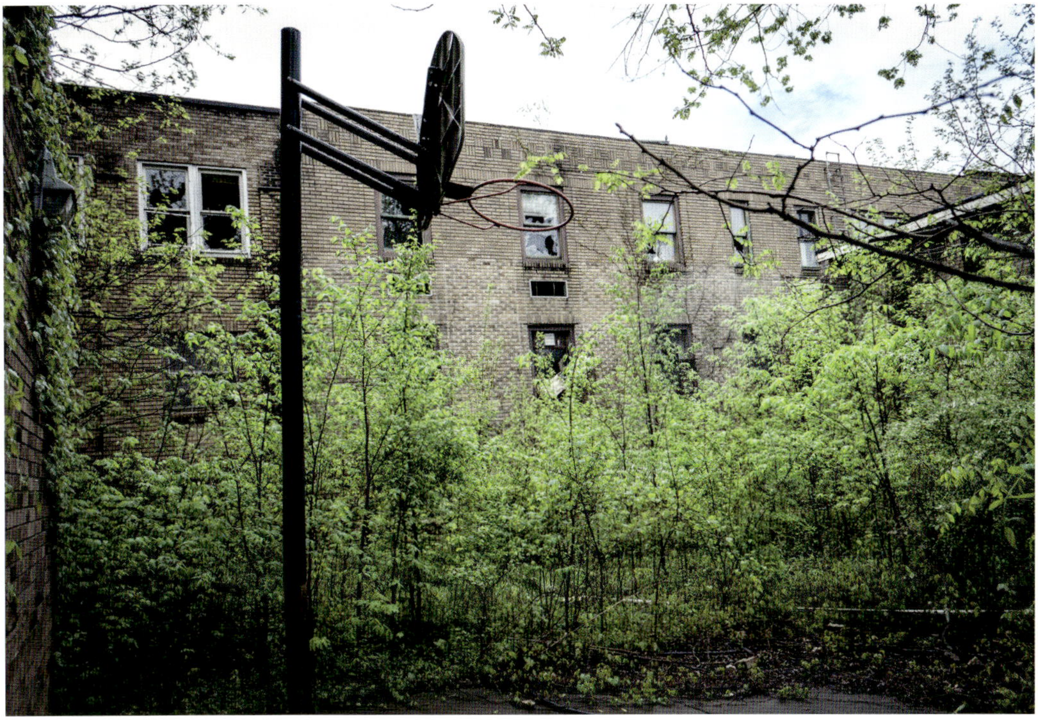

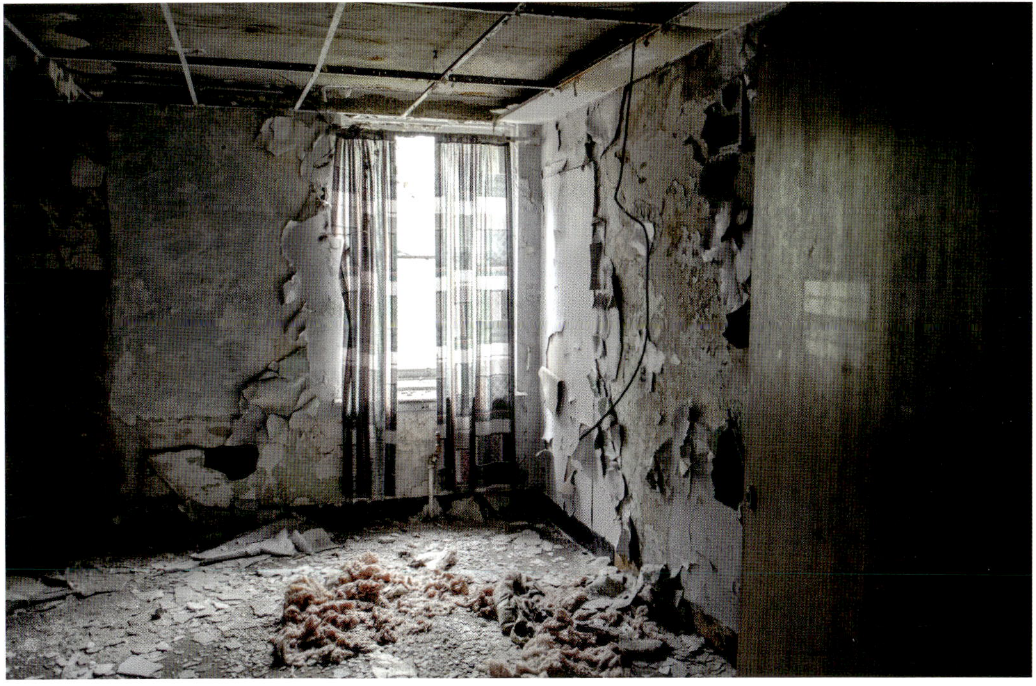

There were so many windows in the courtyard, I couldn't help but wonder how often they had basketballs go through them over the years.

A surprising number of curtains were still up in this place. Those don't usually last when the rest of the building is at this level of decay.

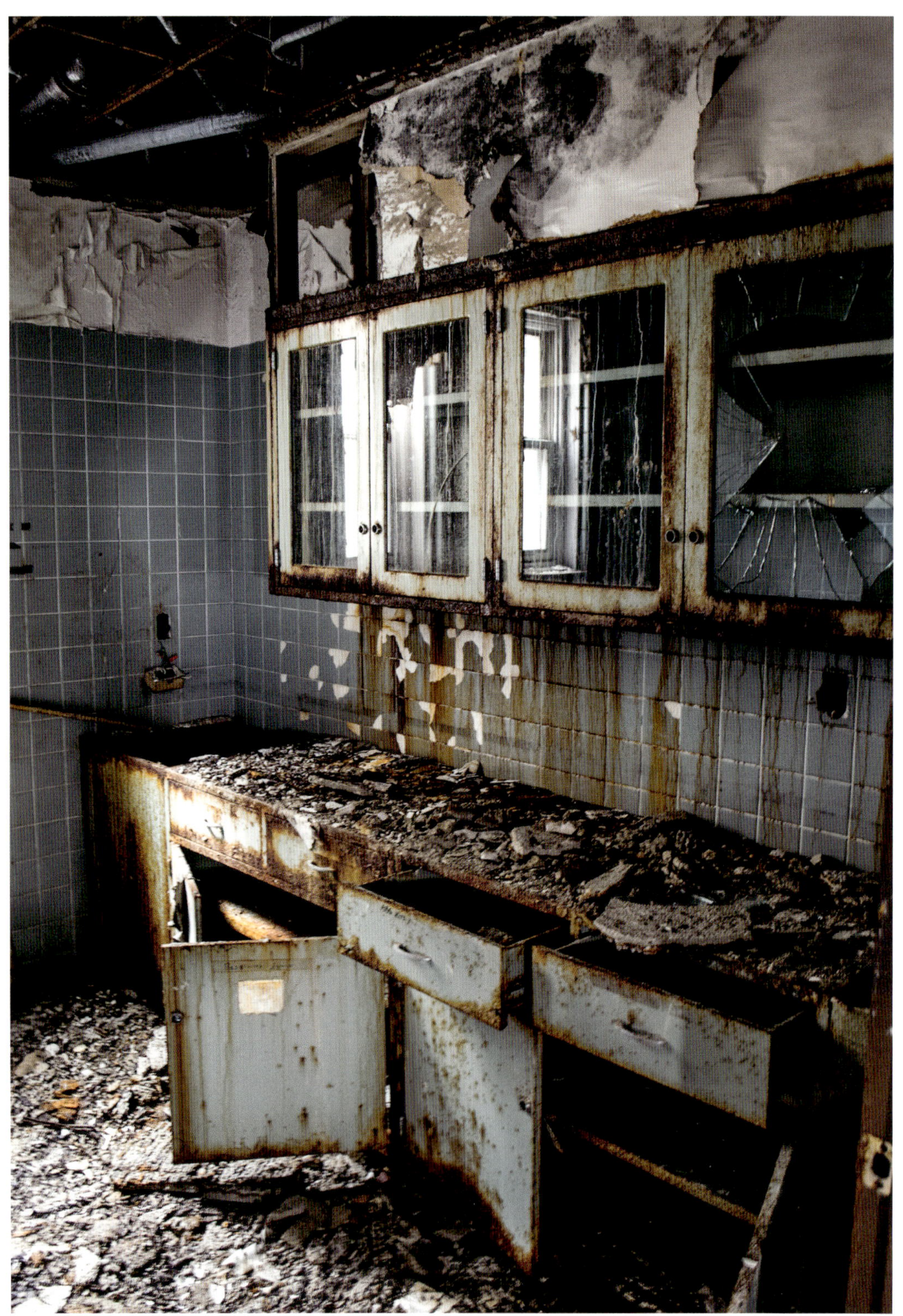

You can almost smell this place just from this photo.

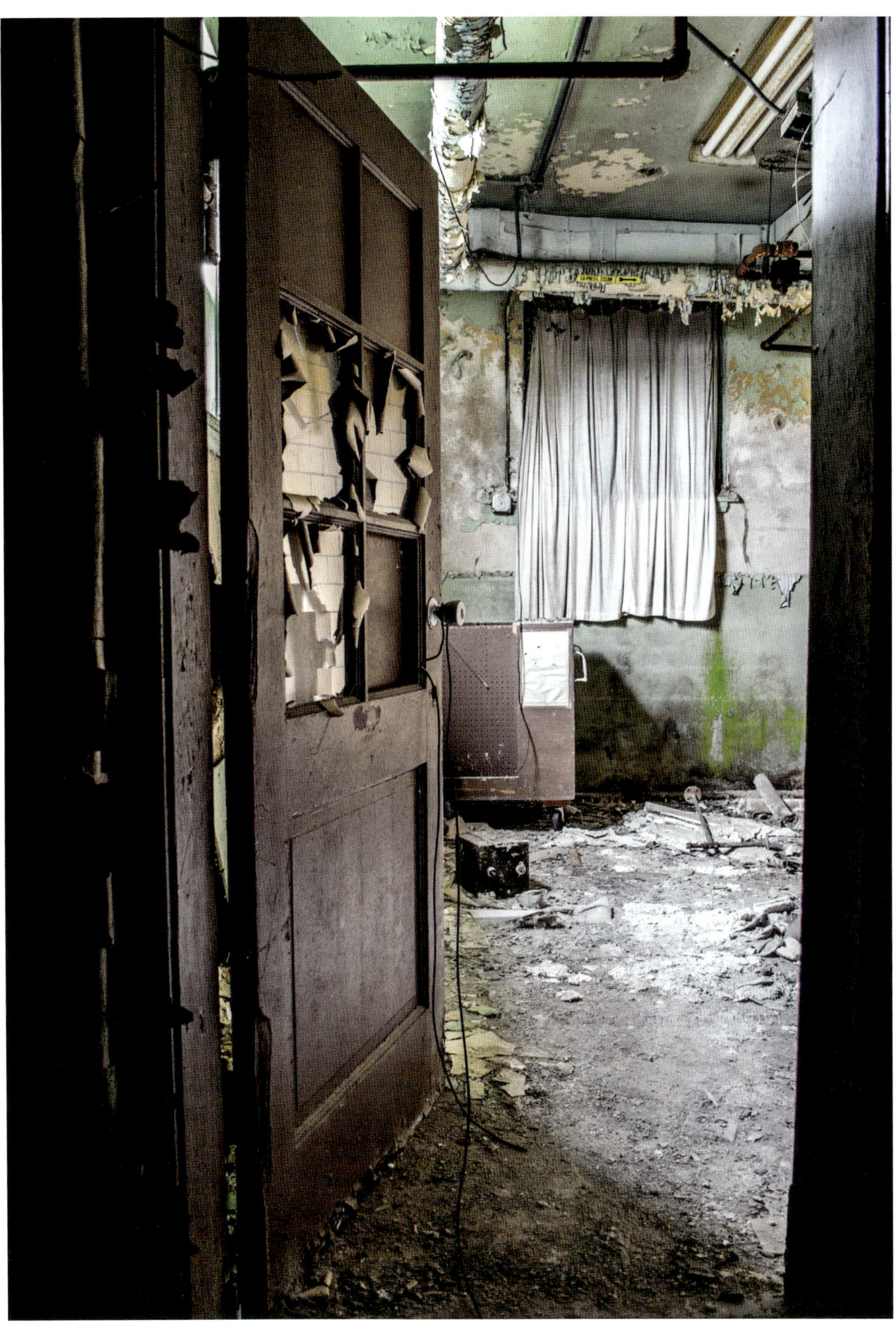

We got lost trying to get back out of this hospital. You would think it would be easy to retrace your steps, but apparently not. At least we got to see some cool spots in the basement.

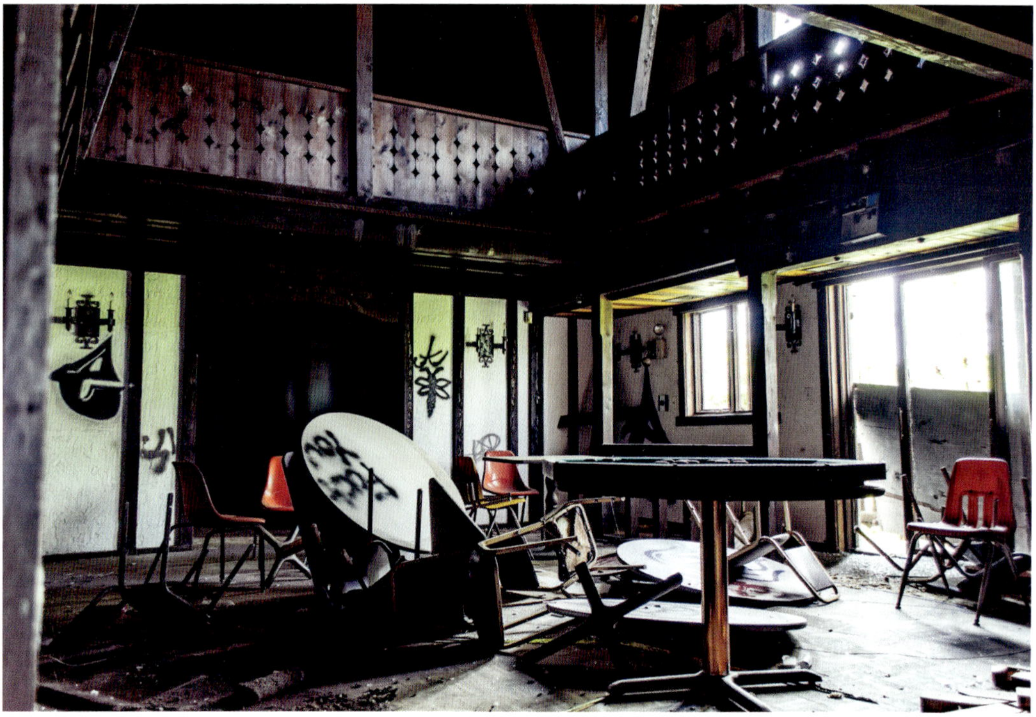

There was a lot of cheesy 70s faux-Swiss in this place, but in parts it was well done.

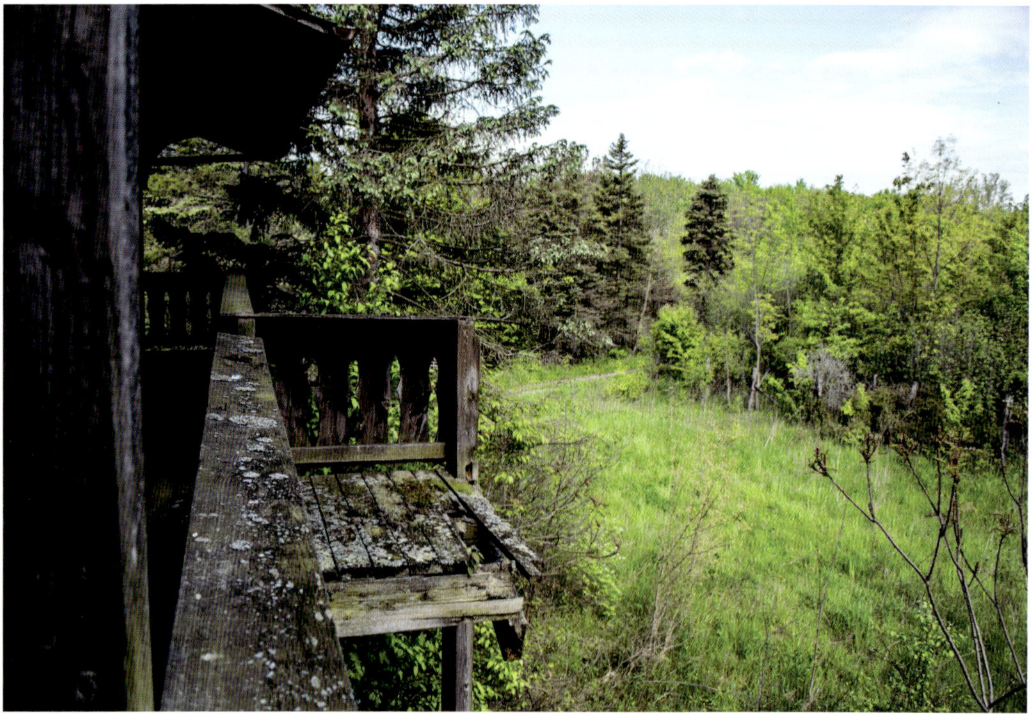

There was no rubble where these stairs had been, so it's possible this happened before the place was boarded up. It was a great view from up there though. This must have been a great little getaway in its day.

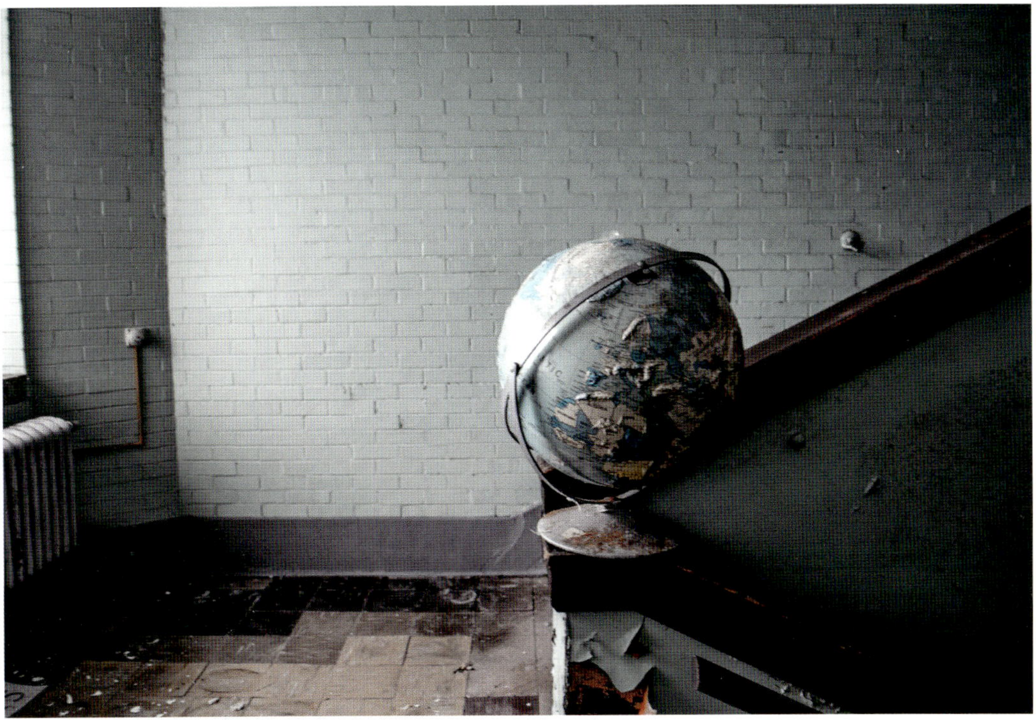

This globe was just sitting there, and the color matched the walls so perfectly that I had to have a photo.

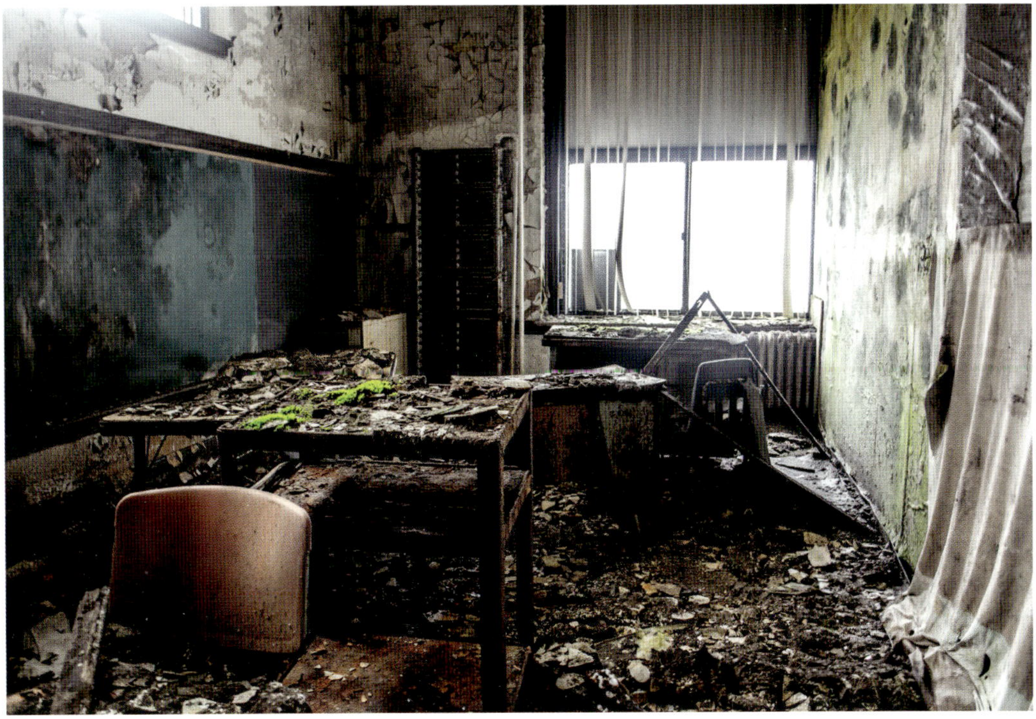

If exploring has taught me one thing, it's what water damage and moisture can do to a building. A little bit gets in and it's just a matter of time before the whole place goes.

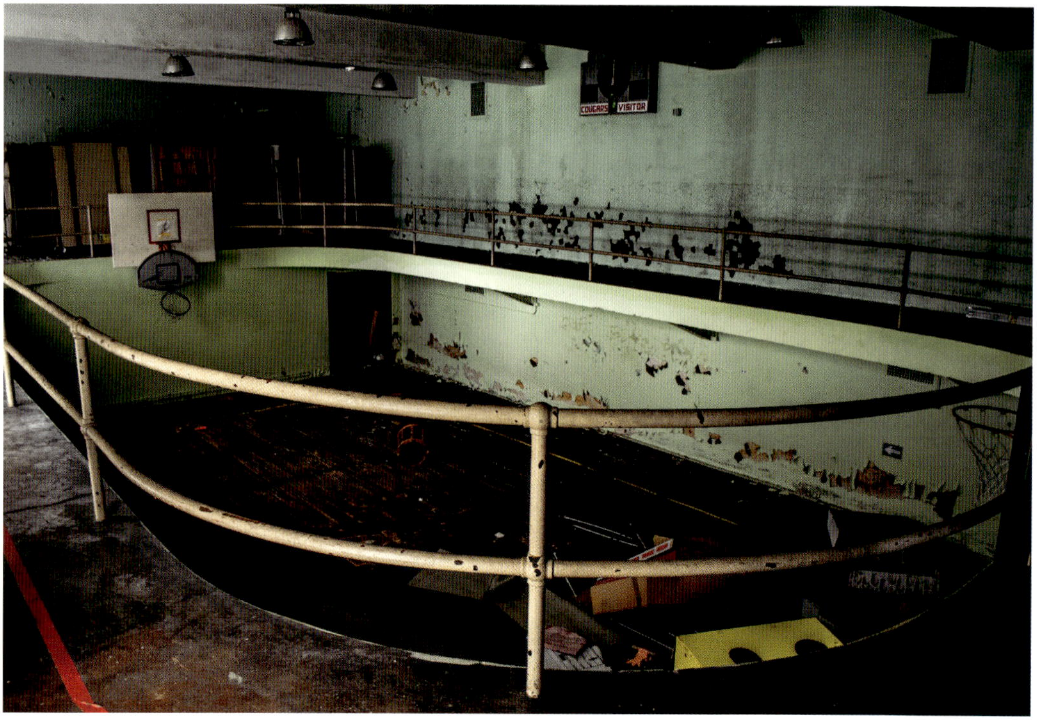

The windows here weren't boarded up—there was just very little natural light in here. It seemed like a kind of miserable place to hold gym class, but it made for a good photo.

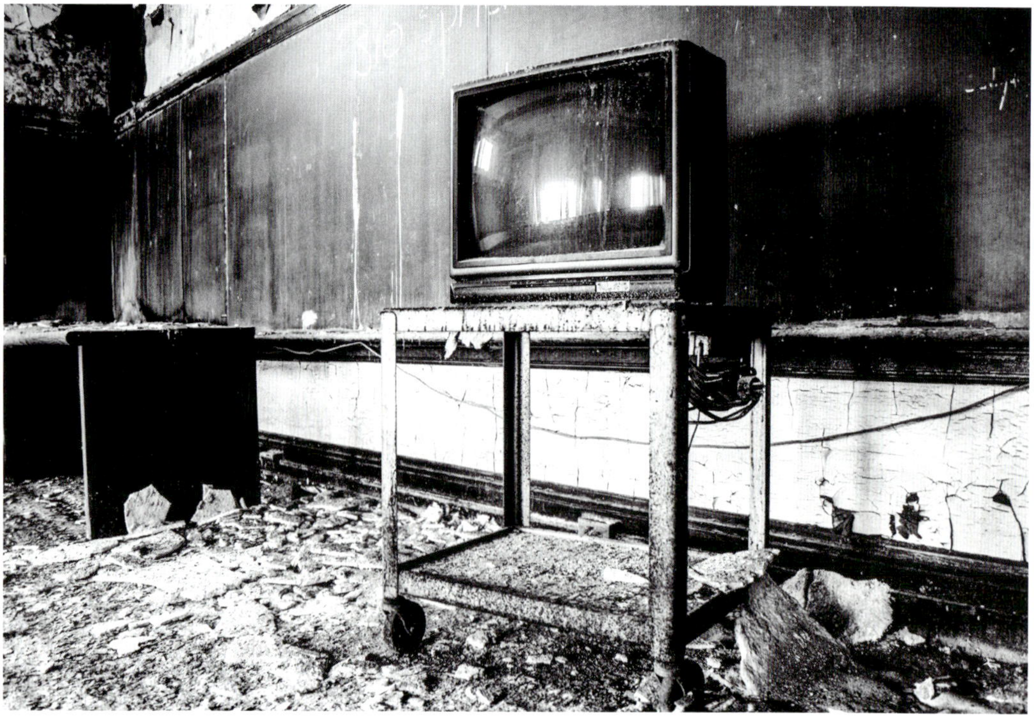

An intact TV in an abandoned building—one for the history books.

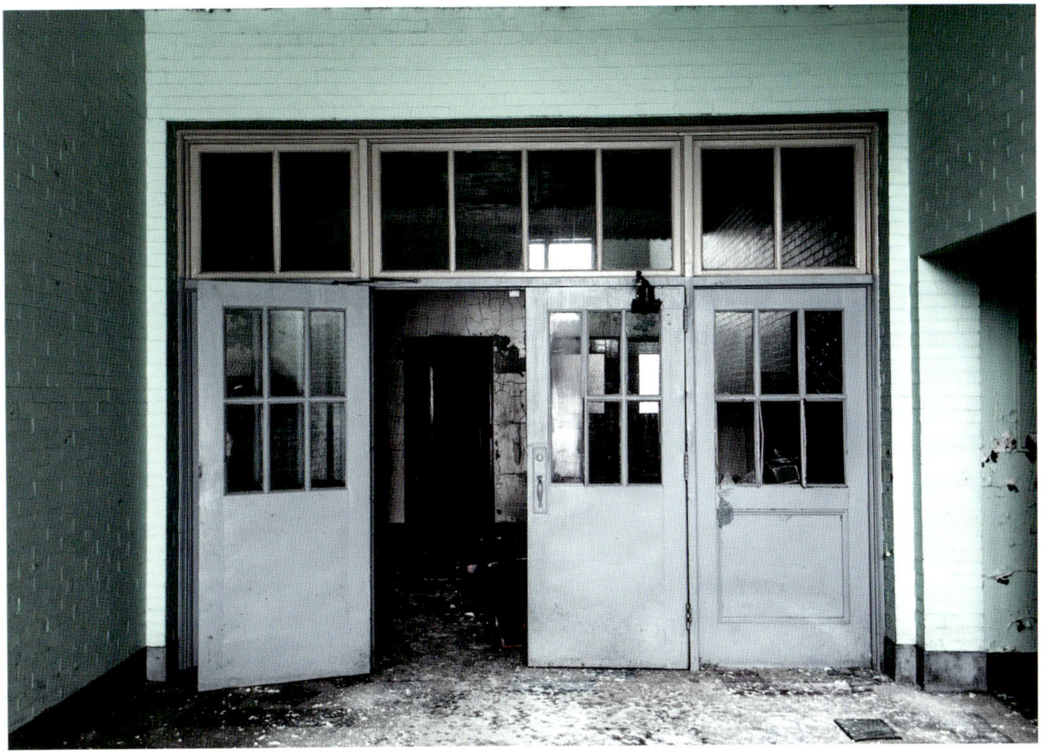

I don't think they picked the paint colors for this school with urban explorers in mind, but I found them very pleasing.

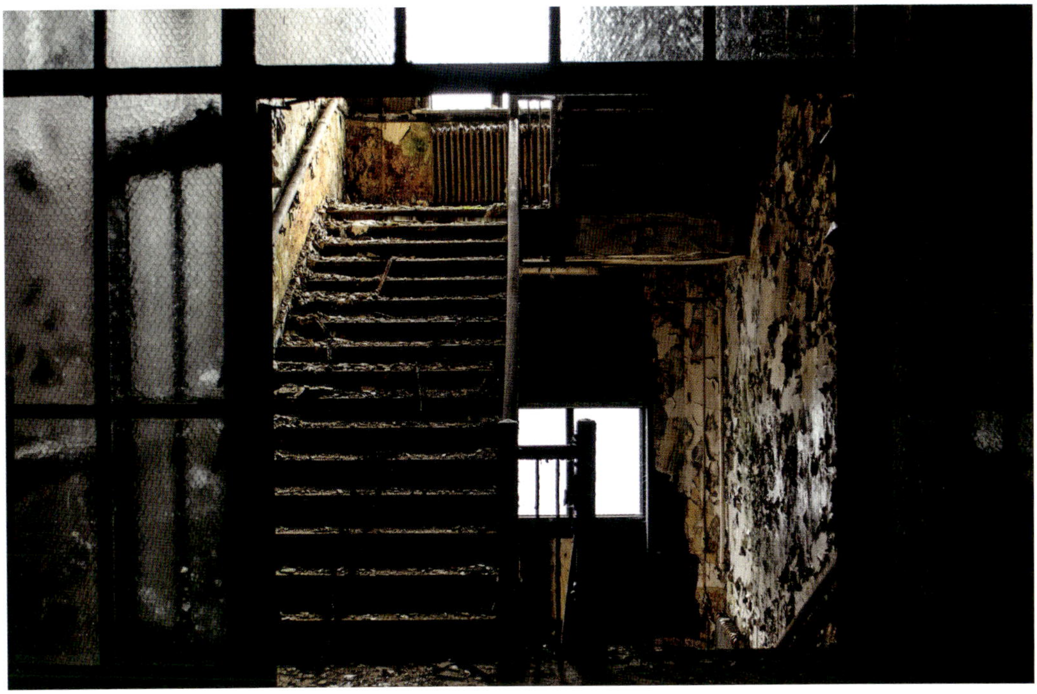

The detritus that you find on the floors of every abandoned building is usually mostly paint that has peeled off the walls.

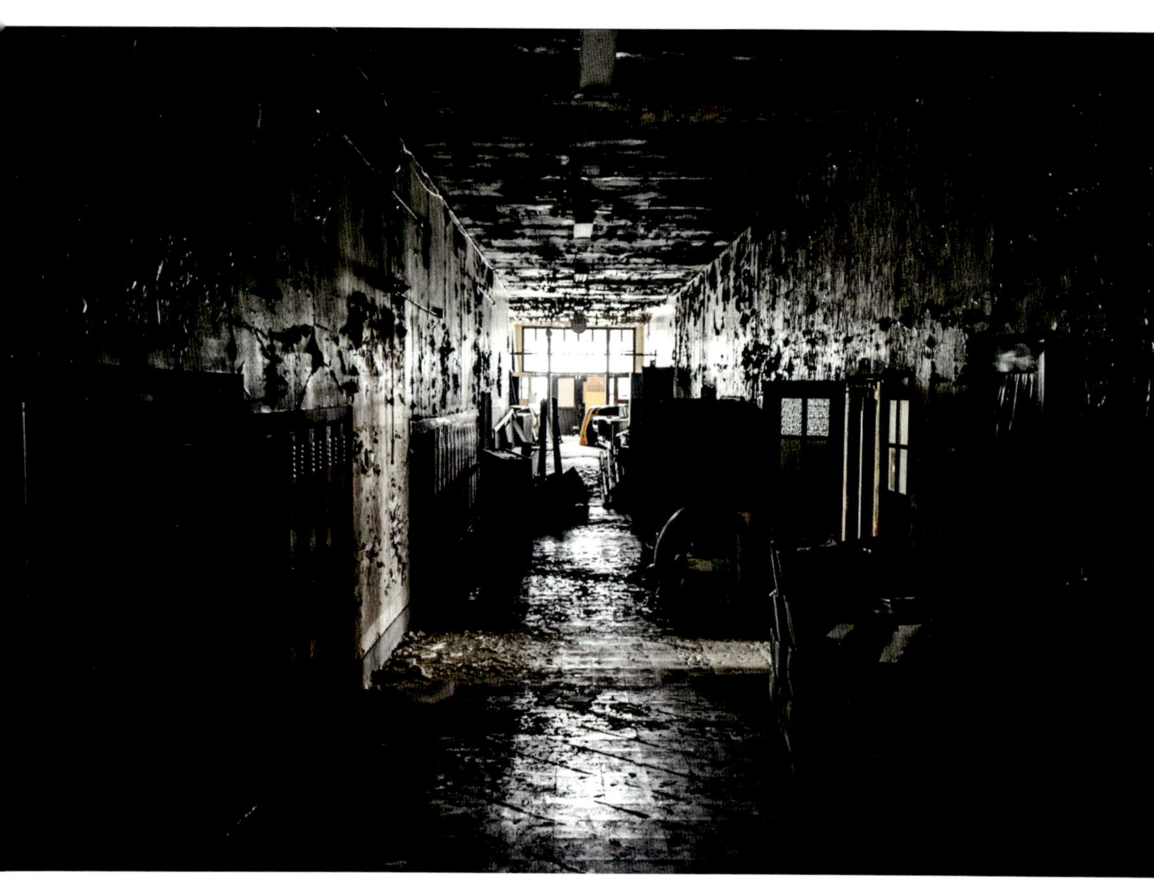

It's not easy to see, but in the far doorway there's an entire hood of a school bus. I believe the school district was using this part of the school as storage for a while, before abandoning it completely.

Opposite: This was quite a well-appointed church, given how small it was. I think this must have once been a nice part of town.

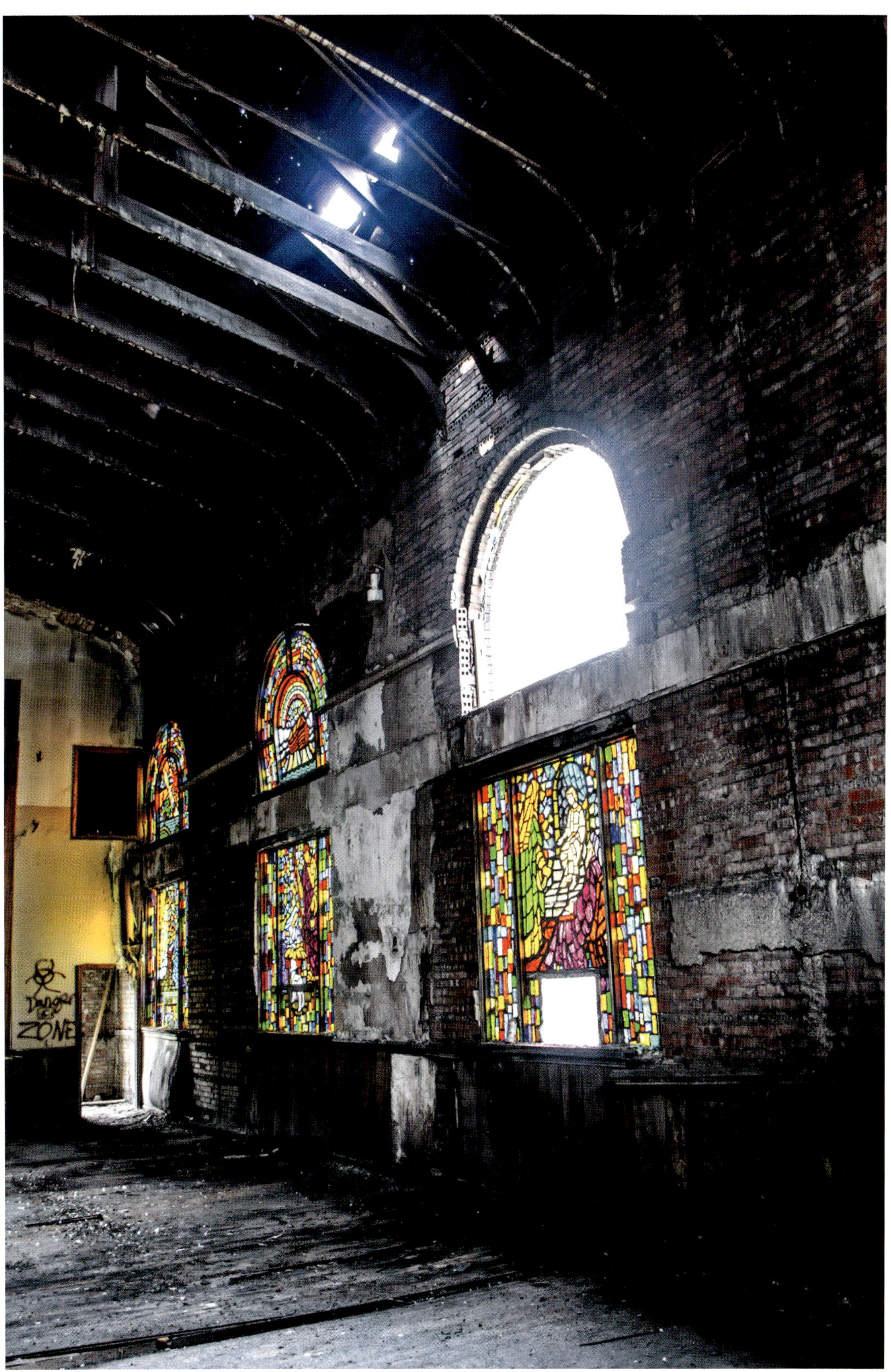

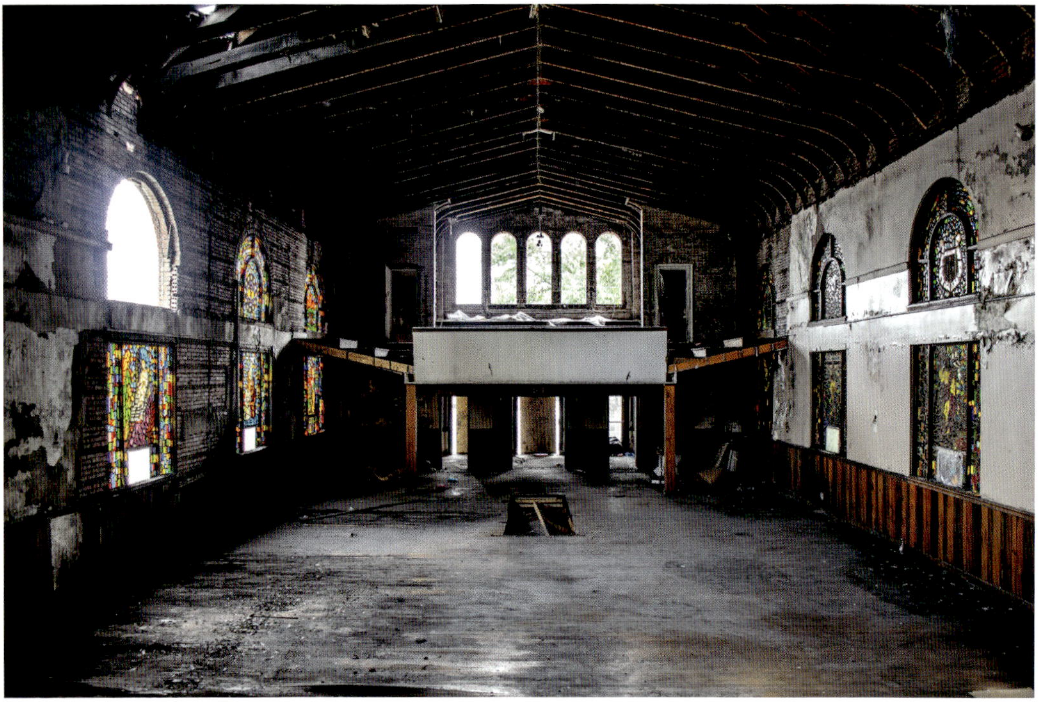

This was a tricky shot. The light from outside was so bright and only penetrating a few spots. My exploring companion said I was wasting my time trying. It did take several tries.

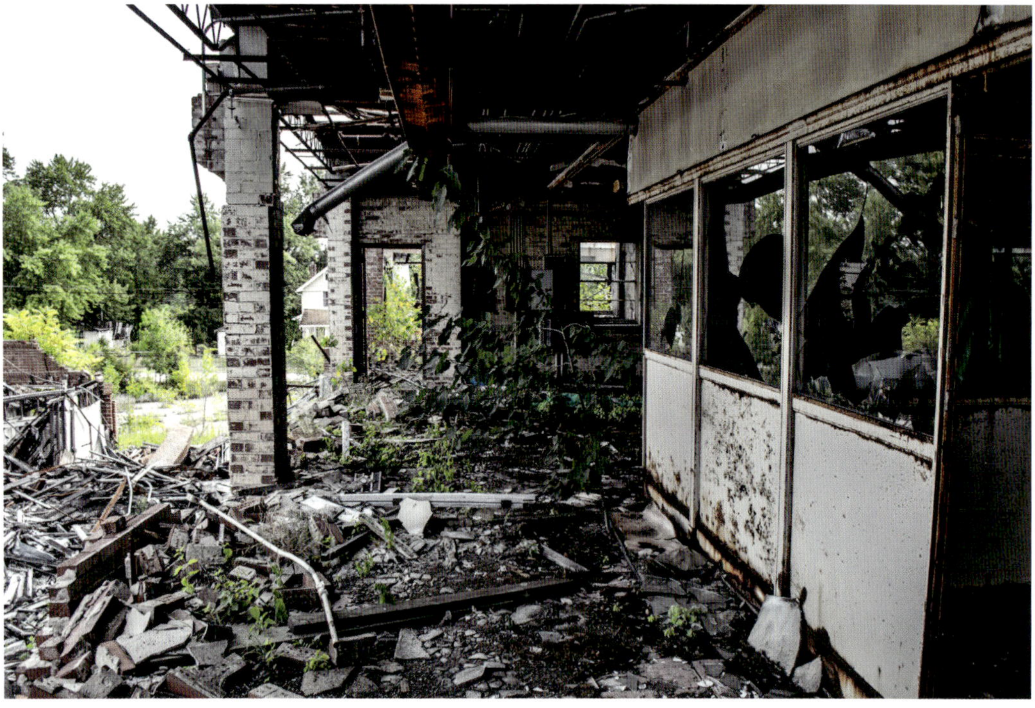

I had to step very carefully on the second floor of this building. Fortunately, there wasn't very much of it, so the anxiety-inducing experience didn't last long.

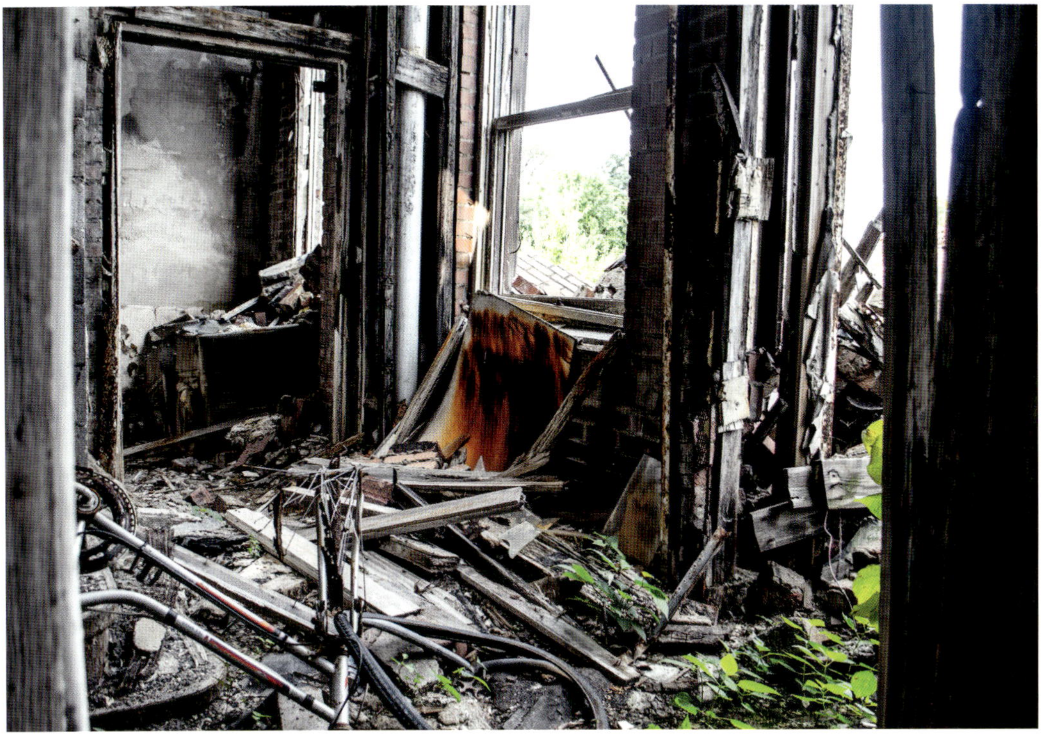

This was still the most intact stairway in the place.

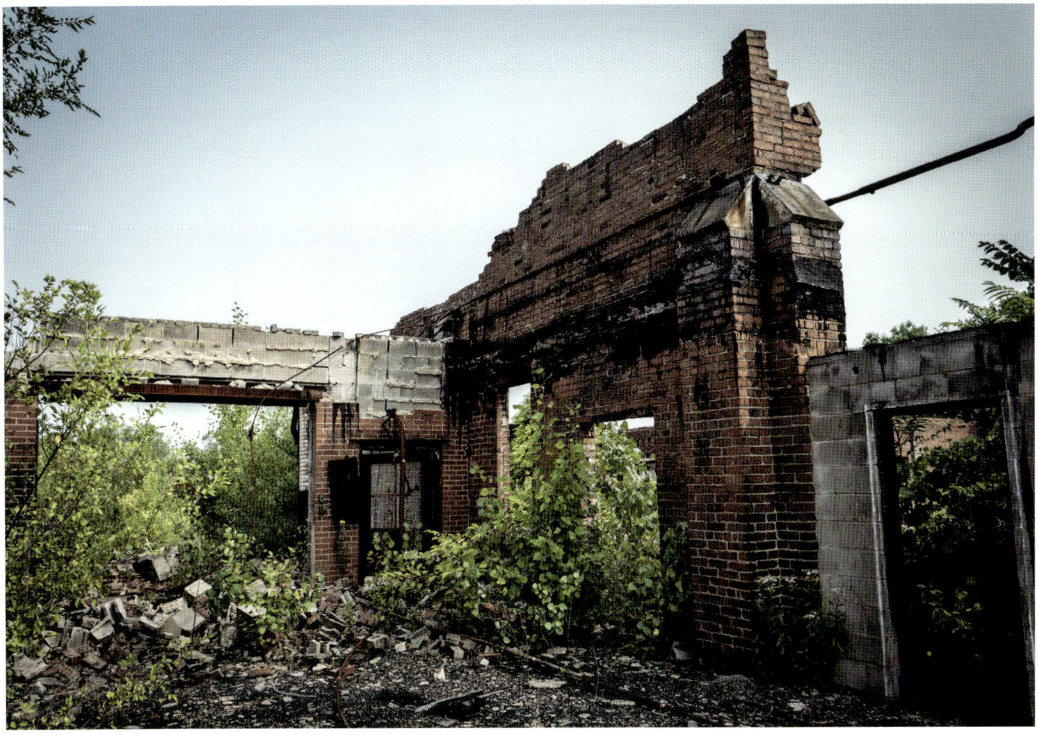

I don't know when they gave up on tearing this place down, but it must have been long ago for it to be so overgrown.

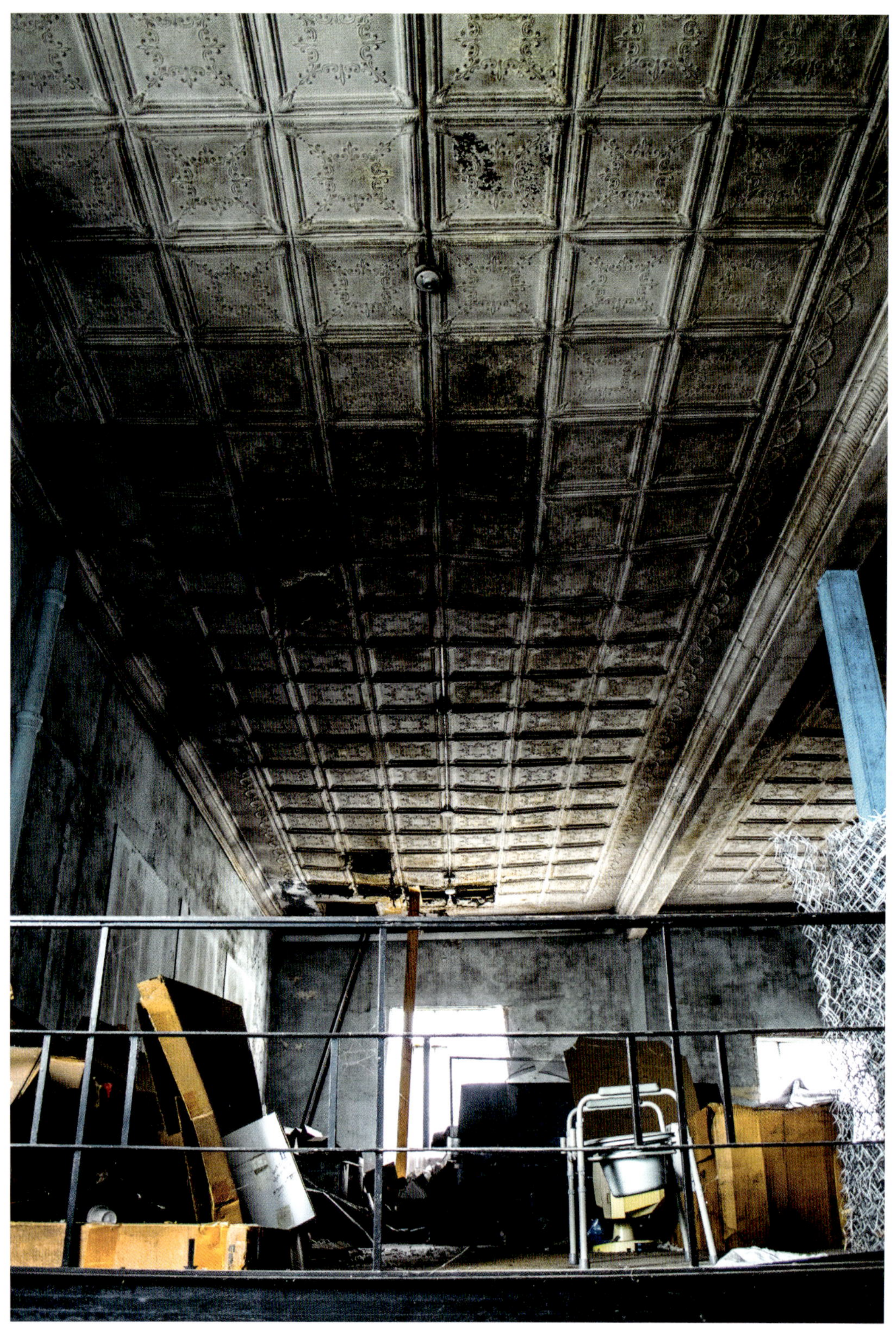

The ceiling was the only thing in this place worth photographing.

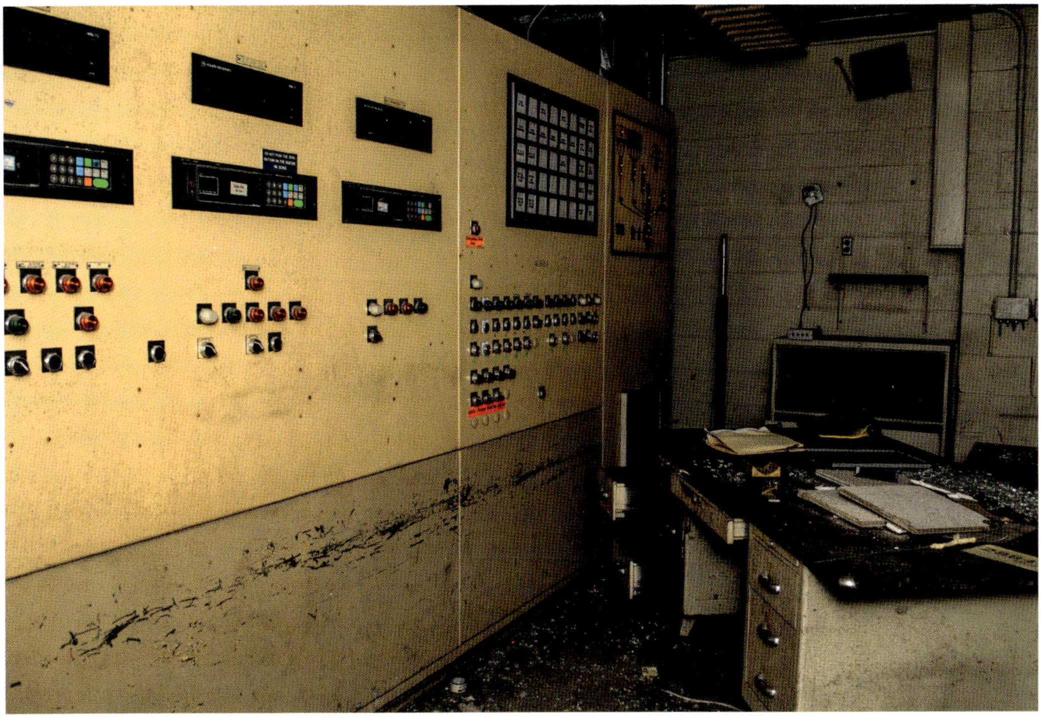

I have no idea what this did, but I'm going to bet it was important.

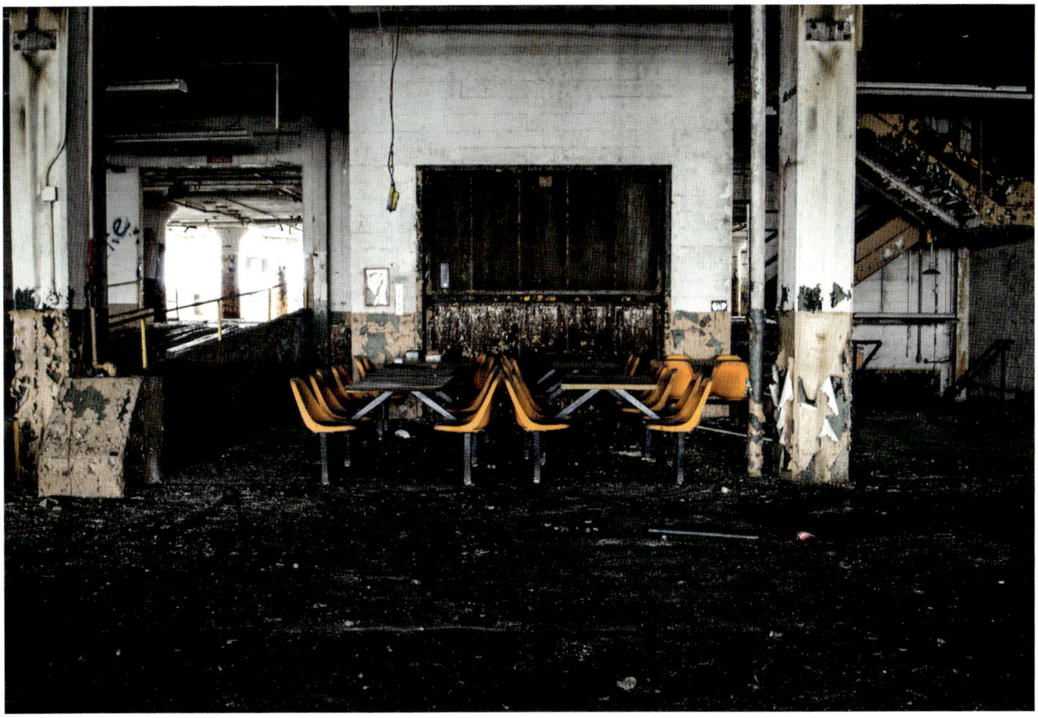

I don't think this was actually a break area, given that it was blocking the freight elevator, but what a miserable place to put it if it was.

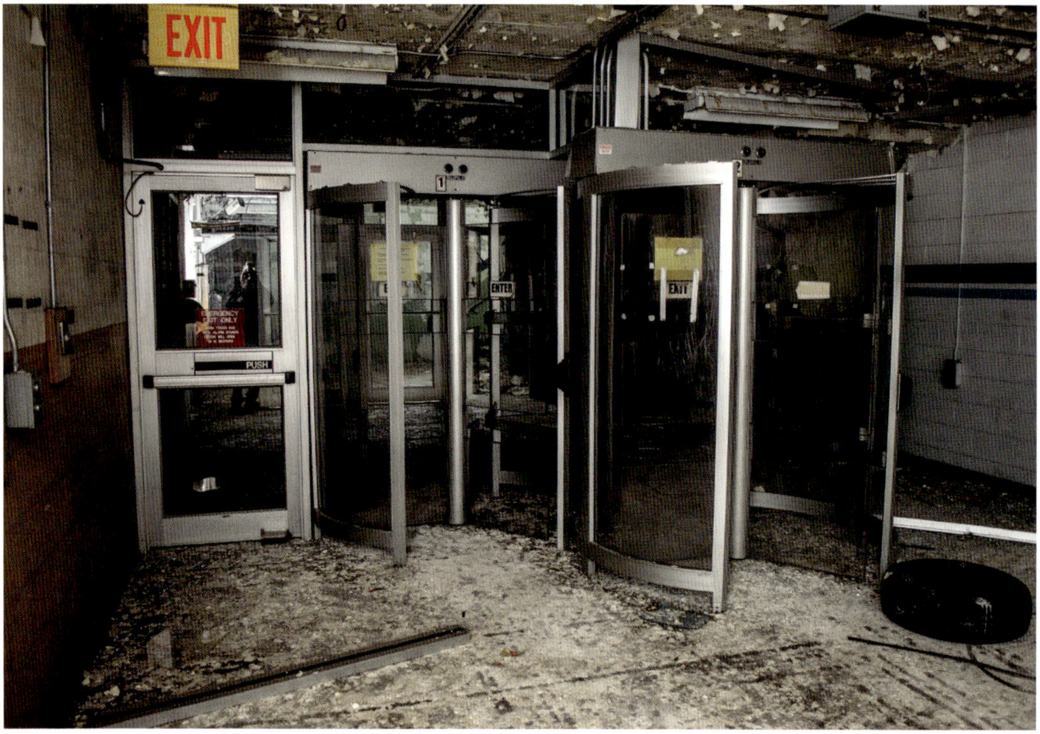

I was surprised to see all this intact. I'm guessing this was some very thick glass.

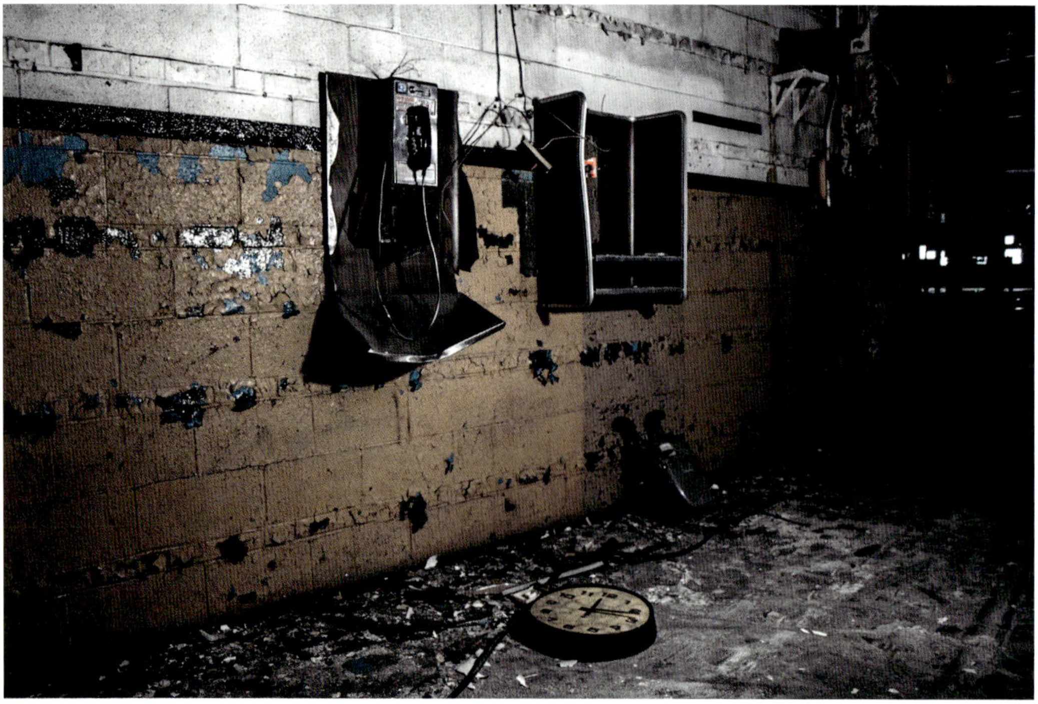

These were just off to the side of the factory floor. It must have been exceedingly difficult to have a conversation on them with all the noise.

6

THE COMPANY TOWN

I wanted to give the last group of photos here their own chapter, as they came from a different sort of exploring. They come from an entire neighborhood in Campbell, Ohio, which is a suburb of Youngstown. Campbell was built initially as a company town for Youngstown Sheet and Tube, around 100 years ago. Most of what you see here is the company housing that was built for the 5,000 or so workers employed there. The factory closed in 1977, and even though Youngstown is just down the street, few people live in the area anymore. Whole blocks are sitting empty, and even those with residents are still mostly empty. But unlike many areas with a lot of empty and abandoned housing, crime isn't such a concern here. In fact, preservation work is even being done by the Iron Soup Preservation Society, which is who we contacted for permission to explore and get more in-depth looks at this near-ghost town.

This type of row housing isn't especially common in North America, even a 100 years ago when it was built. The houses were also a lot smaller than most Americans would be used to, but the layout of the neighborhood would be familiar to anyone familiar with modern planned communities. Part of the area, particularly those sealed off and watched over by the Preservation Society, were like time capsules. And you can see from the photos that a surprising number of relics from the early days of the neighborhood are still around.

Campbell remains one of the biggest highlights of my time exploring. It was fascinating, and even after spending all day there, I don't feel like I've seen all there is to see. This seems like an appropriate way to close the book. I hope you've enjoyed it.

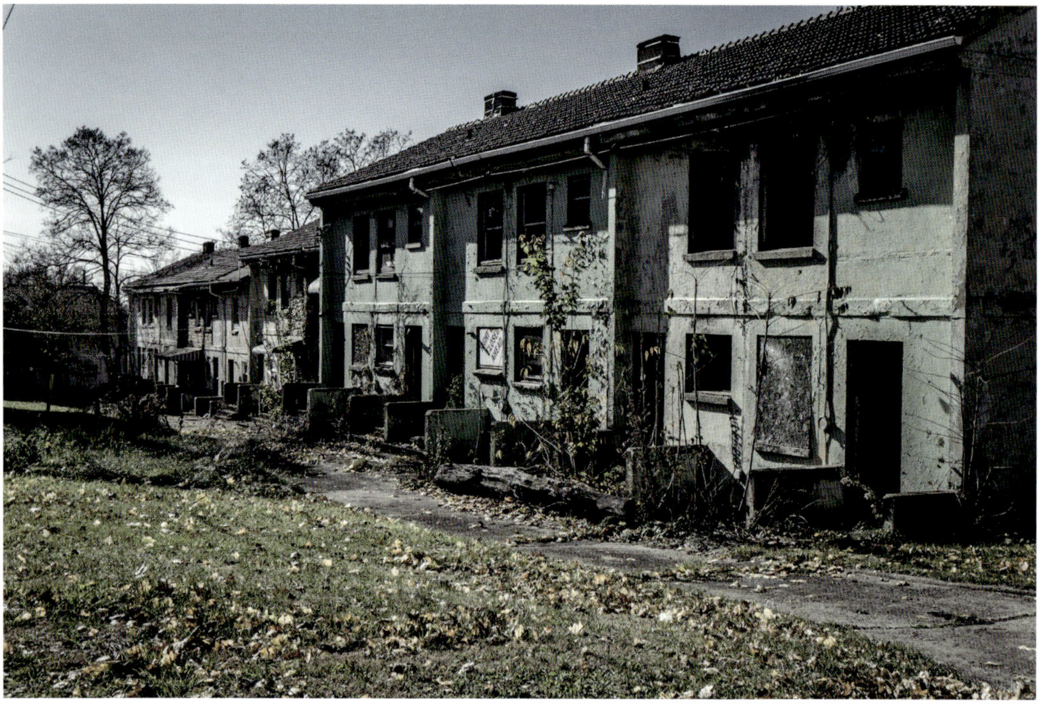

There was probably a time when these houses didn't look quite so grim, but as you can see, they were made to be very basic. Sturdy, obviously, but unadorned with much of anything.

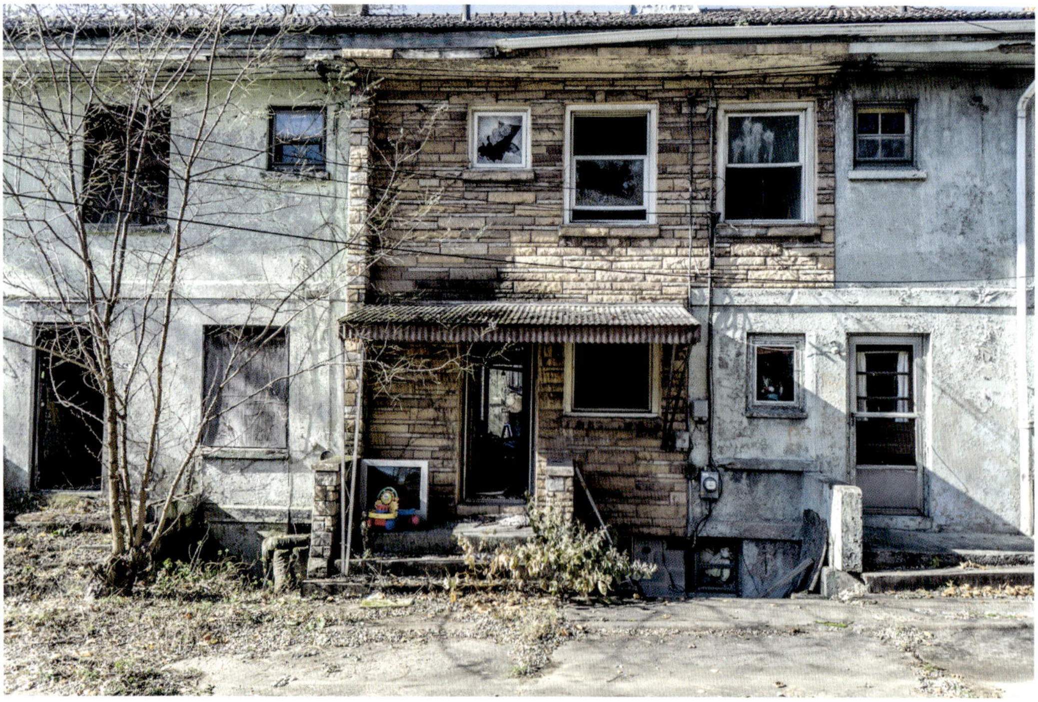

This was one of a couple of units that had been spruced up a bit, and had probably been lived in more recently than the other ones in this row. Still, it had also been abandoned for a while by the time we saw it.

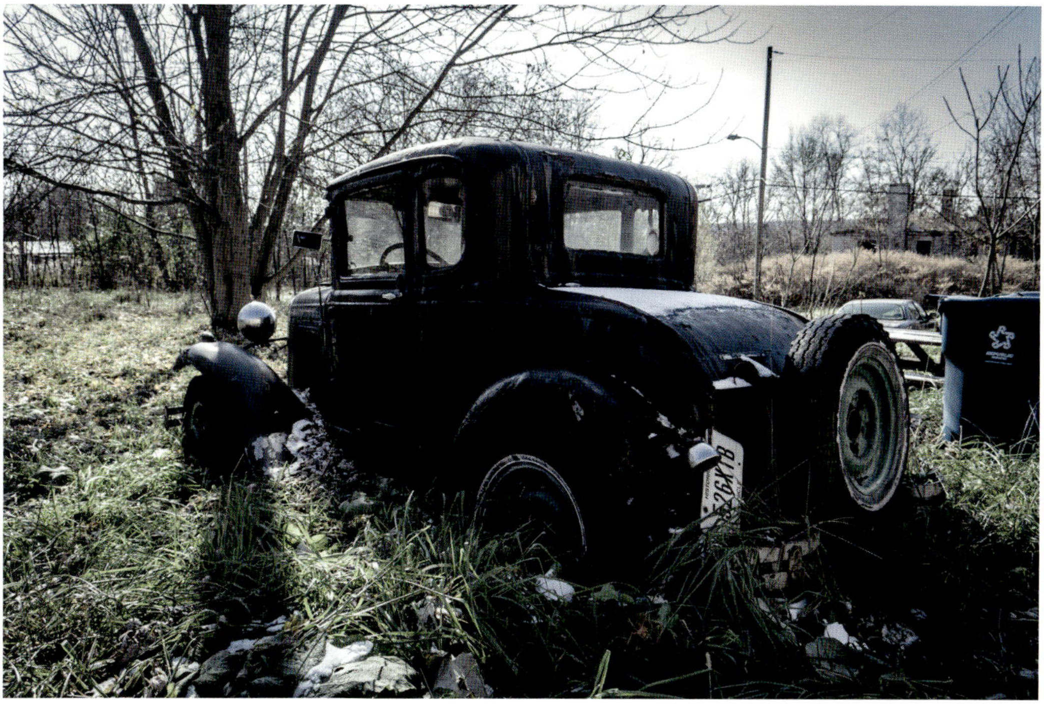

This car isn't really abandoned. It's registered, has historic plates, and the owner lives in a row house just outside of this shot. But the snow and stark-naked trees in the background made it too hard to pass up.

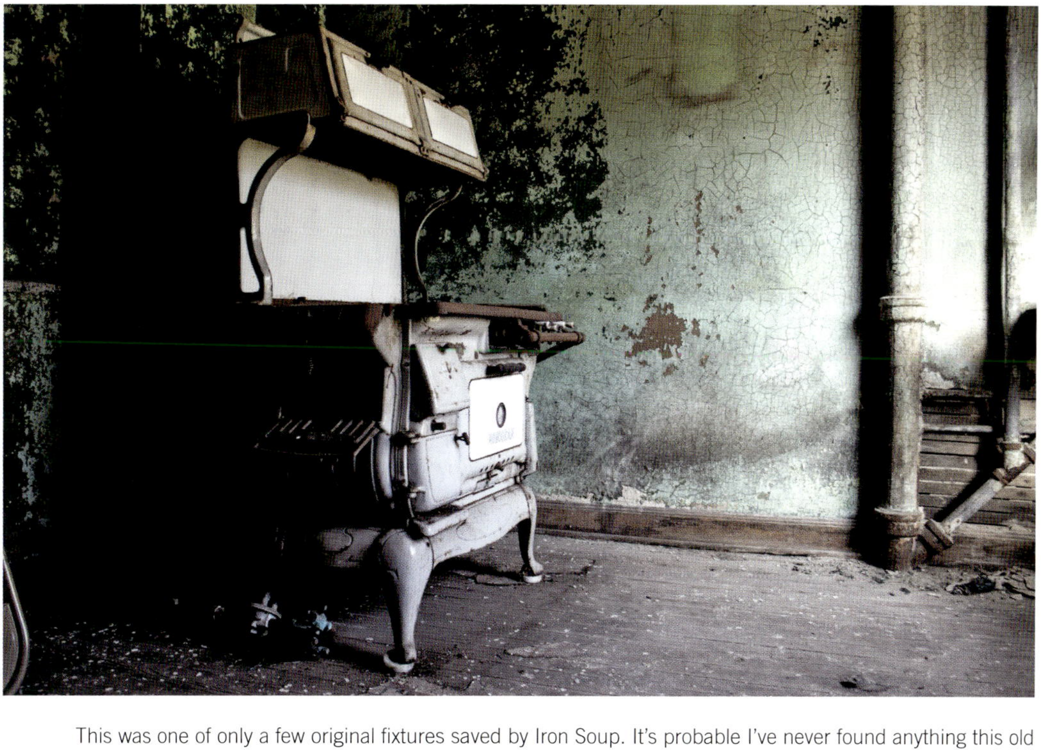

This was one of only a few original fixtures saved by Iron Soup. It's probable I've never found anything this old that's still in such good shape in all my exploring.

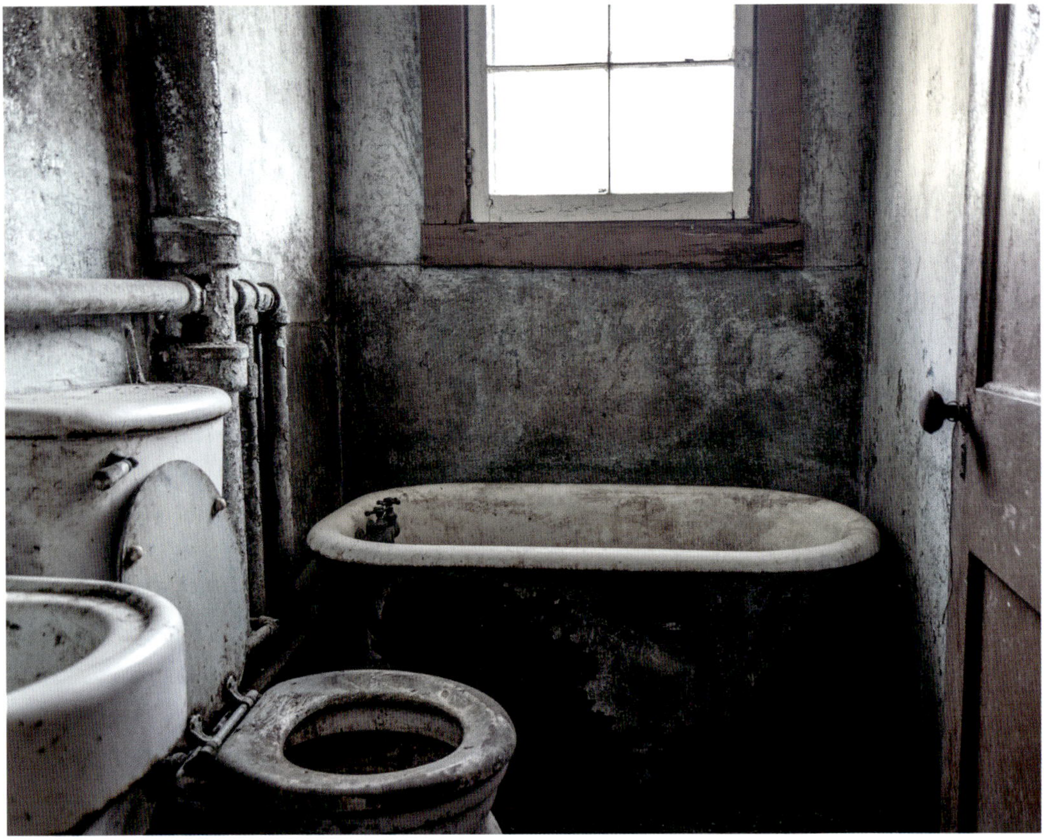

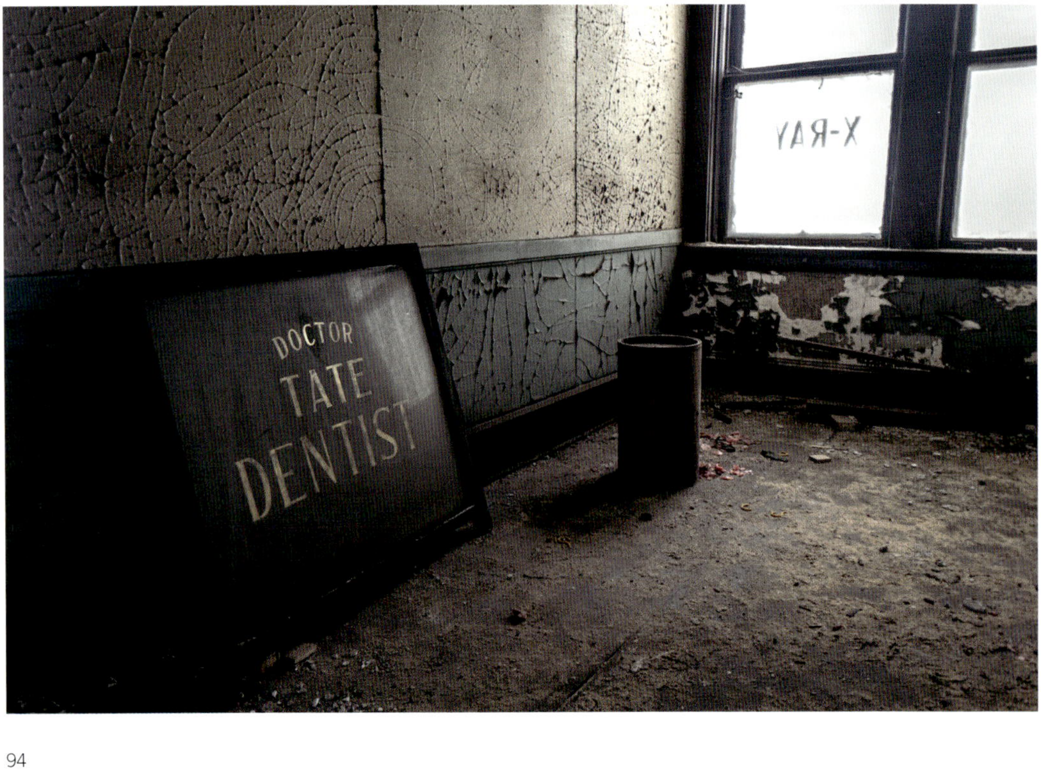

X-RAY

DOCTOR
TATE
DENTIST

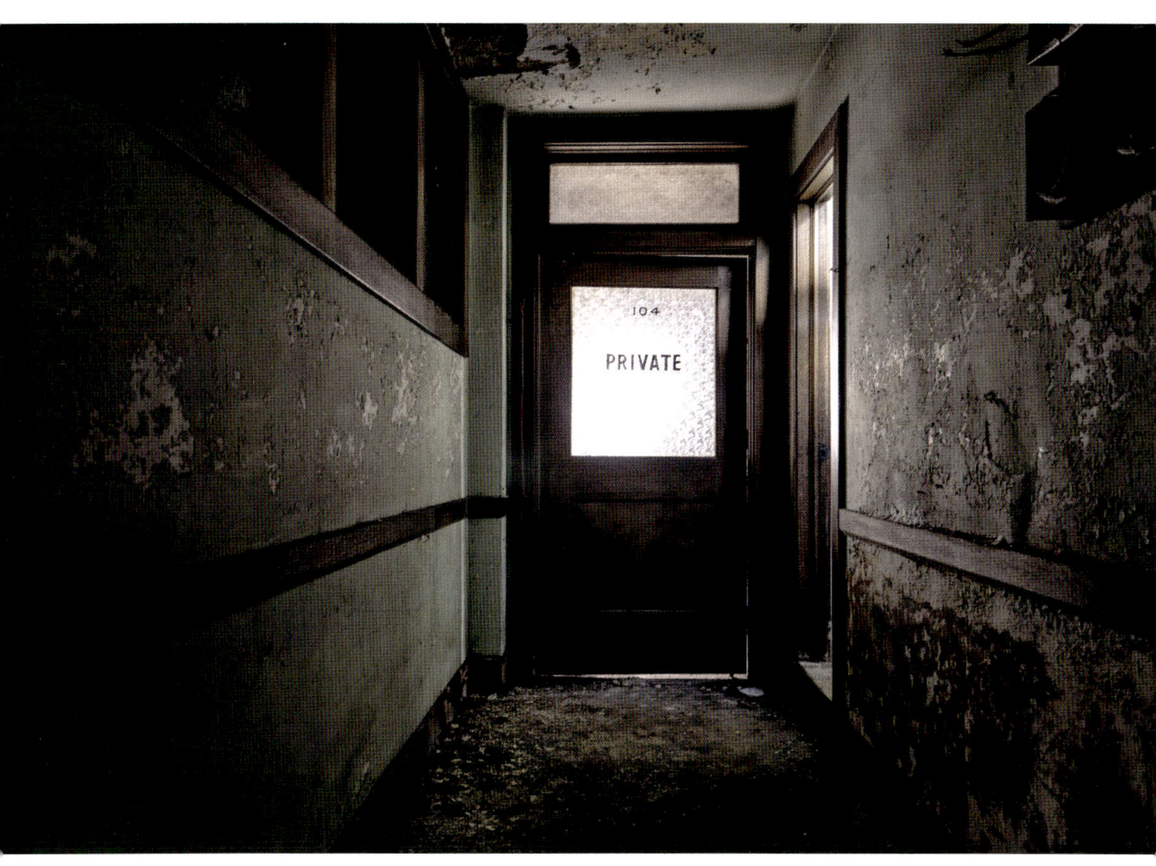

All we found in this room was a table with a pair of baby shoes on it. It was weird.

Opposite above: This unit has been converted into something of a museum by Iron Soup, a kind of model home for a century-old community. But you will be relieved to hear that this was not meant as a functional bathroom.

Opposite below: There was one commercial building left in this area: a bank with rental office spaces above it, all of which looked to have been abandoned earlier than the homes. We couldn't tell what most of the space was used for, but this unit was clear.

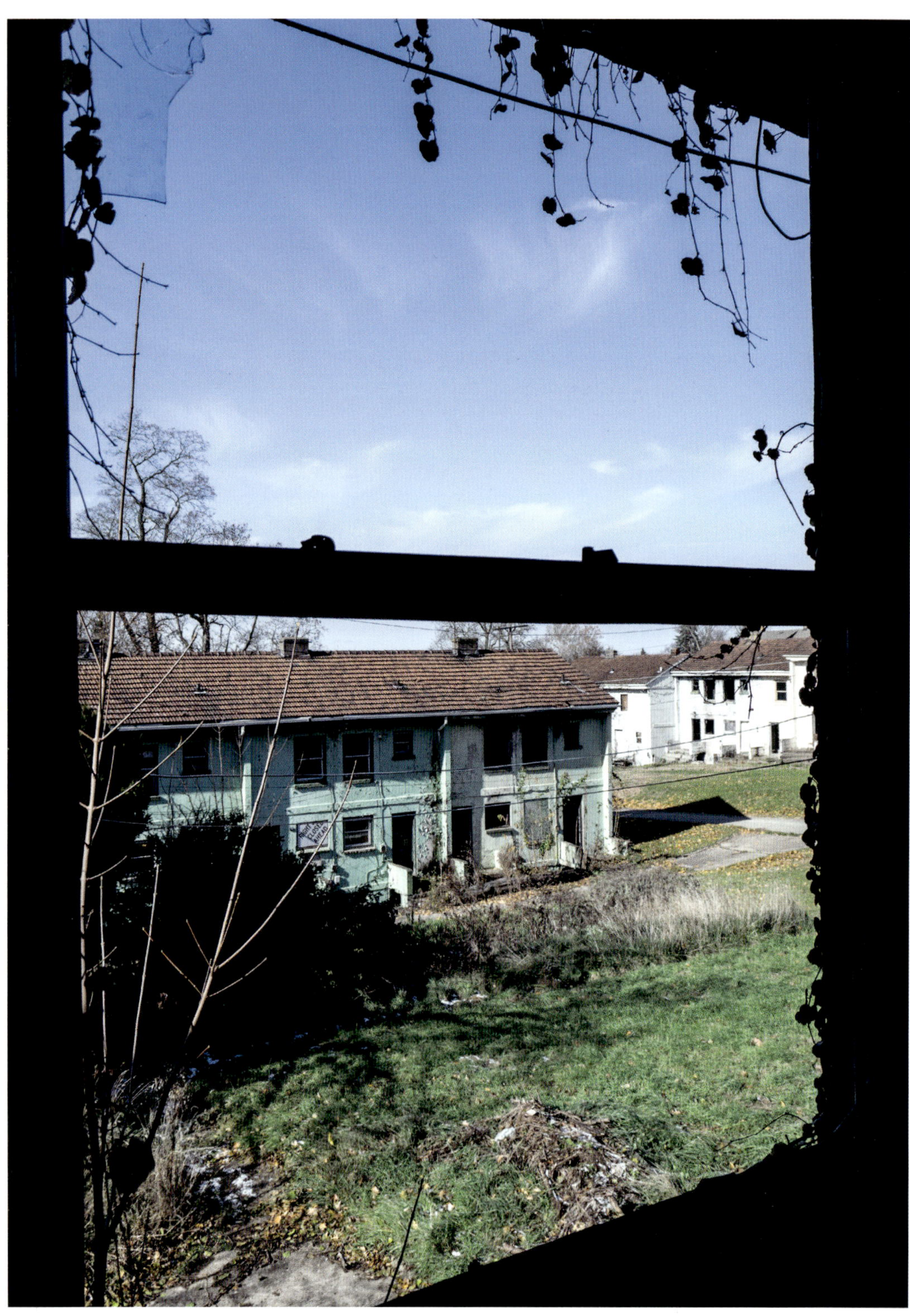

Because of the layout of this neighborhood, it's impossible to show the scope of it from one photo, but it was massive. There were at least a couple of dozen rows of houses and hundreds of units. This is decades after the factory closed; there used to be even more.